THE INVISIBLE HEART

Also by Nancy Folbre

The Ultimate Field Guide to the U.S. Economy
(with James Heintz and the Center for Popular Economics)

The War on the Poor: A Defense Manual
(with Randy Albelda and the Center for Popular Economics)

Who Pays for the Kids?
Gender and the Structures of Constraint

THE INVISIBLE HEART

Economics and Family Values

NANCY FOLBRE

The New Press
New York

Published in the United States by The New Press, New York, 2001
Distributed by W.W. Norton & Company, Inc., New York

Grateful acknowledgment is made to the following for permission to reprint previously published material:

BMG Publishing Ltd: Excerpt from "The Milkman of Human Kindness" by Stephen William Bragg, copyright 1987. All rights for the U.S. on behalf of BMG Music Publishing Ltd. administered by BMG Songs, Inc./ASCAP. All rights reserved. International copyright secured.

Random House, Inc.: "Occidental" from *The Panther and the Lash* by Langston Hughes, copyright © 1967 by Arna Bontemps and George Houston Bass, Executors of the Estate of Langston Hughes. Used by permission of Alfred A. Knopf, a division of Random House, Inc.

Susan Stinson: "Whole Cloth" from *Belly Songs: In Celebration of Fat Women*, Orogeny Press, copyright © 1993. Reprinted by permission of the author.

LIBRARY OF CONGRESS CATALOGING-IN-PUBLICATION DATA

Folbre, Nancy.
   The invisible heart : economics and family values / Nancy Folbre.
     p. cm.
   Includes bibliographical references and index.
   ISBN 1-56584-655-9 (hc.)
     1. Economics — Moral and ethical aspects. 2. Feminist economics.
   3. Social justice. 4. United States — Economic policy — 1993–
   5. United States — Economic conditions — 1981– 6. United States —
   Social policy — 1993– 7. United States — Social conditions — 1980–
   I. Title.

HB72 .F637   2001
306.3'0973 — dc21   00–062207

The New Press was established in 1990 as a not-for-profit alternative to the large, commercial publishing houses currently dominating the book publishing industry. The New Press operates in the public interest rather than for private gain, and is committed to publishing, in innovative ways, works of educational, cultural, and community value that are often deemed insufficiently profitable.

The New Press, 450 West 41st Street, 6th floor, New York, NY 10036

www.thenewpress.com

Printed in the United States of America

2 4 6 8 10 9 7 5 3 1

Thanks to:

Caren Grown, Barbara Rifkind, André Schiffrin, Helen Smith, and Susan Stinson, for urging me on.

Paula England, Julie Nelson, Lee Badgett, Tom Weisskopf, and Ann Ferguson, for coauthoring papers that helped develop many of the ideas presented here.

The John D. and Catherine T. MacArthur Foundation and the French-American Foundation, for financial support.

Helen Smith, Susan Stinson, and Bill Weye, for superb research and editorial assistance.

Peter Bohmer and his students at Evergreen College, Paul Goren, Carol Heim, Terry McDonald, Julie Nelson, Jennie Romich, Myra Strober, and Ruby Takanishi, for detailed comments and criticisms.

André Schiffrin and Marc Favreau for editorial assistance.

Bob Dworak for unstinting technical and not-so-technical support.

CONTENTS

Introduction   xi

*The invisible hand of markets depends upon the invisible heart of
care. Markets cannot function effectively outside the framework of
families and communities built on values of love, obligation, and
reciprocity.*

I. The Economics of Care

   1. The Milk of Human Kindness   3

*Women have traditionally been assigned disproportionate
responsibility for the invisible heart, but are no longer willing to
accept it. Feminism has successfully challenged the double
standard, demanding that care should be equally shared. But it
hasn't given us much advice on how much care we should
provide, or to whom.*

   2. The Care Penalty   22

*We can't rely on the forces of supply and demand to meet our needs
for care. Competitors can't always afford to be nice. It's often
hard to measure the benefits of care. Furthermore, the benefits of
caring for other people are not limited to those enjoyed by parties
to a specific transaction, but often spill over to society at large.*

3. Measuring Success   53

Competitive pressures in the health, child care and elder care industries have the effect of lowering the quality of care. Our entire accounting system misdirects our attention. The Dow Jones and other indices of stock prices are lousy indicators of our collective welfare. Developing human capabilities, good communities, and a healthy environment are better long-term goals than maximizing the Gross Domestic Product.

II. Good Government

4. The Nanny State   83

The welfare state has problems. We don't want to tempt people to slack off. We don't want to absolve them of responsibility for themselves and their family members. We don't want to create entrenched bureaucracies that are resistant to change. But one of the reasons that the welfare state emerged was that neither families nor the market can fully provide the care we need. We should try to improve social welfare programs rather than dumping on them.

5. Children as Pets   109

Pets provide considerable gratification for those who care for them. Children do this and more; they provide benefits for the rest of us. They qualify as public goods deserving of greater public support. Our current family support system, a patchwork of welfare and tax programs, is inadequate and unfair. It both reflects and encourages anger toward mothers living in poverty, who have been unfairly caricatured as welfare queens. Most European countries provide much better social support for families and so should we.

6. Robin Hood School   136

Education requires care and care takes money. We can't accurately measure the effects of educational spending on students by looking at standardized test scores. Taking equal opportunity seriously means reforming our system of school finance. Increased school choice could also help but not if it takes the form of vouchers that destabilize existing public school systems.

7. The Golden Eggs   159

Contrary to conservative rhetoric, progressive taxes support family values. They encourage people to spend less time advancing their personal careers and more time taking care of kids, parents, friends, and neighbors. Money can't buy happiness. But money can help meet people's basic needs and help create the kind of level playing field that healthy competition requires.

III. Between the Devil and the Deep Blue Sea

8. CorporNation   185

Just like people, corporations dream of an island paradise where they can get away from it all. Globalization is increasing the intensity of competition among countries, as well as among firms. Both immigration and capital mobility allow employers to free-ride on the contributions of parents, friends and neighbors. If they're not willing to pay, they should be kicked off the bus.

9. Dancing in the Dark   209

Jaded debates about capitalism versus socialism are holding us back. Progressive economists have cool ideas about alternatives like market socialism and participatory democracy. These might actually work if we could combine them with a better system of organizing and rewarding care for other people.

Notes   233

Index   257

INTRODUCTION

When everything is for sale, the person who volunteers time, who helps a stranger, who agrees to work for a modest wage out of commitment to the public good, who desists from littering even when no one is looking, who forgoes an opportunity to free-ride, begins to feel like a sucker.

—ROBERT KUTTNER,
Everything for Sale

When everything is for sale, women in particular begin to wonder why so much of the work they do goes unrewarded. Our modern economy has weakened many forms of patriarchal power that once gave women little choice but to specialize in caring for others. But it has also intensified competitive pressures that penalize women, men, and institutions for engaging in activities that don't improve the bottom line.

I am an economist who studies the time and effort that people put into taking care of one another. Caring labor is done on a person-to-person basis, in relationships where people generally call each other by their first names, for reasons that include affection and respect. Some of this work is compensated, at least partially, with a paycheck or a share of someone else's paycheck. Some of this work is not compensated by money at all. Economists use the adjective "nonmarket" to describe work that is not directly paid for and therefore difficult to put a price on. Much of this work is done on behalf of family members—cooking meals, changing diapers, mowing lawns. Much, though not all of it, has an explicitly compassionate dimension. None of it is counted as part of our Gross Domestic Product, and economists generally don't pay it much attention.

Caring labor is a particularly important kind of work because it has a direct effect on our emotional well-being. When you hire someone to clean your house or mow your lawn, it's pretty easy to figure out if they are doing a good job. When you hire someone to look after your infant or elderly parent, you can never be sure about the quality of care they provide. You will probably look for somebody who not only has the requisite skills but also seems to genuinely like taking care of other people. Just because care is paid by a wage doesn't mean that it isn't motivated by love as well as money. A great deal of caring labor is provided through the market. Daycare workers, home health workers, teachers, and nurses, among others, often develop loving personal relationships with the people they take care of.

I have long been curious about the ways that the responsibilities and rewards for caring labor—whether paid or unpaid, in the market or in the home—are distributed. The editor of the *Wall Street Journal* once put me down as a "feminist economist who studies nonmarket production (a.k.a. socialism)." Maybe he considers families socialistic. If he does, that's one idea we agree on. In general, however, the *Wall Street Journal* underestimates the importance of forms of work motivated by affection and respect for others, rather than pure pecuniary gain.

"Family values" means different things to different people. To me, the term conveys the ideas of love, obligation, and reciprocity. The first word implies feelings; the second morality; the third, rational calculation. I think my parents understood it this way: loving and being loved are essential to a meaningful and happy life. Each of us has some obligations for the care of other people, whether we like it or not. Moreover, if we take care of other people, they are more likely to take care of us.

Adam and Me

When the eighteenth-century economist Adam Smith extolled *the invisible hand*, he was referring to the decentralized, automatic, self-regulating forces of supply and demand in competitive markets. These are places or, more broadly, situations in which there are many buyers and many sellers, none of whom can conspire with each other. Sellers don't care who buys from them, and buyers don't care from whom they buy. Both parties know what they are getting in terms of quality, so they wrangle only over prices and quantities. No long-term relationships are involved. These conditions hold for the production of many goods and services. But they do not hold for the provision of caring labor.

Adam Smith believed that competitive markets could transmute the selfish desires of individuals into outcomes that served society as a whole. He concluded that it was not only unavoidable but even beneficial for individuals to pursue their own interests. In the 250 years since Smith wrote *The Wealth of Nations*, this widely believed prescription has almost certainly contributed to technological change and economic growth. The role that competitive markets play in our lives has steadily expanded. And encouragement for individuals to pursue self-interest has expanded with it, sometimes at the expense of care for others.

Adam Smith, a great thinker, anticipated this problem. But he didn't take it seriously, because he optimistically assumed that people were not all that selfish. He considered love of family, duty to others, and loyalty to country the hallmarks of an advanced civilization. The book that launched his career was entitled *The Theory of the Moral Sentiments*. In it he wrote, "However selfish soever man may be supposed, there are evidently some principles in his nature, which interest him in the fortune of others, and render their happiness necessary to him, though he derives nothing from it, except the pleasure of seeing it."[1]

The reliability of these moral sentiments was crucial to Smith's argument that the pursuit of self-interest should be given free rein. If people are unselfish at heart, they—like ideal family members—make other people's interests their own. Under these circumstances, self-interested behavior is not necessarily selfish behavior. Smith was so confident of human benevolence that he never asked where moral sentiments came from or if they might change over time. Like today's *Wall Street Journal*, he ignored the possibility that the expansion of an economy based on self-interest might weaken moral sentiments.

Smith's invisible hand is actually fairly visible. Almost by definition, market transactions can be recorded. They have price tags. They leave trails. The less direct effects of these transactions, however, are harder to trace. They can reshape human motivation, hardening some sentiments and softening others. The actions of the hand affect the feelings of the heart, though it is often difficult to say exactly how. It's easier to understand costs and benefits than likes and dislikes. It's easier to figure out how to get what we want than to determine whether we want the right things.

Most economists appreciate the importance of social norms of honesty and trust: these are norms that enable markets to function. Without them, the unbridled pursuit of self-interest can lead to deception and extortion. It's always easier to cut a deal with someone if you're sure they're not going to cut your throat. The invisible handshake helps the invisible hand. But what about the invisible heart, the feelings of affection, respect, and care for others that reinforce honesty and trust? Economists sometimes acknowledge emotions like altruism, but usually treat them the way Adam Smith did the moral sentiments—as givens. This is a big mistake.

Supplying Care

Traditionally, most, if not all, societies have assigned women primary responsibility for the tasks of caring for children, the sick, and the elderly. Indeed, for centuries, women were largely denied opportunities to pursue their own interests, discouraged from even thinking of themselves as autonomous beings. The growth of competitive markets for labor helped to disrupt and destabilize patriarchal power—and I, for one, am grateful. But the new forms of power we have been putting in its place sometimes threaten a different extreme: our absolution from responsibility for anyone else.

Restrictions on women's rights were oppressive, but they lowered the cost of caring labor. Women who had few opportunities outside the home were willing to specialize in providing family care. Those who sought paid employment were crowded into traditionally female jobs such as teaching and nursing, lowering the wages offered in those jobs. As career opportunities for women have expanded, the amount of money they stand to lose by devoting time to care has increased. Many women are taking advantage of opportunities to earn more money. So far, so good.

But the increased cost of care has several negative effects. First, it means that more people, especially children, the elderly, and other dependents, cannot always afford the care they need. Second, increased pressure to cut costs leads to reductions in the quality of care, a process already evident in many schools, hospitals, and nursing homes. Reliance on competitive markets in these areas puts pressure on providers to meet visible targets and generate cash revenues at the expense of results that are more difficult to quantify. Just as standardized tests can't tell us whether or not students have developed the motivation to learn on their own, so too the number of occupied beds in a hospital says nothing about patients' sense of being cared for.

Third, and perhaps most ominous, caring for people who can't pay the market rate—and that includes most children and many other dependents—begins to seem impractical, even quixotic. Our increasingly competitive economy seldom honors or rewards care for others. In its emphasis on the efficiency of markets and impersonal exchange, it sends the message that nice folks finish last.

Nice Countries and the Family State

Intensified global competition is now sending the message that nice countries finish last too. Economic development entails a transfer of economic activities from family and kin-based systems to larger, more impersonal institutions. One aspect of this process is the emergence of nation-states, which function as metaphorical families—our fatherlands, our mother countries. We speak of "what's good for the country" much as we speak of "what's good for the family," recognizing that individuals who often disagree are nonetheless sometimes willing to cooperate. Over the last century, the government has begun to play an increasingly important role in the provision of services such as education, health, and a social safety net.

The term "welfare state" surfaced in Great Britain after World War I as a positive alternative to the "warfare state." Today, however, many people associate it with inefficiency, bureaucracy, and waste. Perhaps we need another phrase to convey the underlying ideal. I like the term "family state," not because the state should replace families, but because it should promote familial values of caring and sharing as well as duty and responsibility.

The realities of both the family and the family state fall short of our ideals. But we will not be able to reform them unless we can also defend them against the competitive pressures of unencumbered individualism. In today's economy, both familial and social responsibilities have begun to seem like luxuries. The nurturance, education, protection, and care of dependents requires money and time. Individuals who don't want to pay these costs are finding it easier to opt out than they did in the past. Likewise, businesses that don't want to pay taxes or a living wage are finding it easier to relocate to other countries.

Deadbeat dads, angry that their families haven't met their expectations, often refuse to pay child support. "I don't have enough control over how the money is being spent," they say, moving across state lines to evade enforcement of their responsibilities. Corporations sometimes say the same thing when they move their operations overseas. Complaints about our minimum wage laws and environmental protection rules sound like teenagers threatening to leave home and never look back: "If you don't stop telling me what to do, I'll just move out."

Globalization is a way of leaving home. It may be an inevitable stage of economic development. But there's nothing inevitable about the way it's done or what happens to those who get left behind. Family values demand love, obligation, and reciprocity. They also demand putting the hand in service to the heart. The economist John Maynard Keynes once pointed out how hard it is to wait for the future. "In the long run," he wrote, "we are all dead." He was right. But in the long run, if we are careful, our children and our students will survive. We need to think harder about what being careful means.

The Visible Heart

The year I was born, my father went to work for the McFarlin Oil Company, handling the personal as well as business affairs of a small dynasty of the sort made famous by the television show *Dallas*. He oversaw their investments, minimized their taxes, retrieved them from drinking binges, got them in and out of mental institutions, advised them on their philanthropy, coordinated their divorces, and soothed their ruffled feelings. Never did I hear him express any resentment of the often quite onerous tasks he was required to perform. But many times I heard him say, usually with a chuckle, "Money—it sure doesn't buy happiness."

I always found it to difficult to reconcile this apparent wisdom with the behavior of most people—including, occasionally, my father. More than simply a source of privilege, money is the most widely used yard-stick of success and competence. It is the great common denominator, rendering all things comparable: apples and oranges, right and wrong, principal and interest, principle and convenience. The almighty dollar, the demon dollar, funny money, small change—everyone has a price. The first time I ever asked my father what he did every day at the office he said curtly, "I make money." What he really did was take care of a bunch of nutty millionaires.

One of his favorite responsibilities was making the hunting arrange-ments, a Texas thing. He would obtain a deer hunting lease, set up a camp with either a tent or a small trailer, and put a temporary fence around it to keep out the cows. (In Texas, there are usually cows.) On late fall and early winter weekends, my dad would take E. B. McFarlin, whom we called Mr. Mac, down to the lease to hunt. Mr. Mac was the founder of the family business. He and his uncle, Mr. Chapman, chanced to buy the right set of mineral rights to the right piece of land in Tulsa, Oklahoma, at the right time. Oil. Or, as they used to say on *The Beverly Hillbillies*, liquid gold.

When I was about eight years old, Mr. Mac was in his seventies, deaf as a doorpost and half blind. A diabetic, he was ordered not to drink, but he depended on his wife Myrtle to enforce this prohibition. When he came with Dad to the hunting lease, though, Myrtle didn't come along and Mr. Mac would usually bring a flask of bourbon in her place. My father, subject to female supervision of his own alcohol intake, was sympathetic. He sometimes speculated that if the old man had just been allowed to have a nip or two during the week he wouldn't get so hopelessly drunk at the hunting camp.

But where gun safety was concerned, my father had strong opinions. It drove him crazy when Mr. Mac took a flask along on the hunt. Even when he was sober, the tip of Mr. Mac's gun would swing every which way. No matter what happened, my father would stand between me and it. If I got in front, or if Mr. Mac turned around, my father would yank me behind him so I'd be shielded if the gun went off, trying not to make it too obvious that he didn't trust the boss.

I think my mother made my father promise to do this. At least once, I heard her complain that his job was putting her youngest child's life at risk. I always loved going hunting, though, partly because I could run around and chase cows and look for snakes, and partly because I enjoyed watching my parents act like kids. One night my mother fixed a really nice dinner on the camp stove. Steak, green beans, potatoes, biscuits, and gravy. We were all sitting at a fold-up table with a kerosene lantern on it. I distinctly remember that my head barely reached the table, because that put me at exactly the right angle to notice when Mr. Mac started sopping his paper napkin in his gravy and raising it to his mouth. I tugged at my father's sleeve and whispered, "Dad, Mr. Mac is eating his napkin!"

My startled father must have assumed that this problem was not in his department, since it had to do with dinner. He whispered to my mother, "Eleanor, do something. Mr. Mac is eating his napkin." She refused the responsibility. "I'm not going to tell him," she whispered back. "It's your job. You tell him." By this time, most of the napkin was gone—chewed, savored, swallowed and on its way to digestive conclusion.

You would think a scene like this wouldn't bear repeating. The following year, under similar circumstances, we were eating hamburgers, and all the fixings were on the table: mayonnaise, mustard, ketchup, pickles. Darned if Mr. Mac didn't pick up the mayonnaise jar and start sucking it down as though it were milk. The second time around, it was just as funny.

A few years ago when I was helping my father clean out a desk at the McFarlin Oil Company, I came across two photographs of Mr. Mac in his prime. In one, he stands on a dock holding a long fishing pole; a giant sailfish hangs behind him. Big and ruddy, he looks like a combination of Ernest Hemingway and Teddy Roosevelt. In another, he proudly wields his hunting rifle in front of about twenty dead bucks. Both these images remind me of my favorite photograph of myself at the hunting camp. In it, I am a skinny ten-year-old holding a dead rattlesnake that is taller than I am. (My mother had let me shoot it with my .22 after she ran over it with the jeep.)

This personal history helps explain why I never considered economics a dismal science. I learned at a tender age that some very successful men couldn't always tell the difference between milk and mayonnaise. Almost everything I studied in economics courses connected one way or another to some of the more puzzling experiences of my childhood. One of my favorite economists has written a book entitled *If You're So Smart, Why Aren't You Rich?* I always wanted to ask Mr. Mac, "If you're so rich, why aren't you smart?" and, "If you're so rich, why aren't you happy?"

My parents lived on a modest middle-class scale, but they had more fun and more love in their lives than the McFarlins did. Going to the hunting camp increased my appreciation for family values. Of course, going hunting also increased my tomboy confidence with guns and snakes. That I grew up to become a college professor instead of a cowgirl Amazon revolutionary is probably a tribute to my family's redeeming tolerance and affection.

What's Next

I tell some personal stories in this book, because I want to reveal how my own family background has shaped my point of view. Each chapter focuses on an important aspect of the relationship between economics and family values. The chapters are grouped into three sections. The first deals with theory, the second with policy, the third with strategies for the future.

The theoretical chapters debunk the conventional economic assumption that we're all automatically better off if we each pursue our own self-interest. For most of our history, women have been carefully prevented from doing any such thing. No society oriented exclusively toward individual success—to the exclusion of care for the next generation—can reproduce itself. Rules of obligation to other people must be enforced. It may be convenient for one group to enforce them upon another, but this arrangement is unfair, and ultimately inefficient. The costs of fulfilling values of love, obligation, and reciprocity should be more evenly distributed. We should also develop better ways of monitoring and improving the quality of care services.

The second section explores the evolution of relationships between family and government, describing both conflicts and complementarities. A general history of social welfare programs such as Social Security leads into a description of how men and women, as well as other groups, scuffle over who should pay for what. Next come some specific complaints about our public assistance programs, our public schools, and our tax system. The gist of the argument is that more caring and sharing would be an excellent idea. If we could better allocate the costs of investing in human capabilities, we might actually enjoy a pretty good rate of return.

The final section turns toward the future, considering the impact of increased international competition and its implications for both families and governments. We need to establish democratic control over the process of globalization. We also need to move beyond the old capitalism versus communism debate and find more creative ways of balancing freedom and obligation, achievement and care. Some kinds of care for others cannot be bought and sold. But they can be strengthened—or weakened—by the way we organize our economy.

———◆———

We may discover that the best things we will ever do for our own families, however we define them, is to get involved in community or political action to help others.

—STEPHANIE COONTZ,
*The Way We Never Were: American Families
and the Nostalgia Trap*

The Economics of Care

The invisible hand represents the forces of supply and demand in competitive markets. The invisible heart represents family values of love, obligation, and reciprocity. The invisible hand is about achievement. The invisible heart is about care for others. The hand and the heart are interdependent, but they are also in conflict. The only way to balance them successfully is to find fair ways of rewarding those who care for other people.

This is not a problem that economists—or business people—have taken seriously. They have generally assumed that God, nature, the family, and "Super Mom"—or some combination thereof—would automatically provide whatever care was needed. The following chapters explain why this assumption is wrong. Both the quantity and quality of care for other people are coming under increasing economic pressure.

THE MILK OF HUMAN KINDNESS

If you're lonely, I will call.
If you're poorly, I will send poetry.
I love you.
I am the milkman of human kindness.
I will leave an extra pint.

—BILLY BRAGG

Investors are fascinated by bulls, as in a "bull market" and "Merrill Lynch is bullish on America." Cows, sows, and nannies are associated with socialism, as in "everyone wants to milk the common cow," or "sucking on the government teat." Margaret Thatcher taught a whole generation of politicians to deride the "nanny state." Ditto Rush Limbaugh, who suggested we replace the eagle, our current national symbol, with a "huge sow that has a lot of nipples and a bunch of fat little piglets hanging on them, all trying to suckle as much nourishment from them as possible."[1] The implication seems to be that real men don't drink milk and shouldn't offer any to other people.

In our culture, milk often serves as a metaphor for kindness, and motherhood embodies both. Partly as a result, our ideals of love and care for others have often been defined differently for women and men. When I graduated from high school in 1969, I was warned not to seem too smart or too ambitious. Some family friends capped this advice with a quotation from Shakespeare: "Be good, sweet girl, and let those who will be clever." I remember my mother giving me a big wink. As someone who had reconciled herself to goodness, she secretly urged me on to mischief. Over time, I've seen discomfort about female accomplishments diminish. Norms of appropriate behavior for women have changed.

In a 1977 poll, about two-thirds of the Americans surveyed agreed that "It is much better for everyone if the man is the achiever and the woman takes care of the home and family." By 1998, only one-third agreed: the proportions had reversed.[2] Women are now far more likely to work outside the home than they were twenty-five years ago. Partly as a result, they are less bound by family obligations, with more permission—indeed, encouragement—to pursue their own interests. Men's work hasn't changed nearly as much. The amount of time they devote to housework and child care has increased by a negligible amount.

This chapter explores the connections between masculinity, femininity, self-interest, and care for others. In the United States today, men and women have equal rights before the law. With respect to the care of children and other dependents, however, our cultural norms still reflect greater expectations for women than for men. Economic theory offers vivid examples of this cultural double standard. The history of feminism reflects a sustained effort to challenge it.

Liberal feminism has demanded greater individual rights for women. Social feminism has demanded greater social obligations, especially for men. For reasons that have to do with our economic system, as well as our political history, liberal feminism has enjoyed relatively more success in the United States than in the more traditional societies of Europe. Its very success has contributed to a dilemma. Women know they can benefit economically by becoming achievers rather than caregivers. They also, know, however, that if all women adopt this strategy, society as a whole will become oriented more toward achievement than care.

◆

Most advice books for men concern money and sex and say virtually nothing about caring for their elderly parents or small children. Books for women, such as Helen Gurley Brown's *Having It*

All or Sonya Freeman's *Smart Cookies Don't Crumble*, now also glamorize a life for women that is relatively free of the burden of care.

— ARLIE HOCHSCHILD
"Ideals of Love" in Karen V. Hansen and Anita Corey, eds.,
Families in the U.S.: Kinship and Domestic Politics

———————◆———————

Coercion and Care

It is often assumed that women are naturally more altruistic than men, especially toward their own offspring. Biologists borrow an economic concept, pointing out that mothers have a greater biological "investment" in children than fathers do, since they carry the fetus within their body and nourish the infant with milk from their breasts. Maternal love, however, has always had limits. The varied circumstances in which we have evolved have forced mothers to make hard choices, to evaluate the effect that one child might have on another child's—and on her own— chances of survival.[3]

Any time that costs and benefits are taken into account, outcomes hinge on who pays the costs and who enjoys the benefits. Precisely because mothers pay a disproportionate share of the costs, fathers often worry less than mothers about the prospect of too many offspring. Furthermore, the more that women specialize in child rearing, the more dependent they become on adult men for assistance. As a result, fathers generally acquire power along with the responsibility for caring for their families. The biological division of labor sets the stage for an array of social and cultural forms of control over women, some of which may give patriarchal societies an edge over more egalitarian societies.[4]

Conservative social thinkers, including many economists, insist that women are naturally suited to child care, and that this, in turn, gives them a comparative advantage in providing care to others, including the sick and elderly. Specialization, after all, increases efficiency. But specialization also affects the development of human capabilities and the exercise of bargaining power. In the short run, it may be efficient for one country to specialize in producing sugar and bananas while another country specializes in producing computers and guns. In the long run, however, the country that specializes in producing sugar and bananas is unlikely to be able to defend its own borders or develop its own technology. The same may be said of a person who specializes in rearing children and taking care of other dependents.

Historical scholarship details the many laws that gave fathers and husbands property rights over daughters and wives, enforced male control over female wealth and income, restricted women's access to education and systematically excluded them from access to lucrative jobs.[5] It is difficult to explain why such coercive rules evolved, if not because of some big differences between what men wanted women to do and what women would have chosen on their own. A nineteenth-century Prussian law actually gave husbands the right to determine how long their wives should breast-feed their infants.[6]

In some areas of the world, women's relative position has improved over the last two centuries. Economic development and technological change have increased the importance of brains—including women's brains—relative to brawn. Equally important has been the decline in fertility and the shift of focus from the quantity of children to the quality of their upbringing. Looking back, it seems pretty clear that traditional patriarchal rules did more than increase women's specialization in child rearing. They also increased women's specialization in the provision of other kinds of care services. Economic dependence made women's welfare contingent on the welfare of their fathers and husbands—a powerful incentive to pay attention to other people's needs. Those who are denied a cultural conception of themselves as individuals may not even think of themselves as separate persons.[7]

Many systematic forms of violence seem designed to decrease women's ability to perform directly productive work. Foot-binding in ancient China made it difficult for women to walk. Strict rules of exclusion, such as purdah in many Islamic countries, limit women's opportunity to earn a market income. Genital mutilation, still practiced in many areas of Africa, poses serious risks to women's health. Domestic violence, still rife in many areas of Europe and the United States, makes it more difficult for a wife or mother to get dinner on the table and children off to school. All these practices lower productivity and enforce subordination, encouraging women to put others' needs above their own.

Of course, you can't force somebody to love you. Subordination doesn't always lead to high quality care. It can create tension, resentment, even fury. Greek mythology tells of Medea, so angered by her husband Jason's betrayal that she murdered their two sons and served them up for dinner. Less extreme threats have often given women informal power. We value love most when it is freely given. People who have a voice in defining their commitments to other people probably fulfill those commitments more gracefully. Allowing women new choices improves the quality of care and, in this respect, everybody benefits.

But choice is a funny thing, affected by both moral values and by social pressures. Often what we choose depends on what we think other people will choose. It's harder to stay honest if we see other people cheating. It's harder to engage in teamwork if other team members are shirking. It's harder to take on responsibilities for the care of other people if those responsibilities don't seem to be shared. This is why too much choice—or too little social coordination of choice—can lead to outcomes that can be just as problematic as having no choice at all.

Work versus Care

In the seventeenth century, a number of English political theorists began to argue that men should govern themselves rather than automatically accept the authority of a king. They also laid the conceptual foundation for an economy based on contract rather than coercion. John Locke emphasized two basic economic principles. First, a man should have ownership of himself; no one else should have dominion over him. Second, a man should be allowed to claim the products of his own labor, thus guaranteeing incentives for him to work hard and well.

None of these principles were initially extended to anyone except adult male citizens. The notion that women should have a right to vote was thought preposterous. The idea that they should have control over their own decisions was also ruled out. Fathers had authority over daughters until they married. Once married, women were required to obey their husbands. Women exercised some choice over whom they would marry but a decision not to marry at all was impractical, given the restrictions on their access to education or well-paid work. As to the right of control over the products of their own labor—the main product of women's labor was children, and female control over grown sons would have violated men's presumed right to self-determination.[8]

In retrospect, this double standard seems as outrageous as it is inconsistent. At the time, however, it was justified by the claim that women's activities—primarily, caring for children and other dependents—did not amount to real work. Unlike men's activities, they did not involve the rational calculation of costs and benefits or responses to economic incentives. Rather, what women did was both instinctive and moral, performed for natural and God-given reasons. Women who declined to accept this responsibility were treated as unnatural and wicked.

Although such views were widely held, they were by no means universal. Early critics of the double standard pointed out that women seemed to be penalized, rather than rewarded, for assuming the responsibilities of motherhood. Mary Astell, a largely self-educated merchant's daughter who eked out a living for herself as a writer, issued in 1694 a salvo entitled *A Serious Proposal to the Ladies for the Advancement of Their True and Greatest Interest*. Astell played famously upon the inconsistencies of John Locke's theory, pointing out that it was a bit difficult to understand how, if kings had no God-given authority over their subjects, men could claim God-given authority over their wives.

She complained that men seemed to consider the nursing of children as low and despicable even though no activity deserved more honor, or greater thanks and rewards.[9] Astell located the source of women's subordination in their responsibilities for care: "Such the generous offices we do them: Such the ungenerous returns they make us."[10] About a hundred years later, Mary Wollstonecraft would pick up the argument in *A Vindication of the Rights of Women*. Few people realize that feminism as an intellectual tradition reaches to the beginnings of liberal political theory. It may not have received much attention or respect at the time, but it was present, foreshadowing things to come.

Adam, But Not Eve

As the scope for individual choice expanded, philosophers began to argue that selfishness served the greater good. Adam Smith is best known to us for offering, in *The Wealth of Nations*, the first systematic explanation of "trickle-down" theory. Encouraging men to pursue their own self-interest would, Smith argued, promote economic growth that would benefit everyone, and provide for those in need. "It is not from the benevolence of the butcher, the brewer, or the baker that we expect our dinner," he wrote, "but from regard to their self-interest."[11]

Just a minute. It is not usually the butcher, the brewer, or the baker who fixes dinner, but his wife or mother. Does she act out of self-interest too? Smith would have been horrified by the very idea. Self-interest was appropriate only to the impersonal world of the market. The moral sentiments, he believed, were firmly rooted in the family and the home. Smith considered all forms of labor that provided services to other people to be unproductive (though certainly not unimportant).

Thomas Robert Malthus was even less interested in the work that went into rearing the next generation and far more worried about the possibility of overpopulation. Like Smith, he was a great believer in the redemptive power of self-interest. Indeed, he went beyond Smith to argue that benevolence and charity toward others could have destructive effects. Specifically, he maintained that provision of public assistance to poor people would make them worse off, because this would prompt them to marry earlier and have—God help us all—more children. In the long run, the resulting increase in the supply of labor would push wages down and make poor families worse off. Men, he argued, should pursue their self-interest by delaying marriage.

But, Malthus argued, any effort to avoid births by using "the improper arts" would be unnatural and immoral. His injunctions against birth control applied nominally to both men and women but whether married or unmarried, men of Malthus's day had recourse to prostitutes and therefore a means of separating sex from reproduction.[12] And women, of course (whether prostitutes or not), were left with the responsibility for children if they became pregnant out of wedlock. The sexual double standard both reflected and reinforced the line drawn between the male world of self-interest and the female world of responsibility for care.

Some of Malthus's contemporaries bravely risked public censure by advocating birth control. But those who advocated forms of contraception that women could use, such as the vaginal sponge, faced particularly strong prosecution. At the age of seventeen, John Stuart Mill was arrested for handing out handbills on this subject. Later, inspired by the convictions of his deceased wife, Harriet Taylor, Mill wrote the most famous feminist tract of the nineteenth century, "On the Subjection of Women." In it, he argued not only that women were being deprived of equal rights, but also that they were being forced to assume disproportionate moral and economic responsibility for care:

> If women are better than men in anything, it surely is in individual self-sacrifice for those of their own family. But I lay little stress on this, so long as they are universally taught that they are born and created for self-sacrifice. I believe that equality of rights would abate the exaggerated self-abnegation which is the present artificial ideal of feminine character, and that a good woman would not be more self-sacrificing than the best man: but on the other hand, men would be much more unselfish and self-sacrificing than at present, because they would no longer be taught to worship their own will as such a grand thing that it is actually the law for another rational being.[13]

Mill was naive to think that such a transformation would automatically ensue; it never occurred to him that overall levels of self-sacrifice might decline. But he clearly recognized the links between gender, sub-ordination, and restrictions on self-interest. Though he failed to con-vince his contemporaries that women should be given equal rights, he laid a strong foundation for later, more successful efforts. And he cer-tainly encouraged many women to be clever as well as good.

Separate Spheres

In my family, the men took charge of making money while the women figured out ways to give it away. I remember my mother, a restless housewife, taking on sizable responsibilities for the local Junior League, the United Fund, and the Girl Scouts. She died of cancer when I was eighteen, and my father remarried about a year later. My second mom was a high-powered businesswoman who helped start a small manufac-turing firm, but lost interest once it was bought out by a multinational corporation. She then turned her attention and her energy to running a local San Antonio philanthropy.

The family that my father worked for had a similar division of labor. Mr. Mac's aunt, Leta McFarlin Chapman, grew up in a small Texas town named Pecan Grove where she attended school with a number of Na-tive Americans. She always claimed that the experience had given her a lifelong concern for minority groups and underprivileged people in general. Over her lifetime, she gave well over a hundred million dollars to churches, colleges, and hospitals—far exceeding her nephew's gen-erosity.

The notion that women should be more altruistic than men has a long history. In the nineteenth century, it became a virtual obsession. The growth of capitalism increased the scope of impersonal exchange, par-ticularly the sale of labor power to strangers in return for wages. This process created enormous apprehensions. Would society become so atomistic, so competitive, so individualistic that it would fall apart? Conservatives like Edmund Burke urged a return to feudal principles of respect for royal and paternal authority. Socialists like Robert Owen be-gan to imagine new forms of social organization based on the family writ large, in which men and women would work together as brothers and sisters.[14]

A more common response to apprehension about the growth of markets was the romanticization of family life. By devoting themselves to their husbands and children, women could hold civilization together. In both Britain and the United States, a burgeoning literature of domesticity explained how women could become angels of the home. No one painted a more panoramic view of this process than Catherine Beecher and Harriet Beecher Stowe, whose 1869 book *The American Woman's Home* became so popular that it remained a textbook for my own grandmother's generation.

The Beecher sisters sought to create home as a haven in a heartless world. Women's greatest mission, they argued, is "self-denial."[15] They didn't believe that women were innately altruistic, but rather that they were destined to preserve the values of the home so threatened by the impersonal business world. "A man that has been drawn from the social ties at home and has spent his life in the collisions of the world," Catherine Beecher explained, "seldom escapes without the most confirmed habits of cold and revolting selfishness."[16] Only a devoted wife and mother could civilize such a man and buffer the disruptive effects of competition on society as a whole.[17]

The Beecher sisters focused on women's moral obligations. Other advocates of this "separate spheres" approach recognized the need to ensure that women would not be distracted from their historical mission. In the late nineteenth century the famous English economist Alfred Marshall praised the efficiency of the forces of supply and demand in the labor market—as far as men were concerned. He explicitly warned that higher wages for women in the labor market might tempt them to neglect their duties as wives and mothers.[18] As a professor at Cambridge he opposed admitting women to study for degrees because they might become more preoccupied with developing their own capabilities than those of their future children.[19] He attributed the declining birth rate in England—which he considered a serious problem—to "women's selfish desire to resemble men."[20]

The separate spheres doctrine was appealing to economists for a variety of reasons. It relieved them of the responsibility for analyzing love and altruism, while reiterating their principles of morality. It excused them from considering the economics of family life, without suggesting that this aspect of life was unimportant. Most conveniently, the separate spheres doctrine helped men explain just why they should be self-interested, while women should be altruistic. It was, for them, a comfortable way of seeking the best of both worlds.

Reproductive Rights and Wrongs

In late nineteenth-century Britain, it was not difficult for men to separate sex from fatherhood. Prostitution was more than legal: it was regulated by the government, which, trying to reduce the number of cases of venereal disease, required regular medical examinations of prostitutes.

Much of the social resistance to contraception came from a fear of what would happen if women were allowed to separate sex from motherhood. Sex, after all, was about personal pleasure; motherhood was about responsibility.

In London in 1877, Annie Besant and Charles Bradlaugh printed a tract that included advice on birth control. They were promptly prosecuted for obscenity and, while they got off on a technicality, others who followed their example went to jail. In the United States, the 1873 Comstock Law made it illegal to ship any information or devices that could be used to prevent conception. The first application of the law came with the incarceration of the feminist activist Victoria Woodhull, an event that effectively ended her political career.[21] More than forty years later, Margaret Sanger, considered the pioneer of family planning in this country, was jailed under the same law.

Even more significant than legal and political efforts to repress contraceptive information and technology were the moral exhortations to women to have more children. Concern about fertility decline among the educated women of the upper classes prompted anxiety about "the future of the race." Authorities in Britain proclaimed that the Empire was at stake. If the number of cradles did not exceed the number of coffins, civilization itself might be imperiled. Petitions were circulated stipulating that only women who had borne at least four children should be allowed the vote. In the United States, President Teddy Roosevelt complained that Anglo-Saxon women's selfish desire to limit motherhood was weakening the nation. Women's emancipation is a great thing, he conceded, but immediately added that it shouldn't be taken too far.[22]

Advocates of birth control did more than argue for sex education and legalized contraception. They also insisted that women should pursue their own self-interest because voluntary—rather than mandatory—motherhood was better for everyone. Margaret Sanger regarded birth control as the key to reconciling the larger social conflict between altruistic commitment and individual autonomy. In retrospect, she was over-optimistic. That conflict remains with us today. If anything, it has intensified.

Crybabies

The last two decades of the twentieth century witnessed a conservative backlash against feminism, driven by a fear that women were becoming less altruistic. Rush Limbaugh panics at the thought of women acting in their own self-interest, explaining that women's jobs are to "establish enduring values that are crucial to the continuation of mankind."[23] George Gilder proclaims that the beautiful thing about femininity is its "civilizing" influence.[24] Allan Bloom argues that the American mind is doomed unless men take responsibility for achievement, and women take responsibility for care.[25] It's quite flattering, really, until you realize the dimensions of the burden. Civilization in not entirely women's responsibility.

This kind of conservatism demeans men by assuming that they can't possibly help out. The argument seems to be that women must not stop behaving in traditional ways, because men are incapable of offering more love and tenderness. The sacrifice of mothers—but not fathers—is held forth as an imitation of Christ. Conservative activist Connie Marshner asks: "How can we possibly imitate the Creator in our relationships if we can't learn from our mothers to give of ourselves, to offer ourselves in love to another, and to control our fleshly impulses for the sake of another?"[26] Marshner wants women to be more unselfish than men—a double standard that seems inconsistent with her own Christian ideals.

Much of the rage about abortion reflects a larger anxiety about maternal care. According to the so-called pro-life perspective, women shouldn't have a choice to care or not to care for a developing fetus. From the so-called pro-choice perspective, such a choice is crucial to the meaning as well as the quality of caring. Anti-abortion activists are often explicit in their attacks on what they consider female selfishness. As one doctor put it, "I think women's lib is on the wrong track. I think they've got every [possible] gripe and they've always been that way. The women have been the superior people. They're more civilized, they're more unselfish by nature, but now they want to compete with men at being selfish. And so there's nobody to give an example, and what happens is that men become more selfish."[27] Here's that anxiety again, that fear that men simply can't be altruistic unless women are more so.

In 1993, a journalist named Barbara Dafoe Whitehead wrote an article entitled "Dan Quayle Was Right."[28] The brouhaha started when then–Vice President Quayle criticized an episode of the television show *Murphy Brown* in which the heroine, played by Candice Bergen, decided to have a child out of wedlock. Never mind that the child had actually been conceived while Murphy was married to his father. Television was undermining family values by sanctioning divorce and holding a single mother up as a positive role model. Whitehead took up Quayle's campaign on a more serious intellectual level, arguing that public policy should explicitly discourage divorce and births out of wedlock.

She told a joke that pretty well captures the fear our society feels about the loss of feminine altruism. Two female praying mantises are having a conversation in the garden. The first one says, "It's tough being a single parent, tougher than I thought." "Yeah," says the second. "Maybe we shouldn't have eaten our husbands after all." The lesson is that women should stop being bloodthirsty feminists and return to our traditional self-sacrificing roles as wives and mothers. While we're at it, maybe we should also ask for a big pay cut as child care workers, secretaries, nurses, and teachers. That way, we could help out in the business world as well as at home.

Conservatives love to tell mothers that they should continue to be unselfish nurturers.[29] But few seem to worry about encouraging unselfish nurturance outside the home, or reducing poverty among other people's children. Greed is good, especially for guys. Rush Limbaugh calls people who disagree "liberal compassion fascists."[30] Once Mom and Dad go to work, efficiency should rule. Want to improve the bottom line? Lay off some employees. Family values? Leave them at home.[31]

The cultural debate over feminism is at bottom a debate about the meaning of family values. Conservative activists like Beverley LaHaye offer a narrow definition: "Family values is a married mother and father and children. It is passionately pro-life, virulently anti-homosexual, hostile to feminists. Period."[32] Most Americans disagree. In a 1995 poll, a majority of women defined family values broadly as "loving, taking care of, and supporting each other." Only 2 percent felt it meant "family coming first."[33]

The same poll asked men and women what social issues they were worried about, allowing them to choose among the following categories: people not caring for others; health care; whether education can prepare young people for the future; domestic violence; the increasing number of poor people. More women than men—70 percent compared to 52 percent—put top priority on people not caring for others.[34] Still, a clear majority was worrying about a problem that neither Adam Smith nor Alfred Marshall nor any other economist has ever considered significant. Family values are inconsistent with the principle that greed is good for everyone except Mom.

—————————◆—————————

The contemporary attempt at a solution to the cultural contradictions of motherhood is to ideologically separate the world of motherhood from the larger social world and therefore make women responsible for unselfish nurturing while men are responsible for self-interested profit maximization.

— SHARON HAYS,
The Cultural Contradictions of Motherhood

—————————◆—————————

Trucks versus Dolls

In an era of rapid social change it is genuinely difficult to define our values. Feminists have long struggled with a dilemma framed as "equality" versus "difference." Should women concentrate on attaining success in male terms, demanding the right to compete? Or should women value the qualities that make them different from men and try to reduce the ways in which society penalizes femininity? Liberal feminists have often fought for the right to behave in more masculine ways. Social feminists have often fought for rules that would require men to take on more traditionally feminine responsibilities both within the family and beyond.

In the United States, at least, a liberal and highly individualist form of feminism has prevailed. Everybody has heard of "Take-Your-Daughter-to-Work Day," an event promoted by the Ms. Foundation to encourage young women to think about their careers. No one has ever heard of "Teach-Your-Son-How-to-Babysit Day." Even women who earn considerably more than their husbands seldom persuade their guys to put more hours into family work. Highly educated women are moving into traditionally masculine professions. But men recognize that moving into traditionally female occupations would probably entail a significant loss of pay and status. It takes courage and conviction for a man to go to nursing school.

Our culture continues to define care in feminine terms. Perhaps as a result, many women feel uncomfortable with the notion that masculine ideals are somehow better than feminine ones. It's a view that has been nicely summarized by a bumper sticker: "Women who want to be as good as men lack ambition." Some people think that girls should be encouraged to play with blocks and trucks rather than dolls, the better to compete with boys. But as one reader put it in a letter to the *New York Times*, "If we continue to promote 'rewardable' skills over those related to nurturing, who's going to take care of us when we're too old, young or sick to be out pursuing rewards?"[35]

Of course, if women are going to pursue this strategy, we must ourselves continue to play with dolls. And that is a risky business. A lot of feminist economists are downright opposed to it. "I just don't see any good evidence for the 'difference' perspective," says Myra Strober of Stanford University. "It glorifies existing stereotypes of female behavior." Barbara Bergmann of American University strongly opposes any efforts to count housework as part of the Gross Domestic Product, one proposal for valuing a "different" kind of contribution: "Anything that romanticizes housework and childcare," she growls, "is bad for women."[36] Strober and Bergmann are right—unless and until we can distribute responsibilities for care more equally and reward caring more generously. The challenge for social feminists is to show how we might do this—in practice as well as in theory.

Sharing Care

There is nothing natural or inevitable about the way we associate femininity with altruism. Most fathers also care for their children. They change diapers, get up in the night to warm their babies' bottles, and go to work to earn the money to buy the milk and bicycles and computers their children need. Nowadays fathers are being encouraged to play a more direct role. Sharing care for children, however, is not enough. Other dependents, including the sick and the elderly, require attention. Most adults need to be cared for in the emotional sense, even if not in the economic sense of relying on another to take responsibility for them. Our need for love may ebb and flow, but sometimes it comes in tidal waves. As the biologist Franz de Waal explains, "Absorption of parental care into adult human relationships is evident from the widespread use of infantile names (such as 'baby') for mates and lovers. . . ."[37] Traditionally, scientists have drawn a sharp distinction between altruism toward kin and toward non-kin.[38] More recently, they have begun to argue there is a continuum, rather than a gulf.[39] Kinship, after all, is a relative concept. Human beings share a common genetic heritage. Altruism toward immediate kin fosters altruism toward others who are less closely related. We are often altruistic toward our mates, who share responsibility for our actual or potential offspring. Our brothers, sisters, nephews, and nieces, as well as our children, share our genes and will combine them with those of other people when they have children of their own. Kin-based altruism reinforces our concerns about the future. Worrying about the future impels us to worry about those who will inhabit it, alongside our immediate kin.

Emotional connections to other people reinforce reciprocity and trust. Groups that elicit solidarity from their members may be able to out-compete those that don't. Organizations often refer to their members as symbolic kin. Feminists appeal to a larger concept of "sisterhood." Trade union members, like fraternities and sororities, frequently refer to each other as "brothers and sisters." Patriots vow to love the mother country or the fatherland, and so on.

Empathy for other people is a powerful force—so powerful, in fact, that we often take steps to avoid letting it develop.[40] Is empathy a siren song? According to Greek mythology, Odysseus knew that his boat would be passing by the island of the sirens, whose beautiful voices tempted sailors to hurl themselves into the surf and approach them, only to be dashed against the rocks. A famously wise man, he filled his sailors' ears with wax to deafen them, but devised a way to safely listen to the music himself. He instructed his sailors to bind him to the mast and to refuse to release him until the boat had passed the island. The preemptive measure protected him against loss of self-control as he swooned with pleasure from the song.

Maybe Homer misleads us. Maybe the surf is not so dangerous after all. Maybe the sailors could use a bit of a swim, and seeing the sirens face to face would make Odysseus a better man. We might want to listen for the music—even turn up the volume—instead of shutting it out. There are ways of encouraging empathy for others, rather than trying to repress it. To come back to the gendered double standard: if we can reinforce caring behavior in women, we can also reinforce it in men. Doing so, however, will be costly. That's why we need some good economists on the case.

◆

Instead of importing into the household principles from the marketplace, perhaps we should export to the wider society the relations suitable for mothering persons and children.

> —VIRGINIA HELD,
> "Mothering versus Contract" in Jane J. Mansbridge, ed.,
> *Beyond Self-Interest*

◆

Unacceptable Choices

Many feminists have fought patriarchy with individualism, demanding new rights for women and conducting a process of consciousness-raising that has encouraged women to become more assertive. That the results can be uncomfortable and inconvenient for men is obvious. It is becoming increasingly apparent that there can also be some negative consequences for dependents, such as children, the sick, and the elderly. Patriarchy was not simply a means of privileging men. It was also a means of ensuring an adequate supply of care. By increasing the pressure on women to be altruistic toward members of their families and communities, it helped to minimize the retaliatory logic that can lead to the War of All Against All.

We cannot base our critique of impersonal market-based society on some romantic vision of a past society as one big happy family. In that family, Big Daddy was usually in control. Today, patriarchal coercion is unacceptable. On the other hand, pure selfish individualism is both ugly and unviable. Without at least some altruism, we cannot reproduce ourselves. If we believe we have obligations to care for one another, we should decide what these are and how they should be enforced. Since we can't depend entirely on human nature and/or divine assistance, some rewards and punishments will probably be required. The milk of human kindness does not flow from some natural, inexhaustible source. Nor is it produced according to the laws of supply and demand.

THE CARE PENALTY

Once upon a time, some very powerful goddesses decided to sponsor a competition, a kind of Olympics, among the nations of the world. They agreed to award a wonderful prize—health and prosperity for all—to the nation that could collectively run the greatest distance in a set period of time. This was not an ordinary race, in which the distance was set and the winner was the runner who took the shortest time, but rather a contest to see which society, acting as a team, could move all its members forward.

Each nation that decided to compete had a giant scoreboard placed in the sky to count up all the miles traveled per person. But the goddesses did not tell them how long the race would last—the participants had to guess. When the starting gun went off, one nation assumed that the race would not last long. Its leaders urged all citizens to start running as quickly as possible. It was every person for themself. Very soon, of course, the young children and the elderly fell behind, but none of the front runners stopped to help them; that would have slowed them down.

At first, those who were out in front were exhilarated by their success. As the race continued, however, some of them became tired or hurt and fell by the wayside. Gradually all the runners grew exhausted or sick, and, with no one to replace them, began to realize that they would lose. Attention turned to a second nation, one that had adopted a slightly different strategy. The leaders of this nation sent all their young men, the fastest runners, out ahead to compete, but required all the women to come along behind, carrying the children, the sick, and the elderly, and caring for any runners who needed help. They explained to the women that this was a natural and efficient arrangement, from which everyone would benefit. Oh yes, one incentive offered to men for running fast was the reward of authority and power over the women.

At first, this seemed to work. But then the women found out that they could run just as fast as the men, provided they were not burdened with extra responsibilities. They began to argue that the work they were doing—caring for the runners—was every bit as important as the running itself and that they deserved equal rights. The men (whose brains may have been impaired by the stress of running) found this claim ridiculous. "What incentive," they asked, "would men have to run, if they couldn't stay in charge?" The women looked at one another, then went out on strike. Chaos ensued. Eventually it became clear that this nation too was losing the race.

Now everyone looked to a third nation, which, like the tortoise in competition with the hare, was making slow but persistent progress. Its strategy was different: everyone was required both to run and to take care of those who could not run. Both men and women were urged to compete, to run as fast as possible; but the rules required them to carry equal shares of the weight of care. Jogging with a heavy load, these citizens became strong as well as fast. Their freedom and equality fostered their solidarity. Of course they won the race. What did you expect? It was a race that goddesses designed.

I've told this story to many different kinds of people. Some say it's a utopian fairy tale, because the ending is way too happy. Some say there's truth to it, because long-term sustainability matters more than short-term success. Still others say that offering a prize is the same as paying a bribe, and that competition and compassion are not at all compatible. This last response is the one I disagree with most. Competitors prefer to offload their responsibilities onto others. That doesn't mean we can't discourage them from doing so. In any case, the moral of the story is much simpler: short-term strategies don't necessarily lead to long-term success.

This maxim may seem obvious. But few students in introductory economics classes have ever heard of it. They are instructed, as per Adam Smith, to pursue their own self-interest because everyone will benefit as a result. Not surprisingly, economics students tend to express more selfish attitudes than do others.[1] At the other extreme, students in introductory ethics classes are introduced to a long philosophical tradition of defining right and wrong in abstract terms, with more attention paid to motives than to costs.

Combining care with competition requires combining ethics with economics. In general, people want to do the right thing. But whether we like it or not, our evolution as a species has programmed us to take into account the cost of doing the right thing. If our ancestors hadn't been sufficiently worried about this, we wouldn't be here today. If we don't worry about it, our kids won't be here tomorrow. This much we've known for a long time. What's new is that our evolutionary context is changing. We are no longer simply responding to the pressures of our natural environment. We are creating a new economic environment, a new social ecology. Individualistic competition for wealth offers no rewards for the work of care.

This chapter explains why. It begins with a discussion of the Nice Person's Dilemma—the worry that opportunists will take advantage of those who are generous and cooperative. Such risks are probably reduced when people know and care for one another, but they are never entirely eliminated. Part of the problem can be traced to the very nature of caring for other people. It is difficult to gauge its quality or measure its effects—partly because these have important emotional as well as physical dimensions. Caregiving is inherently risky, because it is difficult to capture or claim the effects, which are embodied in people who cannot be contractually bound to pay them back. Caregiving produces many unintended side effects, benefits that are passed on from person to person in surprising and complicated ways. The difficulty of capturing or claiming the rewards of care is one of the reasons why communities—whether local, state, national, or international—play a crucial role in stabilizing market economies. And it is one of the reasons why market economies can have the effect of undermining the very families and communities they depend upon in the long run.

Reciprocity and Contracts

Biologists have a good explanation of the risks of altruism toward non-kin. A kind and generous creature who gives up some of its own resources in order to help another, unrelated creature reduces the resources available for its own offspring. But its own offspring are the ones carrying the genes for kindness and generosity. Altruistic genes, it seems, suffer a competitive disadvantage. Now, this kind and generous creature is not necessarily dumb. It may correctly calculate that there are benefits to altruism if other creatures reciprocate. But what if they lie, cheat, steal, or simply fail to cooperate? If altruists can't distinguish selfish opportunists from fellow altruists, the selfish opportunists will generally win.[2]

The same risks operate, though not as forcefully, on altruism toward kin. Sociobiologists argue that a male who wants to propagate as many as possible of his own genes as possible will try to impregnate many females while minimizing demands on his own resources. In some environments, this strategy will backfire, because without committed assistance from a father, the offspring will not survive. In some environments, however, mothers may be able to raise offspring without paternal assistance, and they may find it difficult, if not impossible, to tell the good dads from the bad dads (at least, ahead of time). In these situations the bad dads' genes are likely to prevail.

If the altruists could all get together and exclude the opportunists, or if the women could identify the men likely to be bad fathers and send them packing, altruism would be rewarded. The problem comes from mimicry, the wolf in sheep's clothing. Neither the general altruists nor the good dads are clearly labeled, so how can they be identified? Economist Robert Frank points out that emotions offer a cue: people can't turn them on and off at will, and often find it difficult to conceal them.[3] If someone persuades you that he or she loves you, you're more likely to trust and care for him or her. Unfortunately, as any jilted lover will tell you, emotions are not only hard to read but also too volatile to rely on.

Another risk to good behavior comes from the difficulty of enforcing reciprocity. Here, we humans have an advantage over most other creatures because we can make explicit agreements: "If I give you X, you will give me Y." This kind of reciprocity is what markets are all about. However, some such agreements are more difficult to enforce than others. If both parties know exactly what they are giving and what they are getting—so that the exchange is transparent—then both are likely to be pleased with whatever exchange they agree on.

This is what economists have in mind when they emphasize the efficiency of competitive markets. They work particularly well when products are standardized, their quality easy to ascertain. We put seventy-five cents in a vending machine, and we trust we'll get a soda in return. Of course, things can go wrong, even here. Now and again, the vending machine takes our money and doesn't deliver the goods. In this situation, we often feel justified in giving it a kick. These machines, however, are engineered to work well (and to withstand a certain frequency of kicks) precisely because they won't keep making money unless they do.

Things are a lot more complicated when we buy something less standardized. Appearances can be deceptive. When we buy a car or a computer, we know that something could go wrong with it (probably the day after the warranty has expired). We are taking a risk. Knowing that the seller has a good reputation and a vested interest in future sales that depends on maintaining that reputation helps minimize this risk.[4] We further lower our risk by buying a brand we trust, or by sticking with a well-respected business that will stand by its products. In this situation, abstractions like trust and respect—which are left out of introductory economics textbooks—become important.

Not all things we buy bear brand names. Sometimes we get involved in transactions with individuals or businesses—as when we hire accountants or lawyers—where the quality of future services is hard to guarantee. They could take our money up front and then do a sloppy job. But by the time we figure this out, it could be too late to void the transaction. In this situation, we tend to ask for personal advice from people we know we can rely on. We have more confidence in the invisible hand of the market if it is joined by an invisible handshake that conveys not only trust but good will. A long-term personal relationship improves the efficiency of the short-term transaction.

On the other hand, personal relationships do not guarantee reciprocity. Consider the contract called marriage, which is based on a formal agreement between two people to love and care for one another. This agreement sometimes breaks down. Some aspects of it can be made indissoluble. For instance, laws can specify that a person who marries one person can never marry another unless his or her first spouse dies. Laws can specify that two married people are mutually responsible for economic support, and must share their property. Laws cannot, however, and do not specify exactly how two people should cooperate and collaborate within a marriage.[5] Moreover, laws cannot require that one person love another.

Some services—especially those that have personal and emotional content—simply cannot be bought and sold. Contracts for these services often take an implicit rather than explicit form, making them difficult to enforce. Therefore, the provision of these services is inherently risky (at least, for people who don't have confidence in a hereafter in which all the accounts of love are balanced). If you love someone, you can never be sure they will love you back. If you care for your daughter, you can never be sure that when she grows up, she will reciprocate. If you offer kindness to a stranger, you can never be sure that you will be offered kindness in return.

Perhaps none of these services would be offered if they were based on rational cost-benefit decisions. But emotion and reason are not always as separate as they are assumed to be. Most people pay attention to the possible costs of developing affection for others. We are all dimly aware of subtle ways in which rewards and penalties may shape our feelings, as well as our rational decisions. We think about the ways in which our feelings might affect certain formal contracts, and we also think about the ways certain formal contracts might affect our feelings.

Affection can encourage reciprocity, and vice versa. Both, however, remain vulnerable to the temptations of defection.

The Nice Person's Dilemma

Economists have a parable that emphasizes the difficulties of cooperation. It is called the Prisoner's Dilemma. Two men who have committed a crime are swiftly apprehended by the police. They are taken to separate interrogation rooms. The prosecutor doesn't have enough evidence to convict either without a confession. If both suspects deny any involvement in the crime, they could get off free. Each man knows that his best strategy is denial, if he can be sure that the other will do the same. Each has promised, ahead of time, never to rat on his pal.

But is there honor among thieves? The risk is obvious. Once nailed by the police, the suspect in the other room may opt for an opportunistic strategy, telling everything he knows in return for a short, suspended sentence. An individual who remains loyal while his partner defects suffers the greatest penalty. The cops know this and do everything they can to sow seeds of doubt. The prisoners lose faith in one another and confess at the same time. Both go to jail without any credit for helping condemn the other. From the cops' point of view, it's the best possible outcome. From the prisoners' point of view it's the worst possible outcome. The opportunistic strategy, which entails breaking a promise, ends up making both prisoners worse off.

The economist Amartya Sen has long argued that the Prisoner's Dilemma is really misnamed, because it applies to many situations that have nothing to do with crime, situations in which everyone would benefit from cooperation, but is afraid that someone else will defect or cheat.[6] An arms agreement is an obvious example, or an effort to protect a common resource, such as a fish population. These agreements work only if everyone cooperates. For students, the best example is a study group. They can have more fun and get more done by collaborating, but they feel ripped off when some people show up just to copy down what the others have figured out.

We could call it the Nice Person's Dilemma. A person does something to help another person. If the other reciprocates, both will end up better off; if not, the nice person loses. Nice gals and guys finish last. It has long been observed that such dilemmas are easier to resolve among people who know each other well than among strangers. Many communities come up with pretty effective ways of governing access to common resources.[7] Identification with a community is important because it encourages members to care about others in the group, emphasizing their common interests and restricting their contact with outsiders.

A kind of virtuous circle comes into play. Efforts to increase the probability of cooperation increase the payoff to it. As Jane Mansbridge puts it in her classic essay, "On the Relation of Altruism and Self-Interest,"

> Arrangements that generate some self-interest return to unselfish behavior create an "ecological niche" that helps sustain that unselfish behavior. Arrangements that make unselfishness less costly in narrowly self-interested terms increase the degree to which individuals feel they can afford to indulge their feelings of empathy and their moral commitments, as well as their readiness to foster empathy and moral commitments in their children.[8]

The big question is how such "ecological niches" for unselfishness are established and defended. Biologists explore similar concerns when they consider the ways in which groups or teams, rather than individuals, may compete. In some circumstances, the group or team with the highest level of cooperation is likely to win.[9]

Both biologists and economists tend to assume that solidarity and generosity are completely natural within families. As the previous chapter emphasized, however, there was nothing natural about rules and laws that forced women to specialize in family care. Now that women have gained rights similar to those of men, they are entering a world in which they have more freedom to consider the penalties imposed on unselfish behavior.

Consider the Good Parent's Dilemma. Two people decide to rear a child, but one of them makes more sacrifices than the other. Usually it's the mother who agrees to take time away from her career to stay home with the baby, and to move wherever the father's career dictates, so he can earn money to support the family. "Later on," she might say, "it will be my turn. We'll put *my* career first, and *you* can be the Good Parent." Sometimes, this implicit agreement works just fine. Sometimes it doesn't, because it involves one of those aspects of the marriage contract that is not enforceable by law. The only thing the Good Parent can do if the other parent refuses to take their turn is to end the relationship, which can have unpleasant consequences for both parents and children.[10]

This risk of default on an implicit agreement is not limited to couple dynamics. It also faces parents in their relationships with their children, which also involve an implicit contract: we take care of you, and when you're grown you will take care of us—if and when we really need your help. Most children respect this implicit contract, though teenagers have been heard to mutter "I didn't ask to be born into this family." They're right, of course. Precisely because they feel they have not been given an individual choice, some adult children default on responsibilities to parents. If and when that happens, there's not much parents can do about it unless they have enough wealth to threaten disinheritance.[11]

Fairness and Care

Individual decisions are made in a social context. What we want and how we will behave is strongly affected by our perceptions of what other people want and how they are likely to behave. Moral values and social norms probably evolved because they encourage cooperative behavior that is productive in the long run. Norms of fairness and reciprocity are surprisingly robust.

Economists have developed an experiment that illustrates their impact. You can play it with your friends more easily than most card games. Take two people aside and give one of them ten one-dollar bills. The person with the cash is required to make a take-it-or-leave-it offer to share part of this money with the other person. If the other person accepts the offer, they both can keep the amounts agreed upon. If the other person refuses the offer, however, the money must be returned. For instance, if I start out with the cash, I might offer you three dollars. If you accept, you get three and I get seven. If you refuse, neither of us gets anything.

It's called an "ultimatum game." Where a windfall is concerned— money that wasn't earned or deserved in any way—most people think that a fifty/fifty split is fair. Furthermore, a significant percentage will turn down a less-than-equal offer, even though this leaves them worse off than they would have been had they accepted. In the example above, many will turn down the three dollars offered, on the grounds that it is unfair. They want a fair share, or they want nothing at all, as if they intend to punish those who offer less.

When I have conducted this experiment in my own classes, students have been skeptical, insisting that there would be less concern for fairness if larger—and actual—amounts of money were involved. As one cynic put it, "You should change the ten dollars to ten million and watch the fairness freaks crumble." But ultimatum games have been conducted in many different places, and under many different conditions, with very large sums of money. The results are remarkably consistent.[12]

Most of the economists who conduct such experiments are interested in the way people think strategically. I am more interested in how the players feel. Does concern for other people's welfare affect perception of their own payoff? Think back to the Nice Person's Dilemma. If you love the person you are helping, then you are less likely to be inhibited by fear that you will be ripped off.

But love, affection, and connection are aspects of the cooperation game that experimental economists have largely neglected.[13] Consider the maxim traditionally known as the golden rule: "Do unto others as you would have them do unto you." This is not exactly a rule of reciprocity. It's a rule of empathy. It asks you to think about what it would *feel* like to be in the other person's situation. It is related to another prescription for altruism: "Love thy neighbor as thyself." In this context, it matters whether or not you actually know who your neighbors are. It also matters how much choice you have in determining who they will be. Some neighbors, after all, may be more lovable than others.

Care Trends

Ideas emerging over the past forty years from the economics of contracts and game theory offer a way of reframing some traditional concerns about increasing the scope of individual choice in competitive markets. Social critics like Karl Polanyi have long warned that the growth of market-like behavior, including the increased legitimacy of shopping around, might encourage selfish calculation.[14] One could say that the habits of our hearts are changing. Many scholars today argue that we are experiencing a decline of civic virtue and public commitment.[15]

Social norms of care may be more fragile than norms of reciprocity. The process of economic development seems to lead to a decline in the importance of close personal relationships. Residential mobility goes up as we become more oriented to our jobs. As career mobility increases, we become less loyal to particular firms. As divorce rates go up, personal commitments become less binding. The implications of such trends are difficult to assess. We don't have good measures of what is happening to selfishness over time, and it's hard to imagine how we could monitor it. Furthermore, when many things happen at once, it's hard to untangle their separate effects. Our culture has almost certainly become more materialistic. However, we enjoy much higher standards of living, including health and longevity, than we used to. As we become more affluent, perhaps we shall become more charitable. Adam Smith believed that we would become, at least, more civilized. I haven't seen much evidence of this, but I've not yet given up hope.

Another possibility is that different forms of community are evolving. Most of my academic friends connect with people who are researching similar issues, rather than those who live next door. My parents had a dense network of friends who lived nearby and provided them with close support. I don't, but I do have a geographically diffuse network of friends I stay in touch with through e-mail, conferences, and meetings. Although I don't have children, I devote a lot of time and effort to mentoring students.

We tend to think of altruism and self-interest as opposites; but they often go together. Team sports require individuals to cooperate in order to compete. Commitment to others within our own family, group, or nation enables us to pursue our collective self-interest at the expense of others.

It's easy to say that we should all be more altruistic. It's much harder to explain exactly how we should distribute our altruism. To return to the parable of the race—just whom should we be carrying along? The whole story of the race was based on the assumption that the nation was the unit of analysis, the "team." This is not a good assumption (as I will show in chapter 8).

Another reason to be cautious about generalizations is that it is possible to become more generous about some things and less generous about others. For instance, we can become more charitable with money, but less charitable with time. Such trends could balance each other out. For these reasons, and others, I hesitate to make strong claims about historical trends in altruism, or goodness, or trust—or even honor among thieves. I'm more worried about a smaller but still quite significant subset of concerns: competitive pressures that penalize those who devote resources to the care of dependents, such as children and the elderly.

The Costs of Parenthood

In an economy in which rewards are increasingly based on performance in paid employment, the costs and risks of parenthood are going up.[16] The direct costs of raising children—food, clothing, diapers, medical care, a bigger house, education—are the easiest to quantify. These generally increase along with family income because parents usually spend a percentage of their income on kids, rather than a flat amount. Parents today tend to spend more than they used to because they recognize the increased impact that educational credentials will have on their children's success. More and more young people are seeking university and postgraduate degrees. Partly as a result, they often remain at least somewhat dependent on their parents well past the age of eighteen.

Parenting imposes indirect as well as direct costs. Children affect virtually every decision parents make—where to live, how to spend time, what kinds of jobs to choose. Parents often give up potential income when they decide to cut back on their hours of paid work in order to spend time at home with their children. The effects are bigger than you might think because in today's labor market, taking time out from paid employment tends to hurt career chances and lower future earnings. The larger the potential salary, the greater the potential losses.

If mothers and fathers live together, they share the burden of reduced market income. In fact, fathers may work longer hours on their jobs to make up for it. But today, many women are raising children on their own (about a third of children are born out of wedlock). Plus, the risks of separation and divorce are high (about one-half of marriages are projected to end in divorce).[17] Child-support agreements are difficult to negotiate and even more difficult to enforce. Women who choose to become mothers risk making themselves and their children vulnerable to poverty and other kinds of economic stress.[18]

Whether they actually become mothers or not, women who take time out of the paid labor market to devote themselves full-time to meeting the needs of family members accumulate less labor market experience and earn less money than men with comparable levels of education. As long as she is happily married, a housewife is normally compensated by receiving a share of her husband's income. But if her marriage crumbles or her husband dies, she is left vulnerable. And even if she remains married, her fear of being left to fend for herself may put her in a weak, even subservient, position in the home.[19]

Statistical analysis shows that motherhood tends to lower women's earnings even if they don't take much time out from paid work. The more children a woman has, the less she earns, even if she works the same amount of time and remains with one employer for the same length of time as a childless woman.[20] A number of factors could explain this: employers could have a bias against hiring or promoting mothers; alternatively, mothers might consciously or unconsciously behave in ways that signal less commitment to their careers. What is interesting is that the numbers show exactly the opposite effect for fathers: having children tends to increase men's earnings.

Biological differences in themselves are less important than the tendency that mothers have to take more personal responsibility for children and other dependents, which puts them in a weak position. Even if a woman starts out in a perfectly equal relationship with her spouse or partner, that equality is likely to erode over time. Individuals who specialize in providing care don't control the products of their labor. They acquire valuable experience, but it's not the kind of experience that an employer will pay for.

In the beginning of my course, The Political Economy of Women, I ask students to fill out a survey designed to start them thinking about their present and future earnings. The overwhelming majority of women express no doubt that they will, at age forty, earn the same amount of money as men with similar educational credentials. Yet they also plan to have two children, and (unlike the men in the same class) they plan to take time out from their careers in order to raise them. When I point out that something is wrong with their calculations they aren't entirely surprised. But they seem almost embarrassed by having to consider the issue.

———◆———

> Of course, large numbers of well-meaning moms and dads may still elect to invest large quantities of money and time in child-raising, but for the first time in history their loving energies are not reinforced by enlightened self-interest. Instead, they must rely entirely on large reserves of altruistic love—large enough to last for more than two decades per child. This is a tall order in a society that venerates the market.
>
> —SYLVIA ANN HEWLETT AND CORNEL WEST,
> *The War Against Parents: What We Can Do for America's Beleaguered Moms and Dads*

———◆———

The Costs of Elder Care

Most people can exercise some choice over whether or not to rear children. And certainly it could be argued that we'd be better off in some ways if other people had fewer kids—up to a point. But the same penalties I've described above apply to the care of individuals at the other end of the dependency spectrum. We live in a society in which most of the elderly enjoy an economic safety net known as Social Security. However, many elderly people (especially women) continue to live in poverty and suffer from health problems that require face-to-face hands-on assistance. Money alone, in any case, does not meet their personal and emotional needs. We expect responsible adults to tend to, if not directly care for, their parents and other elderly relatives.

This expectation, however, is not backed up by any economic or legal sanctions, except where the elderly in question control financial assets and can use the promise of a bequest to reward their children's behavior. Sadly, economic research shows that strategic calculations seem to have a small but significant effect on adult children's behavior.[21] A more significant factor, however, is the extent of love, obligation, and reciprocity among family members.

Deciding how to allocate responsibilities for care of an elderly person who needs personal assistance is not easy. Siblings often disagree about who should do what for Mom or Dad. A Good Child's Dilemma comes into play. The first person who volunteers to provide assistance may be stuck with the job forever.

In my own family, things worked out remarkably well. My father cared for my mother when she was stricken with cancer of the pancreas. After she died, he remarried, and when his wife later succumbed to a serious illness, he cared for her, too. The McFarlin Oil Company never offered my father a pension, but he worked well past the age of seventy looking after Mr. Mac's surviving son, John, as well as his oil money, and was rewarded by a substantial bequest when John died. After my father's second wife died, he married again, at the age of eighty.

His new wife, an old family friend, was not much younger than he. Still, she dedicated herself to virtually full-time care of him through a long and difficult period of debility before he died at age eighty-seven. I provided only occasional support and backup. My brother, who lived in the same area as they, stopped by to check up on them once a week. My sister, who had taken early retirement from her job, took on even more responsibility. We never fought or disagreed over who should provide care. I'd say we were pretty lucky.

Virtue is not always its own reward, however. The National Family Caregivers Association surveyed its members in 1997, asking them to describe positive and negative outcomes of caregiving, along with difficulties. An overwhelming majority, 70 percent, said that they had found inner strength they didn't know they had. However, over 67 percent registered frustration and 76 percent were troubled by the lack of consistent help from other family members. Over 60 percent complained of depression.[22] They also paid an economic penalty. A study by the National Center for Women and Aging at Brandeis University and the National Alliance for Caregivers reported that two-thirds of those caring for elderly relatives (i.e., providing more than eight hours a week in unpaid care) had lost out at work by forgoing promotions and training opportunities.[23] Not surprisingly, approximately three-fourths of all home caregivers for persons over the age of fifty are women—spouses, daughters, sisters, and friends.

It is estimated that about 25 percent of all American workers in 1996 provided at least some care for an ailing parent. The demand for this assistance is projected to increase. The demographic pressures are intensifying. Low fertility rates are contributing to an increase in the relative size of our elderly population. Individuals over age eighty-five, the neediest group, are increasing in number. On average, half of this group needs some help with personal care. Wives will probably continue to play an especially important role in caring for aging husbands, because women's life expectancy is greater than men's.

However, there is reason to believe that the supply of unpaid labor for home elder care will soon shrink. Unlike most of the women of my mother's generation, my peers are heavily invested in jobs and careers from which they can not easily excuse themselves. And many of them live a long distance from their parents. The price of providing care has gone up for them. And while they may agree that they have an obligation to care, they are unlikely to agree that their obligation is any greater than that of their husbands or sons or brothers. We are likely to see more and more negotiation over the distribution of elder care responsibilities.

The Prisoner of Love

The costs and risks of caring for dependents have another dimension that has less to do with economics than with psychology. When we spend time with people who need our care, we often become attached to them. An initial decision to care for someone can lead to a cascading level of commitment. It can change our preferences and our priorities. Like Odysseus in his encounter with the sirens, we often make preemptive decisions to avoid emotional commitments. As with the Good Person's Dilemma, our decisions are often shaped by our perceptions of how other people are likely to behave.

Our awareness of the many and various ways we fall in love explains why the decision to bear a child is entirely different from the decision to purchase a consumer durable like a sports utility vehicle. If we aren't satisfied with the product, we can't return it and get our money back, or trade it in for another. Even if we were legally able to do so, and even if a "market" for children developed, our emotional attachments would make it difficult for us to make use of it. Fathers and mothers both know that they are likely to become prisoners of love to their own children. Mothers are particularly vulnerable, if only because they experience such early and intimate physical contact. That's why it is so important to women to have freedom of choice to make this commitment, to ensure that their confinement, as it were, is voluntary.

Forced maternity, as Margaret Sanger described it, is like forced subjugation to the needs of another. Conservatives sometimes seem puzzled that many women choose to terminate unwanted pregnancies rather than carry them to term and put the children up for adoption. The oppressive experience of unwanted pregnancy tells part but not all of the story. Many women fear that they will become emotionally unable to relinquish a newborn child.

Biological dynamics, including breast-feeding, bond the mother more closely than the father to an infant. But social norms, particularly those concerning paternal participation, also have a big influence. Fathers who spend more time with their children bond more strongly with them, and are more likely to develop a relationship that can later endure stresses and strains. This seems like a compelling reason to encourage fathers and/or other co-parents to increase their active participation in caregiving. Strengthening the emotional connections between children and those whom we expect to take economic responsibility for them is a form of insurance: it reduces the probability of default on the implicit contract for care.

Many economists continue to advocate that mothers strongly specialize in child rearing because it's more efficient.[24] The short-run efficiencies are indeed obvious. Mothers enjoy some biological and cultural gifts where infants are concerned. But there are a number of negative side effects to specialization. Fathers, because they are less involved, may become less attached than mothers to their infants. Defining their responsibilities in terms of money rather than time—paying the rent and buying the groceries—may encourage them to believe that they can fulfill those responsibilities just as well at a distance, by sending a child-support check. Of course, once they have moved out of the house, they become even more detached from their children, which helps explain why enforcement of child-support responsibilities remains a serious problem.

This isn't just a mother/father issue. Children and the elderly, like investors, need diversity. In the past, the tasks of care for dependents were spread widely among family members rather than assigned to one Super Mom. Having a portfolio of care providers makes it more likely that a dependent person's emotional needs will be met. More importantly, it ensures that a larger number of people have an emotional stake in providing economic security for the dependent. Their empathy and commitment get revitalized not only by personal contact but also by the

actual exercise of caring. Encouraging people to fulfill their responsibilities to others simply by writing a check may lead them to write
smaller and smaller checks each year, or to stop writing checks altogether.

There's another reason why we should try to share the burdens of
care for dependents. Care providers are not in a very good position to
bargain for more resources, because such bargaining puts the people
they are caring for at risk. Mothers don't usually tell fathers: "Put more
time into being a good parent, or I'm going to reduce the time I spend."
For one thing, this is not a credible threat: such an action would make
the child worse off. Similarly, mothers are often reluctant to threaten
"Pay the child support or I'm not going to let you see Janie," for fear
that loss of contact with the father will harm the child.

People who provide care for pay are also prisoners of love. Nurses
are limited in their ability to go on strike, because job actions threaten
the welfare of their patients. Teachers are reluctant to impose long absences on their students. Auto workers and airplane pilots can make
more credible threats to withdraw their services. Not surprisingly, their
salaries are a lot higher. Even relatively well-paid caregivers, like doctors, work at a disadvantage in today's economy. Many of them hate the
bureaucratic turn that health care institutions are taking, but are forced
to go along because they want to continue caring for their patients.

The prisoner of love also stares out from behind the bars of social
policy. Consider the enormous energy expended on welfare reform in
the 1990s, including the attacks on mothers, labeled irresponsible because they were not working for pay (I'll say more about this in chapter
5). Largely absent from this debate was consideration of certain facts:
most mothers living in poverty could immediately improve their economic situation by insisting that fathers take custody of their children,
putting them up for adoption, or dropping them off at an orphanage.
The per-child costs of public assistance to poor mothers have always
been about a tenth of the per-child costs of a group home or orphanage.
But because they love them and want to be with them, poor mothers can
seldom make a credible threat to abandon their children.

We can't liberate ourselves or others from the various prisons of love, nor should we always try. But some prisoners deserve better treatment than others, and punishment is supposed to fit the crime. Increases in the care penalty, like increases in most penalties, will eventually have a deterrent effect. People will learn to avoid situations in which they might come to care.

Truth and Consequences

Maybe, a long time ago, someone explained the cost of caring to men. That would help explain why they assigned it to women. In any event, women are beginning to figure out just how disadvantageous their traditional responsibilities can be. Birth rates have long been declining in most countries of the world. They are particularly low in countries that provide little or no public support for child-rearing, such as Japan and Italy.[25] These countries have strong pro-family values, but they offer less public support for parenting than do most European countries. Their fertility levels have now fallen below two children per woman, the level required to replace the existing population, and their governments are quite worried about demographic decline.

We're more accustomed to worrying about over- than under-population. But both Japan and Italy are concerned about their future labor supply. Who will take care of their elderly? What will happen to their cultural traditions? Immigration offers a partial solution to the problem, but most countries are nervous about the effects of opening their doors too wide. In the long run, the fertility decline already underway in many relatively poor countries will reduce numbers of potential migrants as well. Reducing the size of the world population is a good idea—for now. At some point, however, we will want to stabilize our population at something close to replacement levels of fertility.

In any case, the number of children being born is less important than the quality of care we provide them and other dependents. It's the quality issue that demands most forcefully that we address the problem of contracting for care. Neither men nor women are likely to freely choose to specialize in an activity that they know will make them economically vulnerable. As Arlie Hochschild writes, "For women, in particular, to take a job is often today to take out an emotional insurance policy on the uncertainties of home life."[26] One can agree that this is a rational choice and still observe that such strategies encourage women (as well as men) to adopt traditionally masculine priorities.

Conservatives seem to think that making divorce more difficult could solve this problem. But making it more difficult to exit marriage would discourage many people from entering it. Moreover, restricting divorce doesn't necessarily improve the position of the person who specializes in providing care. It would provide him or her with more economic security only if it was accompanied by a legal and independent claim on one-half the wealth and earnings of the person who specializes in earning market income. Not even the community property laws in effect in some states go this far: one spouse generally owes only a basic level of support to the other. Specialization in providing care often means that a wife (or the husband, if he assumes this role) has a greater emotional investment in the quality of family life. As a result, she or he suffers more from forced continuation of what has become an unhappy relationship.

Sharing responsibility for caregiving on a daily basis is a better solution. That way, both members of a couple stay emotionally connected to the children, or the sick, or the elderly family members they are caring for. Likewise with community involvement—spending time running a Boy Scout troop or volunteering at a local homeless shelter. If both members of a couple participate, they can negotiate their responsibilities from a position closer to equality, without one becoming more economically dependent on the other. A small but significant minority of families currently organize their lives along these lines.[27] But while individuals can and will make some changes on their own, they must continue to live—and to compete—in an economy in which care for dependents is not well rewarded. This imposes serious constraints on their choices.

Rat Race Effects

Most working people have limited choices about how many hours they work. Their employers usually have more power over this decision than they do. Many people who might like to work fewer than the standard forty hours a week find that the price of dropping back to part time is prohibitively high. Many part-time jobs offer no benefits of any sort; few offer any career track or potential for advancement. Finally, and perhaps most importantly, the effects of cutting back on work, or perhaps simply refusing to work overtime, depend heavily on what other people do. A coordination problem similar to the Nice Person's Dilemma comes into play.

Consider Robin and Terry, two people who work for the same employer and are in competition with each other for a promotion. Both would like to combine a good job with ample time for family work. If forced to choose between these two options they would each choose the good job, but they prefer to have ample time for their families, as well. Suppose their employer desperately wants them to work overtime at the office and holds out the reward of a promotion. If Robin and Terry could coordinate their actions and agree not to work overtime, they would both benefit. Their employer would have to use a different criterion to decide whom to promote. But suppose, as in the Nice Person's Dilemma, that neither Robin nor Terry can be confident of the other's decision. Each will be afraid to refuse overtime for fear that the other will not. They both will work overtime. Still, only one of them will get the promotion.

Robin and Terry are in a situation that faces many young professionals. In prestigious law firms, for example, lawyers who are not yet partners are expected to work extremely long hours for years before they can enjoy job security. Those who do not are fired. Such forms of competition obviously penalize those workers who must find time not merely to eat take-out meals but also to care for family members. Of course, lawyers are pretty well paid. One could argue that their high wages are compensation enough—if one believes that money and time are perfect substitutes for one another.

In a rat race, the rat willing to work the longest hours wins, even though the size of the cheese remains fixed. As any scientist in a white lab coat or corporate executive in a three-piece suit can tell you, it's a good strategy for increasing effort. A lot of competitive games are set up with "winner take all" prizes.[28] The results are not always bad for society as a whole. In the race described above, however, time has been diverted from family care, which isn't directly and immediately rewarded, to paid employment, which offers the immediate gratification of a paycheck.

Rat race effects help explain why most countries regulate the length of the workday for most workers and require companies to pay a premium for overtime. The best-paid jobs in our society, however, are not regulated this way. The competitive pressures required for success in professions like law, medicine, and management filter out many individuals who insist on a life—and a commitment—outside paid employment. In this environment, we shouldn't be surprised to see a new strain of super rats emerging—one that has reduced needs for giving or receiving care.

———————◆———————

To make it possible for both men and women to combine parenthood and gainful employment, a new view of the male role and a radical change in the organization of working life are required.

—SWEDISH MINISTRY OF LABOR

———————◆———————

Pink-Collar Penalties

Women have made very significant inroads in the professions over the last twenty-five years, sometimes gaining full entry into the rat race, and sometimes trying to change it. Still, most women remain concentrated in a relatively small number of pink-collar jobs, working as secretaries, teachers, child care workers, and nurses. Unfortunately, the more women in an occupation, all else being equal, the lower the pay. This pattern probably developed when restrictions limited women's access to lucrative male-dominated jobs, and they were crowded into a few occupations. These restrictions are much diminished today, but many women still move into so-called "women's jobs."

A number of explanations can be offered for this, including the priority that many women place on family commitments and a sometimes explicit desire to avoid rat-race pressures. There are many subtle and not so subtle ways (including sexual harassment) that women can be made to feel unwelcome in traditionally male jobs. Some blue-collar jobs are perceived as almost inevitably masculine, even though women are perfectly capable of performing them. Women may avoid these jobs for fear of appearing less sexually attractive to men and reducing their chances of finding a desirable partner.[31]

Another explanation of women's choices is that many pink-collar jobs involve caring for other people, which women have already been taught to value. Sociologist Paula England finds that jobs that require nurturance are paid less, all else being equal, than other jobs. Jobs that involve exercising authority over other people, on the other hand, are paid more.[30] "That's the beauty of the market," a conventional economist might say. "Workers who provide care for other people get intrinsic satisfaction from doing those jobs, and that warm glow makes up for the low pay. On the other hand, being a boss is *so* unpleasant—that's why the market rewards that kind of work more." This explanation is not too convincing, since low-paying jobs in general don't offer better working conditions or more fun than high-paying jobs. But it's the only explanation that works, if you assume—as many economists do—that nothing affects wages except individual preferences and the forces of supply and demand.

Conventional economic reasoning suggests that it might be good that jobs involving care are poorly paid, because this ensures that the individuals performing these jobs are intrinsically motivated, caring people. After all, a woman who chooses to become a child care worker—even though it pays her less than a job as a parking lot attendant—must really love children. A woman who chooses to be a nurse—even though it pays less than a job as a tree-trimmer—must be full of nurturance. If we paid more for these jobs, we might attract people who performed them simply for the money. Funny how no one seems to worry about high pay undermining intrinsic motives in traditionally male jobs.

Consider some of the negative consequences of offering low pay for caring jobs. Low pay deters job entrants who are educated and skilled enough to have better-paying alternatives. Low pay deters job entrants who need to earn enough money to support their own children. Low pay discourages commitment to training and professional development. Low pay contributes to high rates of burnout and turnover, as workers restlessly seek jobs that might offer marginally better working conditions.[31]

"Not to worry," economists tell us. "If the demand for child care workers goes up, the pay will also go up, and everything will be fine." In the real world, things are not so simple. It's hard to raise wages for child care workers because—in the absence of public subsidies—to do so raises the cost of child care. Most families already have a hard time paying their child care bills. And let's not forget that parental altruism toward children—like that of child care workers toward their jobs—is coming under increasing economic pressure. The same concerns apply to elder care.

I overheard a conversation the other day that reminded me of the ways these pressures accumulate over time. A woman with a new baby asked another mother, with a thirteen-year-old and a fifteen-year-old, a somewhat leading question. "Does your daughter like to babysit?" She got an honest and sincere response. "You know, she does, but I really discourage her from doing it. Experiences like that encourage young girls to go into dead-end jobs." "Oh," the new mother said, sounding disappointed. "What about your son? Wouldn't it be good for him to learn how to take care of a baby?" "Sure, it would be great," the second mother said, "You could probably get him to do it for twenty-five dollars an hour, if you promised to keep it a secret from his friends."

Morality Tales

The pressures that can undermine consideration and responsibility are a subset of a larger set of pressures that can undermine all intrinsic motives. Perhaps you've heard the saying "Everybody has a price." You don't have to second that depressing opinion to agree that a lot of people—even you—have a price for a lot of things. This should make you wonder what happens when those prices start going way up.

Economist Robert Frank has designed a survey to explore how people's values affect the types of jobs they choose. The survey lists pairs of jobs that require the same training and offer exactly the same pay, but have different social implications. Respondents are asked to choose, for instance, whether they would prefer to work as a lawyer for the American Cancer Society or a lawyer for Reynolds Tobacco. Another choice is to take charge of public relations for the Sierra Club, or for Dow Chemical. There are enough variations across different topics (such as health issues and environmental concerns) to highlight the contrast between somewhat redeeming versus somewhat reprehensible jobs.

Respondents are also asked how much more they would have to be paid to take the less noble job. Usually it's a significant amount (and some respondents feel so strongly that no amount of bonus would attract them). In the early 1990s, Frank's students at Cornell declared that they would have to earn $25,000 a year more to work for Reynolds Tobacco than for the American Cancer Society (though some said that they would not work for a tobacco company at any salary). This finding helps explain why institutions (including capitalist firms) that have strong moral values may be able to compete quite effectively with those who don't: they can elicit more loyalty and effort from their workers for less pay. The big question, of course, is how that loyalty and effort hold up over time.

I administered the same survey to my students, with an eye to gender differences. In general, women were less willing than men to say they would accept a morally unattractive job, no matter what the price. If they accepted such a job, they would demand higher pay for it. For instance, the average amount sufficient to induce them to switch to Reynolds Tobacco from the American Cancer Society was $5,000 more than it was for men. What people say, of course, is not necessarily the same as what they do. It's easier to pose as a moral guardian than to be one. But these priorities are consistent with the kinds of jobs that women tend to take.

When women were excluded from the highest-paying jobs, it didn't take a lot of willpower to choose the morally redeeming ones. In some ways, our norms of femininity reflect this tradition of exclusion, what Friedrich Nietzsche disparaged as a "slave morality."[32] These norms are shifting in ways that may benefit women as a group, but they impose new costs on society as a whole. Other economic trends are moving us in the same direction. Increasing inequality of earnings in the United States is making it much harder than it used to be to attract skilled and committed workers not only to family care but also to public service.[33]

Buying Care

We are moving from a system of providing care for children, the sick, and the elderly primarily through the family to a system that relies to a large extent on purchased care. In other words, we are increasing the role of markets—individual decisions to buy this or that, or sell this or that. Markets work pretty well for the provision of some goods and services. Consider home computers: innovative geeks figured out how to produce them and made a lot of money. The profits that they earned attracted others into the industry, and the competition that resulted created big rewards for further innovation that led, in turn, to dramatic decreases in the cost of computing power. Our entire economy has been transformed, in mostly positive ways.

Why can't we rely on the same market forces to provide the services of caregiving? Perhaps we can, to some extent. But keep in mind that care services are at the opposite end of the technological spectrum from computer technology. They are extremely labor intensive. They require face-to-face contact and person-specific knowledge. They cannot be standardized or depersonalized. The possibilities for substituting silicon for sweat and tears are going to remain severely limited unless we come up with some fabulous care robots which, some would argue, would be a contradiction in terms.

As a result, the relative price of care services is likely to go up, leading to the disruptive effects described above. Pressures on quality of care will also increase. Introductory economics textbooks don't worry much about quality issues, because they take consumer sovereignty for granted. They assume that consumers are intelligent and well-informed, and that they can choose among a variety of sellers or service providers. These assumptions seldom hold for children, the sick, or the elderly who need care. Often, care services are purchased on their behalf by others—parents, other family members, insurance companies, or, in some cases, state agencies. Even if the actual decision makers have the most exalted motives and want nothing but the best for those dependent on their choices (a dubious assumption in many cases), it is difficult for them to judge the quality of ensuing care. After all, they are not the ones receiving it.

Some kinds of work result in tangible products: number of widgets produced, number of units sold, number of words processed. Care work can also be measured: number of children supervised, number of days in the hospital, number of aides per resident. But in the face-to-face provision of care services with an emotional content, the quality of interaction can vary enormously. And this quality is difficult to assess. (This is a problem I'll explore in more detail in the next chapter.) "Quality" does not necessarily make the consumer feel good. Sometimes children need to be disciplined. Patients need to be subjected to uncomfortable medical procedures. The elderly need to be pushed to exercise even when they're in pain or not in the mood. Good caregivers are those who genuinely care about other people's well-being. But how do you tell which ones are good?

Even if you don't like the care services that you are purchasing, it's often difficult to find alternatives. Finally, there is the simple fact that many of those who most need care services for themselves or their dependents don't have the resources to buy them. "Too bad for them," you might say. "Tough luck." But some minimal level of care is a necessity, not a luxury. Moreover, when people don't get the care they need, the ill effects can spill over to society as a whole.

Spillovers and Side Effects

Most people work in concert with others, which makes it difficult to identify their separate contributions. This interdependence is especially characteristic of care work. Parents know that the way they raise their children will affect the way their grandchildren are raised. Many of us remember episodes from elementary school that affected our entire lives—how we came to hate math, love spelling, or despise gym. Teachers know that their success in the classroom is greatly affected by their students' home environment. Employers know that physical and emotional health have big impacts on the way people do their jobs. Many of us anticipate that the way we care for our elders will affect the ways we, in turn, are cared for in our old age.

High-quality care creates benefits that extend well beyond the immediate recipients. When child care workers or elementary school teachers do a good job, their students internalize an eagerness to learn and a willingness to cooperate from which subsequent teachers and employers benefit. When doctors and nurses do a good job, patients' families and employers benefit. When elderly folks enjoy a good quality of life, the community as a whole feels more cheerful about its future. Anyone who treats another person in a kind and helpful way creates a minuscule benefit that will be passed along.

Parents who raise happy, healthy, and successful children create an especially important public good.[34] Children themselves are not the only beneficiaries. Employers profit from access to productive workers. The elderly benefit from Social Security taxes paid by the younger generation, a subject I'll discuss at length in chapter 4. Fellow citizens gain from having productive and law-abiding neighbors. These are all examples of positive spillovers and side effects that economists often call "positive externalities" because they are external to the actual decision to provide care.

These externalities offer yet another explanation of why it is so difficult for those who provide care services to charge a price that reflects the value of their contributions. Parents can ask for reciprocity from their children but not from all those who have benefited from their children's capabilities. More generally, the family values of love, obligation, and reciprocity themselves create positive externalities. Nice Persons, Nice Parents, and Nice Children can hope that those they are nice to are nice in return. But they can't hope to capture the cascade effects of their nice behavior, which extend well beyond their ken. Communities, however, can capture these effects and benefit enormously from them. That is one of the reasons why communities are so important.

Care as Commodity

People buy and sell labor services constantly. But people themselves are not commodities—we do not permit them to be bought and sold. Therefore, it's hardly surprising that the work we put into developing and taking care of people is difficult to commodify. The quantity and quality of care work depend heavily on cultural values of love, obligation, and reciprocity—values that are seldom adequately rewarded in the marketplace.

Care, like virtue, can create its own reward. But there are such things as human frailty, vulnerability, and disaffection. Most of us expect some benefits for doing the right thing, and if we don't get them, we experience at least occasional bitterness and anger. The intrinsic satisfaction people receive from caring for others can be eroded by economic hardship. For one thing, money is often a prerequisite for care. A woman willing to endure poverty for the sake of her family may be undone if her children suffer as a result.

But lack of appreciation and reciprocity probably undermines intrinsic satisfactions even more. In personal relationships, we call it heartbreak. In the caring professions, we call it burnout. Goodwill gets exhausted. Cynicism increases. Mothers often warn their daughters against banking too much on marriage, just as Women's Studies professors warn their students of the costs of a career in caregiving. Virtue may be its own reward, but from a social point of view, that reward may not be sufficient to guarantee an adequate supply.

Back to the race, which, after all we—not goddesses—are designing. The effects of competition depend on its rules and rewards. How much do we care for others, including our kin? If we are naturally selfish, it's foolish to constantly exhort one another to be altruistic. But if we are only partly selfish, part of the time, we need to be more careful about the ways we reward selfish behavior. Otherwise, we could drive unselfishness not just out of business, but out of our families and communities as well.

MEASURING SUCCESS

My father-in-law was a volunteer fireman for much of his life. When he died, his memorial service took place in the common room of the firehouse, upstairs from the fire trucks in North Madison, Connecticut. Several people rose to tell stories about fires Karl had fought and families he had helped out in the aftermath. What I remember most vividly, however, was the woman who told how she and Karl kept a regular date to go down to the blood bank to donate blood. His lifetime contribution, she estimated, added up to more than twenty-five gallons. The number stuck in my mind as an indicator of contributions that often go unmeasured.

In his classic book, *The Gift Society*, Richard Titmuss offered a vivid example of the deterioration of quality when self-interested motives come to the fore.[1] He was writing in the 1960s, at a time when our technology for screening blood for such viruses as hepatitis and HIV was poor. He observed significant differences in the quality of the blood supply in Britain, where blood came almost entirely from voluntary donations, and in the United States, where much of it was obtained for cash. Titmuss argued, convincingly, that blood that is bought tends to be of low quality. Individuals who are poor, needy, and likely to carry diseases are far more likely to sell their blood than others. When blood is donated out of a sense of civic responsibility, on the other hand, the quality is usually high.

Technology helped to solve this problem. Today, we identify and throw out bad blood. The quantity that we collect, however, remains a problem. Researchers for the National Blood Data Resource Center warned in 1999 that donations had fallen slowly but steadily over time, threatening the supply needed to provide adequate medical care for the sick and injured. Donations are decreasing by about 1 percent a year, while demand for blood is increasing by about the same amount. About 60 percent of Americans are eligible to give blood, but only about 5 percent do.[2]

There's a simple solution to this shortage. Pay more money to blood donors. Of course, this will raise medical costs. But another reason to feel uneasy about this solution is the possibility that extrinsic motives, like money, can undermine intrinsic motives, like civic responsibility. In other words, we might be alleviating the problem, but we might also be changing ourselves and our cultural values in ways that will cause us problems in the future. The short-term benefits from raising the price are easy to quantify, but the long-term costs are not. In any cost-benefit analysis the things that are easy to measure—dollars, gallons, pounds—will trump the things that are difficult to measure—motives, feelings, values.

Our economy is organized, to some extent, as a game. Any competitive game, in addition to setting rules, establishes ways of keeping score. You get two points for one kind of basket, three points for another. You get six points for a touchdown, but three points for a field goal. The fastest person wins, or the fastest person carrying the most weight wins. The structure of these rewards defines the incentives for the players. In most sports, we try to define success in ways that encourage us to develop our capabilities, to bring out the best in us. Why don't we try this in the economy as well?

We do. But our efforts are seriously hampered by economists who tell us not to interfere with markets, as though any competition, no matter what its form, leads to good results. That's not true. In some areas of the economy, measuring success is pretty easy and can be reduced to a simple bottom line. The company with the highest profits wins. But in other areas of the economy, things are more complicated. Incentives to maximize profits create incentives to minimize costs. Incentives to minimize costs can create a big temptation to lower quality—especially when quality is difficult to measure. In care industries, almost by definition, quality is difficult to define, much less to monitor over time.

The problems emerging in our care industries are a particularly intense version of problems that have long afflicted our economy as a whole. Economists have traditionally measured success purely by market-based measures. The Dow Jones Industrial Average is an index of the value of a set of stocks, considered a leading indicator of the direction of the economy as a whole. The Gross Domestic Product is the value of everything that is bought and sold within the country. Both of them ignore things that accountants can't easily tally. The richer we get, the more important those intangibles begin to seem. It's hard to come up with a single accounting remedy. But it's easy to suggest some alternative measures that reveal a very different picture of our social trajectory.

Cheapening Care

Conventional yardsticks of success are particularly misleading in the paid care sector of our economy, the sector that provides health care, elder care, child care, education, and social services. Government surveys don't officially recognize this category, but with a bit of pushing and pulling, official numbers can be used to construct a category called "professional care services" (using the standard industrial classifications of hospitals, health services except hospitals, educational services, and social services). Employment in this category has increased steadily over time, and it now accounts for one-fifth of the total paid labor force, about the same as employment in the combined sectors of manufacturing, mechanical, and construction industries. Hospitals and schools should now count as much in forming our image of wage employment as factories and construction sites.[3]

Professional care services are disproportionately provided by women. In 1998, women accounted for about 46 percent of the paid labor force over age sixteen, but 76 percent of those employed in hospitals, 79 percent in other health services, 69 percent in educational services, and 82 percent in social services.[4] The ways in which these care industries are structured—including incentives for cutting costs and methods of setting pay and measuring performance—have especially important implications for women workers. They also have obvious implications for the welfare of those being cared for.

In the last thirty years, the overall costs of care have gone up relative to the costs of other goods and services, for a number of reasons in addition to those discussed in the preceding chapter, such as the difficulty of automating this type of work. Changing demographics have increased the relative size of our elderly population. Technological changes in health have created marvelous, but expensive, options for treating disease and prolonging life. The increasing importance of education has intensified demands for higher quality in primary and secondary schools and higher enrollment rates in colleges and universities. As more and more mothers have started bringing home paychecks, families have begun purchasing substitutes for the care they once provided.

When costs go up, pressures tend to intensify. Managers, professionals, and policy makers in the care industries have struggled to devise ways of keeping costs down, often through major institutional restructuring. A good example is the growth of health maintenance organizations (HMOs), which have largely displaced conventional insurance as a means of financing health care. The growing cost of providing public assistance to our elderly population through Medicaid has changed the way nursing home care is financed and regulated. Continued shortages in the availability of high quality child care have contributed to demands for more public subsidies. Dissatisfaction with schools has led to proposals that we dismantle our public education system and simply provide parents with vouchers that enable them to spend a certain amount of money purchasing educational services on the open market (an issue that will be discussed in more detail in chapter 6).

The pressure to cut care costs creates new openings for private, profit-oriented providers that focus on the financial bottom line. Public and nonprofit institutions must compete with these providers, even though they are bound by different rules. Private hospitals, for instance, don't need to provide emergency room care for the indigent, or learning opportunities for interns and resident physicians. Public hospitals do. Private schools can refuse to admit any student who they fear might bring down their average test scores, or expel any student who is a troublemaker. Public schools don't enjoy such privileges.

Even within the private sector, competitive pressures are mounting. Globalization is reducing barriers to trade and capital mobility. Companies can relocate to countries where they needn't provide health benefits for their workers and aren't required to pay taxes to help finance schools and hospitals (more about this in chapter 9). The introduction of competitive discipline can help reduce the escalation of costs in care services. But it can also reduce the quality of services in ways that people may be slow to recognize, and even slower to act upon. Much depends on how we measure, monitor, and defend quality.

Hands-On Health

Much of the cultural history of nursing revolves around ideals of empathetic care, and nursing organizations have tried for years to fend off the growing impersonality of our health care delivery system.[5] They have not been successful, in part because hand-holding has been considered a luxury—as though emotional well-being is subjective, just a transitory state of mind. Evidence suggests, however, that emotions have significant effects on physical health. The most striking examples come from studies of the placebo effect—the seemingly inexplicable fact that patients often benefit just as much from a sugar pill or fake surgery as from bona fide treatment. It seems that the expectation of being treated, the feeling of safety in someone else's hands, has measurably beneficial effects.

Emotional support is a therapeutic force. Journalist Margaret Talbot describes a study on postoperative pain at Massachusetts General Hospital in which patients were randomly divided into two groups. One group was visited the night before surgery by a doctor (an anesthesiologist) who treated them brusquely. The other group was visited the night before by the same doctor, who made an effort to be warm and sympathetic, holding each patient's hand as he sat on their bed. Those in the second group required less painkilling medication after the surgery, and they were also discharged significantly earlier from the hospital. "The placebo effect can occur," as one doctor put it, "when conditions are optimal for hope, faith, trust, and love."[6]

"Optimal conditions" do not include situations where patients lack a personal (much less long-term) relationship with their health care provider. Nor do they include situations in which doctors are under financial pressure to meet a quota of patients per hour or stay under a per-patient limit of diagnostic costs. Yet these situations are increasingly characteristic of health care today. Most health care is provided either by insurance companies, who face increasing pressure to cut costs, or by emergency rooms (the only form of health care that most uninsured folks can afford). In both cases, medical decisions are often supervised by individuals who are not in personal contact with patients, and whose job it is to limit spending.

Health care is costly, and we need to figure out ways to keep those costs down. But in the tug of war between costs and care, it is care that seems to be losing. Unlike traditional fee-for-service insurance programs, health maintenance organizations charge their members a fixed amount of money in advance. In return, they agree to meet the subscribers' medical needs. Not all aspects of this incentive structure are bad. Unlike fee-for-service insurers, HMOs have much to gain by encouraging regular health checkups, good nutrition, and exercise. By improving the overall health of the subscribers, such measures can reduce the incidence, and therefore the cost, of treating serious medical problems.

Unfortunately, the HMO system also creates some unhealthy incentives. Many HMOs provide only limited treatment for mental illness, because it is more difficult to classify than physical illness.[7] Many HMOs discourage their doctors from offering expensive diagnostic procedures or hospitalization. As of July 1999, less than half of all states had laws allowing patients to appeal such decisions. Most of the touted cost savings that HMOs offer derive from lower hospitalization rates than other kinds of programs.[8] Another tactic for saving money is to exclude unhealthy people from membership. It was hoped that, as many elderly people receiving Medicare moved into HMOs, their health care costs would decline. But HMOs realized that the elderly were driving up their costs; in the last few years, many have eliminated coverage for seniors on Medicare. The greater the competitive pressure, the more irresistible the temptations to offload costs.

A study published in the *Journal of the American Medical Association* found that several indicators of care quality are significantly lower in for-profit than nonprofit HMOs.[9] The authors offer a poignant example of the limitations of standardized qualification. A national committee monitors HMOs, collecting data on the percentage of women patients who receive regular mammograms. Hence, administrators have an incentive to encourage doctors to increase the number of mammographies. But, unfortunately, they have no incentive to encourage physicians to take as much time as they need to perform clinical breast examinations, patient education, or other activities that the committee does not monitor.

"Let's face it," says one health care economist, "people went into the for-profit managed care business to make bucks."[10] A law suit filed against six large managed care companies in June 2000 charged them with failing to disclose to members that rewards were offered to doctors and other employees who denied payments for care and limited hospital admissions, thus helping cut their employers' costs.[11]

Hospitals have dramatically reduced the length of stays by sending patients home more quickly than ever before, shifting costs to family members and friends. New portable technologies make it easier to do things like administer intravenous medication at home, which is great. But many family members are now assuming these responsibilities without pay—about 26 million people in 1997, each working an average of eighteen hours a week.[12] Indicators of cost-effectiveness do not take into account these hidden costs. Nor have the health effects been closely scrutinized. Forced cutbacks in hospital stays created so much bad publicity that Congress passed legislation in 1996 prohibiting "drive-through" deliveries, and requiring insurance companies to reimburse at least two days of hospital care for a normal childbirth. Even congressional Republicans recently voted in favor of the Patient Bill of Rights, albeit in an effort to forestall stronger regulation by Democrats.[13]

These well-publicized issues, however, are less troubling than the less visible deterioration in the emotional dimensions of caregiving. As a recent *New York Times* article put it, "critics say 'hit and run' nursing has replaced Florence Nightingale."[14] Bedside nurses have been replaced by unlicenced "care technicians."A survey released in 1996 of over 7,500 nurses reported that 73 percent felt they had less time than previously to comfort and educate patients.[15] A research report that analyzed over 18 million patient discharge records from hospitals between 1994 and 1997 found a 9 percent increase in the average number of patients for which each full-time registered nurse was responsible— from one to every 56.9 to one for every 62.3.[16]

Cutbacks in reimbursements to nurses and to aides who help provide care in patients' homes have reduced the emotional quality of care there, as well. Reflecting on her interviews with workers, Deborah Stone concluded, "The more I talked with people, the more I saw how financial tightening and the ratcheting up of managerial scrutiny are changing the moral world of care giving, along with the quantity and quality of care."[17]

Elder and Child Care

Anxiety about quality also runs high in market-provided elder and child care, the rapidly growing industries that care for the two dependent ends of our age distribution. Nearly all nursing homes are privately run, though most are subsidized with public dollars. Few ordinary elders can afford to pay the roughly $40,000 a year price tag on their own. More than two-thirds of all nursing home residents are indigent and rely on Medicaid to pay their expenses.

They have no choice about where or how they will be cared for; nor are they well-protected by the government. Complaints about abusive treatment are often ignored. According to *Consumer Reports*, about 40 percent of nursing homes repeatedly fail to pass the most basic health and safety inspections. In 1999, the government's General Accounting Office echoed these concerns.[18]

Nursing home profits depend largely on the difference between revenues paid by the government and the costs of providing care. When subsidies remain low—or fail to increase along with prices—the pressure to cut costs is powerful. Wages for workers in elder care are extremely low, and turnover rates are high. Working conditions are difficult. Chronic understaffing contributes to stress and burnout. Injury rates are high. Reform advocates argue that the federal government needs to set staffing ratios, making no aide responsible for more than five residents at a time. To date, only eighteen states have adopted minimum ratios.[19]

Perhaps in recognition of the difficulties facing families who are "comparison shopping" among nursing homes, the Medicare Office now offers a service on the World Wide Web entitled Nursing Home Compare (www.medicare.gov/nursing/Homeasp). At this site you can obtain a list of nursing homes in your local area, as well as some statistics on their performance. An elderly neighbor of mine moved to a local nursing home a couple of years ago and I decided to check it out. I learned that her nursing home had only three "health deficiencies" out of a possible thirty-nine found in the state. The average number of health deficiencies in nursing homes in the United States is five.

Extending my quest to ascertain exactly what a deficiency was, I learned that the nursing home in question, among other things, failed to 1) hire only people who have no legal history of abusing, neglecting, or mistreating residents; or 2) report and investigate any acts or reports of abuse, neglect, or mistreatment of residents. I also learned that only 5 percent of the residents of the home had bedsores (compared to a 15 percent average for the country as a whole) and only 28 percent had behavioral symptoms such as wandering, aggressive verbal or physical behavior, or inappropriate social actions, compared to 37 percent for the nation as a whole.

Better these statistics than no statistics at all. Still, apart from being downright depressing, they are rather limited, revealing nothing about more profound dimensions of care. I can't help but wonder about the emotional and social environment there. Researcher Susan Eaton describes the things companies "can't bill for, but that make all the difference if you're living in a nursing home: time to listen to somebody's story, time to hold their hand, time to comfort somebody who is feeling troubled. And you can't exactly put that on your bill; imagine finding 'holding hands' on the bill. You have to have a 'treatment,' you have to have some formal procedure."[20]

The picture in child care is less bleak. Most kids have parents to advocate for them, and most child care workers genuinely enjoy working with kids. Still, child care, like elder care, is difficult to monitor for quality. My favorite illustration of the problem is the teddy bear with the hidden video camera, a device invented to help parents maintain surveillance over live-in nannies. Only slightly more affordable are Web sites linked to videocameras in child care centers so that anxious parents are only one click away from seeing what their toddlers are actually doing. As of December 1999, some 150 child care centers across the country offered this feature.[21] Most parents obviously cannot afford cyber-supervision, and those who do seldom have the time to carefully scrutinize what they see.

Some home providers and child care centers offer high quality care. Others do not. The workers who actually provide hands-on care earn less than parking lot attendants. Lack of regulation allows the child care industry to draw from a reserve army of relatively unskilled labor—whose members are disproportionately women of color. Only nineteen states have preservice training requirements for teachers.[22] Few states have any training qualifications for family child care providers. In general, hairdressers are required to meet much stricter standards. Fewer than half of all child care workers receive fully covered health insurance for themselves; coverage for their dependents is even more rare.[23]

Turnover rates are well over 30 percent per year in most big cities. It is hard for a young child to trust a caregiver in a revolving door.

Plenty of evidence suggests that high-quality care can improve young children's development. But a recent comprehensive survey argues that the physical and emotional environments in many child care centers remain inadequate in many states because of poor regulation.[24] Voluntary accreditation by the National Association for the Education of Young Children tends to improve quality. A California study, for instance, rated 61 percent of accredited centers as "good" in 1997, compared to only 26 percent of those seeking accreditation the previous year. Nationwide, however, only 5,000 out of the nation's 97,000 child care centers were accredited in that year.[25]

Quality is even more unpredictable among home care providers. In the rush to expand child care slots to accommodate the exigencies of welfare reform, some states have provided child care vouchers that can be used virtually anywhere and are set at extremely low levels. Such policies discourage the development of high quality care, which costs more than public subsidies will cover.

Child care is a complicated business, with a mix of for-profit, family-based, and nonprofit providers. We don't know much about how different institutional forms affect quality of care. What looks attractive to the parent is not necessarily what is best for the child—shiny new toys matter less than the skills and commitment of the caregivers. Studies show that for-profit child care centers do not in general emphasize "curbside appeal" at the expense of aspects of quality which are more difficult to monitor. However, for-profit child care centers that are part of national chains do appear to stoop to this strategy.[26]

It is probably impossible to arrive at an exact understanding of care quality. But it is not hard to think of ways to lessen the economic pressures that can lower quality. Improving the training, wages, and working conditions of workers in care industries would be likely to reduce their turnover and encourage greater personal connection between caregivers and those for whom they care. Indeed, if they had greater opportunities to develop professional standards and some protection

from employer retaliation against "whistle blowers," workers themselves could become leading watchdogs for care quality.

Competitive pressures can have perverse effects. This is why public
provision of care services is sometimes preferable to private provision
and why public regulation of caregiving is almost always necessary. But
the difficulties of measuring success are not limited to the care sector.
Nor can they be solved simply by reorganizing child care, health, and
education. We need to reevaluate—and substantially revise—the
ways we measure and reward success in our economy as a whole.

Doug and Dow Jones

Every night on the evening news we hear what's happening to the Dow
Jones, the average of the price of thirty industrial stocks that serves as a
basic barometer for the stock market. But the Dow is not a very good
indicator of the health of the economy as a whole. Throughout the
1990s, for instance, it soared while average wages remained pretty much
unchanged. In 1998, almost half of American households owned some
stock either directly or indirectly (through, for instance, pension plans).
But the richest 10 percent of all households accounted for 78 percent of
the total value of all stocks.[27]

One of my heroes, the Texas populist Jim Hightower, argues that we
should develop an alternative to the Dow Jones, one that better describes what's happening to ordinary people. It could measure some
combination of changes in unemployment, wages, and benefits like
health insurance—the overall average of what people are earning. He
suggests calling it the Doug Jones, in honor of the working-class guy.
The Doug Jones wouldn't zig and zag as much as the Dow. But which-
ever way it went, it would get folks thinking about what the stock market really means.

It could also push economists to rethink what the economy means.
The indication most relied on is the Gross Domestic Product or GDP.
It represents the market value of all the goods and services bought and
sold within the territorial boundaries of the country. The "gross" part
means that the measurement doesn't take depreciation of buildings and

equipment into account, but only looks at the new stuff produced. In many people's minds, the GDP has literally *become* the economy. When newscasters say "The economy is booming" they are talking about growth in the GDP. When they say, "We're entering a recession," they are referring to two consecutive quarters of the year in which the GDP has declined.

How do you suppose the government measures this? Forms. My favorite example is the measurement of the output of the hair styling industry. The form that surveyors of "Beauty Parlor Services for Females" completed in 1975 included four types of haircut (trim, styling, regular, razor); seven types of coloring (dye, all over; dye, touch-up, rinse, frosting with cap, frosting with aluminum foil, streaking, tipping); six types of wig service, three variations on shampoo and set; other hair services; and other personal care services. The objective: to tally what percent of total sales comes from each of these categories.[28] Determining whether the output of this or any other industry has increased in overall value and productivity is no easy task. It may sound trivial, but in the United States in 1995, consumer expenditures on personal care products and services amounted to about $41 billion, more than twice the GDP of Vietnam and about equal to that of Bangladesh or Algeria.[29]

Guesswork is involved, as well as data collection. For instance, the accounts include a measurement of the annual value of what are called "housing services." Rent is considered a good indication, since it represents what people are actually paying for the privilege of claiming space to live in. But many people in this country own their own homes, so they don't pay rent. This is a problem. If you only counted rent, but not mortgage payments, as part of GDP, then a trend toward home ownership could lower measured economic growth. So, the government bean counters use sample surveys to impute what people who own their own homes would hypothetically pay if they were renting those homes. It seems a bit odd that while they are willing to guess the value of this, they are not willing to guess the value of the people who have traditionally taken care of these homes—housewives.

Dolly Jones

Work is generally something that we would pay somebody else to do for us at least part of the time if we could afford to. Also, it's generally something that creates benefits that are transferable to others. Preparing meals is work. Washing dishes is work. Changing diapers is work. Helping someone eat or get dressed is work. That some people find fulfillment in these activities doesn't diminish their productive significance. The most highly paid workers in the world—movie stars, baseball players, and chief executive officers—usually love their jobs. We treat people's salaries as measures of the value of their market work, whether they love their jobs or not.

Our economic accounts ignore the value of nonmarket work on the grounds that it's just too difficult to estimate its value. This is hardly a credible explanation, given the guesswork involved in imputing the value of other components of GDP, including the value of housing services. The main reason that nonmarket work has traditionally been excluded from the "economy" is that it is considered a moral responsibility rather than a calculated exchange.[30] Some fear that putting a price on it demeans its essential character.

I wouldn't want to reduce the value of everything we do to a dollar estimate, particularly where caregiving is concerned. Purchased services are only partial substitutes for personal services from a family member or friend. Still, the cost of purchased substitutes provides at least a lower-bound estimate of the value of socially important activities, one that we need in order to keep track of how our economy is changing.

The first step is a regular and systematic survey of a large sample of residents that would tell us how much time people devote to work in their homes and communities. It would be similar to the Consumer Expenditure Survey, but it would focus on time rather than money. The United States government has never conducted an official time-use survey, but surveys conducted by academic researchers show that about half of all work takes place outside the labor market, much of it in the form of housework and care for family members.

We can impute a value to this work by asking how much it would have cost to hire someone to do it, or by asking what someone could have earned had they devoted their time instead to earning a wage. Such approximations show that the value of nonmarket work amounts to between 30 percent and 60 percent of the value of all goods and services sold in the market.[31] Studies by groups such as the National Family Caregivers Association show that the value of the services family caregivers provide "for free" (a subset of all nonmarket work) is estimated at $196 billion a year.[32]

What this means is not just that our conventional measure of goods and services produced is way too low, but also that our picture of changes over time is distorted. As one old economist's joke put it, if you marry your housekeeper, you lower GDP. If you put your mother in a nursing home, you increase GDP. As married women moved rapidly into market work over the last thirty years, they reduced the time spent doing work that wasn't counted and increased the time spent doing work that *was* counted. This has probably made economic growth seem more rapid than it really has been.[33]

We don't like to admit it, but we economists are clueless about changes in anything that falls outside our outdated accounting categories. If you think we don't know enough about what has happened to Doug Jones, consider how little we know about Dolly Jones, the representative working mother. We can trace improvements in her labor market earnings over time, but we know little about the organization or outcome of activities that occupy fully half of her total work time— cooking, cleaning, shopping, networking, managing, chauffeuring, volunteering, etc.

Nor do we know exactly how successful Dolly has been at persuading her male family members and friends to assume a greater share of these responsibilities as she has increased her paid work time. The small-scale, intermittent studies of this issue in the United States suggest that she has persuaded men to do a little bit more, but nowhere near an equal share.[34] It would help if the government collected systematic time-use data along the lines of its current surveys of consumer expenditure and labor force participation. Then the evening news could report the Dolly Jones index along with the Doug and the Dow.

———◆———

There is no mainstream liberal program that measures the economics of caretaking for the whole country, that charts the distribution of caretaking work, that assigns weight to care as a value defining national goals. That takes a stand on the importance of family as a source of care, that speaks to the moral dimension of families as a social unit, or that even begins to recognize the ways in which women's equality is bound up with the organization of families and care.

—MONA HARRINGTON,
Care and Equality: Inventing a New Family Politics

———◆———

GDP vs. MEWs

Collecting new numbers, however, is not enough. We need to reevaluate their meaning as well. Exclusive reliance on GDP in comparisons of international economic competition reflects what might generously be called a childish perspective: the country with the most toys at the end wins. It is easier to count toys than it is to engage in philosophical debate, but that's no excuse. We need to grow up and decide on one or two or perhaps even ten Measures of Economic Welfare, or MEWs.

Current GDP indicators put a positive economic value on things that actually do harm. Every time money is spent cleaning up a large oil spill, for instance, GDP goes up. The cormorant or seal who dies coated with oil has no "value" to be subtracted from the accounts, but the wages of the workers hired to vacuum a petroleum-laden beach are added in. When a flood or a hurricane destroys homes and buildings, we put a dollar value on the loss: it represents a depreciation of our capital stock. But when pollution lowers water or air quality or leads to a change in our climate, we don't put a dollar value on the loss, because we never put a value on natural endowments in the first place. When ancient redwood trees are logged from old-growth forests in California, GDP goes up by the amount the resulting lumber sells for. There is no subtraction for the loss of the natural capital embodied in the trees themselves—or for the value of the other plant and animal species that are ecologically dependent on them. These are all considered "nonproduced" goods. We take Mother Nature (like our more immediate mothers) for granted.

I'm partial to trees, because an unsuccessful attempt to defend some big trees marked the beginning of my higher education. In 1969, as a freshman at the University of Texas, I was assigned to a sterile high-rise "megadorm" with a couple of roommates who looked on me as a deviant geek. I used to flee to a towering stand of hundred-year-old cypress trees, a green space alongside the meandering creek that separated the dorms from the football stadium. It was an incidental jungle, a cool informal refuge from the glaring September sun. The cypresses seemed designed for climbing, with large, arching limbs that a Swiss Family Robinson could have built a house in.

I soon learned that they were scheduled for execution. The football stadium needed to be expanded in such a way that the honorary office planned for Lyndon B. Johnson in a new university library would have an unobstructed view of the state capital. A local group of environmentalists felt this was not adequate reason to destroy a much-loved green space. They hired a lawyer and filed for an injunction against the university's plan. When the chair of the board of trustees learned this, he called in a construction company to remove the trees before the judge could rule. This didn't sound like fair play to me.

Along with several other students, I climbed as high as I could in a tree and refused to come down, an act of civil disobedience aimed at delaying any irrevocable destruction, at least until the court could rule. I was wearing a long loose orange dress and a red bandanna; I hadn't planned on climbing a tree. The university called in the fire department with ladder trucks. A crowd gathered. They forcibly removed everyone else, but saved me for last, because I had climbed the highest. Up came two policemen to talk me down. I explained that I wouldn't come voluntarily, but that I would not resist. Below, the firemen held up one of those portable trampolines designed to cushion falls. The policemen handcuffed my hands and feet and carried me down, while news photographers took pictures of my underwear. The trees were sawed off at the ground.

Sometimes tree-huggers are accused of being elitist rich kids, living affluent lifestyles that enable the luxury of concern about quality of life rather than quantity of subsistence goods. But there are plenty of environmentalists in poor countries today, and distortions of GDP are just as relevant to poor countries as to rich ones. Consider the example of Indonesia, heralded as a great success story in the 1970s, with annual rates of GDP growth reaching 7 percent a year. Much of this growth was achieved by the harvest and sale of tropical hardwoods, which were logged at a much faster rate than they were replanted. If you factor in the depreciation of this "natural" capital stock—which you would automatically do if it were man-made capital—it turns out that growth rates were closer to 4 percent per year.[35] Not a great success story after all.

As long as natural endowments seemed infinite and immune to any long-term ill effects of human intervention, we could ignore them. But in the world today these endowments seem even more important than the capital we create ourselves.[36] How different would our measures of economic welfare be if we took the depreciation of our natural environment into account? It is difficult to say, since we are not yet sure what the long-term effects of trends like global warming will be. But we are almost certainly overestimating the improvements in our standard of living. Per capita GDP has risen considerably since 1966. But Sustainable Economic Welfare (SEW), which adds the value of nonmarket services and subtracts the costs of pollution, resource depletion, and long-term environmental damage, shows a very different trend.[37] Per capita SEW was actually lower in 1990 than in 1966.

————————◆————————

Urban forests are fast disappearing, and nobody has noticed. Victims of air pollution, Dutch elm disease, and development, many of the trees that had made American cities cool and green are gone. Like the aging of a familiar face, the decline in city trees has been so gradual as to be almost imperceptible. A booming economy and robust development mean fewer trees. . . . Metropolitan Atlanta, once famed for its trees, lost more than half of its heavy tree cover between 1974 and 1998.

—KATHLEEN WONG,
U.S. News & World Report

Investing in Human Capital

Conventional economic theory concedes that human capital, usually defined in terms of levels of education and workforce experience, is an important factor of production. The importance of human capital offers a rationale for public support for education—the taxpayers as a whole help educate the younger generation because the resulting improvement in their skills will benefit society as a whole. A great deal of evidence suggests that investments in human capital are crucial to economic growth. We owe much of our prosperity to the ways our highly skilled workforce has adapted to enormous changes in technology, learning to use computers with ever more complex forms of software.

If human capital is so important, maybe we should pay more attention to how and where it is actually produced—in families and communities. The way economists treat nature helps explain the way they treat people. Both are taken as "exogenously given." Perhaps Exogenous was a mother. One important contribution to economic growth in most countries throughout the twentieth century was a steady decline in the number of births per woman. This is hardly surprising, since fertility decline involves a reallocation of time and energy from the production of something that is not counted as part of national output (kids) to something that is (the market output that women tend to produce more of when they raise fewer kids). If what we really want to pay attention to is output per capita, this makes sense. Fertility decline offers crucial environmental and economic benefits.

Our current economic accounting system, however, ignores not only contributions to the quantity of our human capital stock—new babies—but also understates contributions to the quality of our human capital stock. We measure expenditures on health and education, but we don't measure the time or effort that families and communities put into maintaining and developing the capabilities of children and adults. Perhaps it's easier to see the contributions that schools make because they develop cognitive skills, at least some of which show up on standardized tests. Families and communities tend to play a more important role in the maintenance and development of emotional skills, which are harder to measure. But as Daniel Goleman points out in his best-seller *Emotional Intelligence*, these emotional skills have a very significant impact on economic success.[38]

Even the way we measure actual expenditures of money on health and education is misleading. Economics is full of rhetoric about human capital, but economists seldom try to measure the value of the existing human capital stock, or ask how it might be appreciating over time. Our national income accounts treat expenditures on health and education as forms of consumption rather than as forms of investment.[39] Economists consider investment rates a crucial indicator of future growth—but investment continues to be defined almost exclusively as dollars contributing to the production of new buildings and equipment. Even the development of new software technologies—which can increase productivity as much if not more than new hardware technologies—is usually excluded from the hallowed category of investment.

Treating spending on health and education as forms of consumption, right along with spending on sneakers and perfume, makes it easy to argue that these are "unproductive" expenditures. Opponents of government spending on health and education often apply this rhetoric, warning that this type of spending slows economic growth. But even the World Bank acknowledges that investments in health and education yield a high rate of return. It just so happens that it is a social rate of return, rather than a private one.

In addition to changing the way we tally the dollar expenditures devoted to the development of human capabilities, we need better ways of monitoring the hidden time and effort expended by families and communities. Human capital is not some kind of Play-Doh that arrives at school to be molded by teachers and then passed on to employers. It's more like a fruit tree that starts with a small seed that needs watering, weeding, and care. Education and job training are like fertilizer that can make it grow faster and stronger only if the sapling itself is sound. We shouldn't measure the cost of the tree simply by the fertilizer, even if that is the only input we had to pay cash for. And we shouldn't measure the output of the tree purely in terms of the fruit that reaches market. Trees also provide flowers, beauty, shade, oxygen in return for carbon dioxide, and places for birds to nest.

———————◆———————

Women's labor is considered a natural resource, freely available like air and water.

—MARIA MIES,
Patriarchy and Accumulation on a World Scale:
Women in the International Division of Labor

———————◆———————

The Human Development Index

Metaphors of investment grab the attention of economists and business people who are trained to think in these terms. But they shouldn't limit us to thinking entirely in terms of costs and benefits. Human capabilities have intrinsic value. As Aristotle put it long ago, the "chief good" is the "working of the soul in the way of excellence."[40] Economic development is only valuable insofar as it enables us to pursue this end. The early nineteenth-century socialist Robert Owen placed the following wish on his list of "conditions for happiness": "To receive from birth the best cultivation of our natural powers—physical, mental, moral and practical—and to know how to give this training and education to others."[41] That sounds to me like the goal that most parents have in mind when they think about their children's futures. But economics textbooks never mention this as a collective goal.

You could argue (and many of my colleagues would) that it's just too complicated and contentious—and it's simpler to concentrate on increasing income per capita. After all, our economic standard of living is an important determinant of our ability to develop our capabilities. In general, rich countries have better health and education systems than poor ones—and more extensive social safety nets. But this generalization doesn't hold as well as you might think, because health and education, like income, can be very unevenly distributed. The life expectancy of black men between thirty-five and fifty-four in New York City's Harlem is lower than that of the inhabitants of the Indian state of Kerala.[42]

In 1989, a group of economists were brought together by the United Nations to brainstorm about developing an alternative to GDP. A variety of measures had been developed to measure health and social welfare, but none had the simplicity of a single index that could be used to rank all the countries of the world. In boiling down their priorities, they settled on three essentials: the capability to lead long and healthy lives, the capability to acquire an education, and the capability to have access to the resources needed for a decent standard of living. They constructed an average of life expectancy at birth, child enrollment ratios and adult literacy rates, and adjusted per capita income and came up with the Human Development Index, or HDI.[43]

Every year since 1990, the UN Human Development Office has published international rankings. In 1995, the United States ranked first in real GDP per capita, but fourth in terms of HDI. Differences were even more striking for developing countries. Costa Rica, with a real GDP per capita about equal to that of Brazil, ranked thirty-fourth in HDI, compared to sixty-second for Brazil. Sri Lanka, with a GDP per capita well below that of Indonesia, scored higher on HDI.[44] The United Nations has devised other measurements as well—a Gender Development Index, a Gender Empowerment Index, and a Human Poverty Index.

Social Concern

You can take the capabilities of a bunch of individuals, add them up, divide by the number of individuals, and get an average. But something about the way that individuals work together usually makes a group more (or less) than the sum of its parts. Love and trust ensure a kind of reciprocity that usually elicits more effective cooperation than would any formal agreement. The pursuit of short-term self-interest can lead to opportunistic behavior that undermines long-term relationships.

The best recent example is what happened to the Russian economy in the 1990s, when a long-repressed hunger for free enterprise exploded into an every-man-for-himself feeding frenzy. Organized crime grew at a rapid rate, making bribes and payoffs a necessary business expense. If they weren't forthcoming, out came the machine guns. Much of the international aid that poured into Russia to help stabilize the economy went right back out and into the Swiss bank accounts of the new managerial elite. The situation became so obviously dysfunctional that even the research economists of the World Bank called for more attention to the social context in which markets operate. A survey they conducted of local entrepreneurs found that crime, theft, and corruption were significant deterrents to investment.[45]

How can we measure the aspects of our social and moral environment that seem to contribute to positive economic outcomes? In a study of Italian communities, the political scientist Robert Putnam sent out a large number of queries to government offices and measured how long it took—and how many phone calls were required—to obtain satisfactory answers. He found that administrations were more efficient in towns where community activities thrived, such as choral groups and soccer leagues. Putnam doesn't explain where high levels of civic participation come from, but he does argue that, once established, they tend to create a virtuous circle that reinforces further cooperation.[46]

He worries that we are experiencing a decline in civic participation in the United States, and points to an increase in the number of individuals bowling alone, rather than in community-based leagues.[47] This indicator is rather idiosyncratic, especially for people who don't know the difference between a candlestick and a bowling pin. One can certainly point to countervailing trends, such as increases in the number of soccer moms. The point is, we should be encouraging researchers to devise broader and more comprehensive ways to measure how we interact with one another.

One statistic that has captured my attention is an indicator of grow-ing economic segregation: more than three million American house-holds now live in "gated communities," places that often feature private security guards and electronic surveillance systems.[48] I live in a rural New England community with far less inequality of income than San Antonio, Texas, where I grew up. Unlike my Texan friends, I seldom lock my house or my car. When my car slides into a snowbank and gets stuck, I am fairly confident that the first person who drives by will stop to help me. If the battery in my car goes dead, I rarely have to call a tow truck, because I can find a friend or colleague to give me a jump start. I actually look forward to some of the unexpected neighborly encounters of winter.

I'd say that my standard of living is higher as a result. Some pretty imaginative research shows that "prosocial" behaviors are more com-mon in small towns than in big cities. If you leave a bunch of addressed stamped envelopes around in random places, someone is more likely to pick them up and put them in a mailbox. Here is a more poignant ex-periment: a child between the ages of six and ten is positioned on a busy street to stop passers by and say, "I'm lost. Can you call my house?" About three-quarters of adults in twelve small towns agreed, compared with fewer than half in big cities.[49]

Economists use the term "social capital" to try to capture the produc-tive elements of a social environment. It makes for a nice parallel with human capital, and the nomenclature insists that social relationships have economic significance. The World Bank's research department, in particular, likes to talk about social capital, not only because capital is what banks are supposed to deal with, but also because it provides a great excuse for socializing. People who are slow to come back into a meeting from a coffee break aren't just shooting the breeze; they are creating trust and goodwill.

Actually, I think the term "social capital" is misleading. It is applied to too many different things. Sometimes it's used to describe the extent of social networks—who knows whom. Sometimes it describes "good" cultural values, like hard work, savings, and risk-taking—who does what. If what you want to get at is who trusts whom, the "capital" metaphor is not particularly appealing. Trust can be accumulated, and sometimes we draw on funds of goodwill. But not everything can be bought and sold, or stored for an indefinite period of time. Trust and goodwill are not easily transferred from one person or one country to another.

I have an even more serious objection. Social capital is seldom defined so as to include feelings or emotions. Yet it is feelings of empathy and concern for others—developed through contact and interaction with them—that provide crucial reinforcement for trust and cooperation. As Dionne Warwick used to sing, "What the world needs now is love, sweet love. That's the only thing that there's just too little of." Why not call it social concern instead of social capital? That nomenclature would make economists squirm.

———————◆———————

Precisely because social capital is a public good, the costs of closing factories and destroying communities go beyond the personal trauma borne by individuals. Worse yet, some government programs themselves, such as urban renewal and public housing projects, have heedlessly ravaged existing social networks. The fact that these collective costs are not well measured by our current accounting schemes does not mean that they are not real. Shred enough of the social fabric and we will all pay.

—ROBERT PUTNAM,
"The Prosperous Community:
Social Capital and Public Life"

———————◆———————

The Dow of Wa

Whatever we call it, there is something quite difficult to measure that is clearly important to the economic success of most institutions. In an economy in which most individuals are paid a wage or salary for their work rather than a share of the output they produce, motivation matters. Workers who feel that they are being treated fairly tend to work better and harder than those who don't. This feeling is important to productivity when work is difficult or expensive to monitor—as when human problem-solving comes into play. It is especially important, as I've argued earlier, where the direct care of other people is involved.

An entire theory of business organization, called Total Quality Management (TQM), insists on the importance of a culture of cooperation. Developed after World War II by an engineer named W. Edwards Deming in conjunction with the Union of Japanese Scientists and Engineers, TQM helped the Japanese rise to global dominance in steel, automobile, and electronics manufacturing by the 1980s. The emphasis on cooperation resonated in Japan partly because it was consistent with their traditional cultural emphasis on *wa*, or harmony. The literal meaning of this word is "circle," but it conveys an ethic of harmony, unity, peace, and wholeness in a social group. Wa builds on *amae*, a feeling of familial affection between associates.

Since the late 1990s, the Japanese have been experiencing serious economic problems, and Western observers have been quick to accuse them of having too much wa, being unable to implement the kinds of tough but painful measures necessary to get their economy going again. I don't agree with this diagnosis of their problems. But in any case, when making comparisons, it's important to pay attention to definitions of success. In 1993, the Japanese experienced 144 crimes per 10,000 population, compared to 548 per 10,000 population in the United States.[50] Even more chilling—especially from the point of view of Japanese tourists—the murder rate of Japanese nationals in the U.S. in 1993 was five times higher than the murder rate in Japan.[51]

The concept of social concern gets at something close to the old-fashioned Western concept of solidarity. This is the good stuff that can bring people together in a worthy cause. I loved the treatment of it in the movie *Independence Day*, even if it was ridiculous: The threat of invasion from outer space by giant, ugly, irredeemably mean bugs heals broken marriages, overcomes racial differences, and successfully unites dancers, drunks, nerds, and warriors against the evil foe.

Solidarity, though, sounds anachronistic, while wa has a New Age ring. It reminds yuppies of the green stuff that they like to put on their sushi. It complements the personal energy, or *chi*, that acupuncturists and massage therapists like to release. I propose hiring some social healers to measure differences in wa across societies and over time, and then to construct a kind of moving average. The evening news could report the Dow of Wa, along with the Doug and Dolly Jones, and the Human Development Index.

Competing Claims

I remember my mother warning me, "Be careful what you ask for, because you may get it." Maybe she worried that I was too oriented toward traditionally masculine measures of success—educational attainment and a professional career. As I've emphasized in the preceding chapters, feminine measures of success have usually been quite different, and with good reason. Historically, most women devoted most of their efforts to caring for other people, a realm in which rankings were hard to come by and standardized quotas did not apply. In the world of care, the most important paybacks are the ones most difficult to measure.

Both women and men have brought strong family values with them into the caring professions. If they had not, the quality of the services we enjoy would surely be lower than it is. Our economy would probably be far less prosperous, measured even in the most conventional terms. If we really care about family values, however, we need to apply them critically to our economy as a whole. We can't continue to visualize the economy as a man's world of cars and trucks and steel, things that can be easily counted and weighed. The economy now encompasses many and varied activities that once took place within families, activities whose quality is defined by personal contact, responsiveness to individual needs, respect, and affection. We need to improve our measures of the kinds of success we care about. Otherwise, we will not be able to reward the kinds of behavior we most value.

———————◆———————

The honesty, trust, and sense of fair play that help economies to function well are not givens that are fortunately abundant or unfortunately scarce. They are not comparable to geological formations or biological necessities. They grow or wither depending on the institutions within which people live and the shared understandings of these institutions. Their content varies widely from individual to individual and from society to society. Economists need to be concerned not only to nurture these vital moral resources, but also to improve them. Better moral principles may enable people to coordinate their behavior better, and they may spread more readily because they command respect and emulation from others.

—DANIEL M. HAUSMAN AND MICHAEL S. MCPHERSON,
Economic Analysis and Moral Philosophy

II

Good Government

Competitive markets may be a useful means of organizing some things, but they are terrible at organizing others. The same may be said of two other major economic institutions, the family and the government. None of the three seems to work very well on its own. We need a better understanding of how each has affected the others in the past in order to combine them more happily in the future.

In this section, I explore the ways that family values—and disagreements over who should pay for them—have shaped policies toward public assistance, education, and taxation in the United States. The next chapter sets the stage with an overview of the historical relationship between these different types of economic institutions. It's an overview that challenges the accuracy of the story that conservatives like to tell about the big bad nanny state.

THE NANNY STATE

What's at issue here is whether we wish for our government to treat us as responsible adults or as child-like wards of the ever-encroaching Nanny State.

      —JAMES T. BENNETT AND THOMAS J. DILORENZO,
      USA Today, November 1998

My own experiences of being cared for as a child and, later, tending to young children as a teenage volunteer in a Head Start-type educational program, were positive ones for me. I'm not sure I would vote for Mary Poppins or Mrs. Doubtfire for president. But I like the idea of people like them playing active roles in government. Conservatives don't. As journalist Michael Novak puts it, "For at least 150 years the great faith of our educated class (or portions of it, at least) has been a worldly dream, a dream of a great maternal redistributive state, egalitarian and fair and just and compassionate."[1] He explains just how dangerous this dream is, using the term "nanny state" to describe any form of capitalism adulterated by social welfare programs.[2]

Many people believe that our political culture puts too much emphasis on individual rights and not enough on social obligations. I agree. But I define social obligations more broadly than conservatives do. I also tell a dramatically different story of how and why these obligations have changed over time. The growth of social welfare programs did not undermine the family; the growth of competitive capitalism did. Most welfare programs began as an effort to strengthen family ties and to improve the economic security of dependents. To a large extent, they emerged as an expression of family values. But because family values are so costly there has always been a struggle between men and women—and between rich and poor—over who would pay for them.

———————◆———————

nanny (naeni) . . . A child's form of address to a nurse; hence, a children's nurse. Also applied to a person or institution, etc., considered to be unduly protective or apprehensive.

— *Oxford English Dictionary*

———————◆———————

How the So-Called Nanny State Was Born

The simple version of the conservative story goes like this: Once upon a time, we all lived in stable, two-parent families, protected by our fathers and nurtured by our mothers. Some of us were poor, but we were all decent and upstanding. Then along came something called the welfare state, invented by well-meaning but weak-willed politicians who wanted to curry favor with lazy, greedy voters. Government started playing a protective role, offering benefits like retirement and unemployment insurance, health services, education subsidies, labor laws, and a social safety net. At first everybody liked this system, because it made them feel secure and loved. But soon they became too dependent. Even grown men started acting like spoiled brats.

Poor mothers fell into a spider web of dependency, sleeping late and watching soap operas while their kids listened to obscene rap music and mugged little old ladies who strayed into their neighborhood. The monthly welfare check was like a drug, an easy out, an effortless high that, in the long run, only harmed its recipients. It also corrupted men, who came to believe that their children didn't need their support. It even corrupted rich people, persuading them that it was no longer necessary to stay involved in church, or local charities, or the Junior League, because the welfare state was taking care of everything. Then, one day, some courageous men and women decided to fight back. Fending off accusations that they were mean-spirited and heartless egoists, they patiently explained that cutting social insurance would actually benefit poor people, as well as society as a whole.[3]

This story is pretty simple. But it includes some reasonable arguments derived from three extremely useful economic concepts: perverse incentives, crowding out, and rent seeking. Perverse incentives are just what they sound like, incentives that encourage people to do unfortunate things. The Englishman Thomas Robert Malthus made them famous about two hundred years ago when he argued that providing assistance to the poor would simply encourage them to breed. It sounded reasonable enough to upper- and middle-class people at the time, inspiring Parliament to implement major restrictions on public assistance to the poor.

In retrospect, however, Malthus's arguments are not convincing. British families started reducing the number of children before the new Poor Law went into effect, and differences in family size between Ireland and England contradict the claim that public assistance had a significant effect. Equally misleading are more recent claims in this country that welfare programs simply encourage poor people to breed. In the 1980s and early 1990s, so-called welfare mothers in the United States had the same average number of children as other mothers. The era of the welfare state is an era of low fertility. Possible perverse incentives do not always lead to unfortunate social consequences.

Consider a less politically charged example. Any form of insurance creates small perversities, sometimes described as "moral hazards." Some drivers get reckless when they're covered by collision insurance, and some hypochondriacs schedule a doctor's appointment only because they know it's covered by their health plan. Some people also succeed in defrauding their insurance providers. Such dishonest behaviors limit the efficiency of all forms of insurance, in the same way that friction limits the efficiency of all physical machines. But the existence of perverse incentives doesn't mean that insurance is a bad idea.

All families suffer from perplexities. One child may demand more love and attention than another. By giving it, you risk penalizing a less demanding child. Sometimes you decide to wash the dishes even though it's not your turn. In doing so, you risk rewarding the household member who is shirking. Sometimes your spouse does something bad and you forgive him or her, even though you know this may give him or her tacit permission to act badly in the future. These are not reasons to reduce insurance or cut back on forgiveness, but rather to think carefully about how they are used.

This similarity between the welfare state and the family should make us worry about the interaction between the two. The term "crowding out" emerged as a way of describing the possibility that government expenditures would not really stimulate the economy because their effect would be canceled out by the resulting reduction in private investment. The same possibility applies to the effects of government programs, such as Social Security, on private transfers. They could lead to "crowding out": grown children might become less willing to help out their elderly parents if they think the state has already assumed responsibility for the task. Similarly, public generosity might crowd out private charity.

But there's a big difference between possibility and reality. Much depends on the specific economic context as well as on the relative size of the effects in question. Social insurance programs developed in large part because they were more efficient and more reliable than family networks.[4] You may plan to depend on your children for support in old age. But what if they die before you (or just move to California and never call)? Sure, you can depend on your local church members to help you out if you lose your job. But what if they lose their jobs at the same time? Pooling risks across a large group makes them easier to manage.

Reliance on family support creates enforcement problems, for the obvious reason that family members sometimes don't come through. Libertarians imply that family virtues would flourish if we simply eliminated the state. Tell that to the many children of unmarried or divorced women who receive little or no economic support from their fathers. We need the government to enforce parental responsibilities that are crucial to children's personal and economic welfare.

On the other hand, enforced responsibility does not always nourish personal relationships. Would you love your parents more if you knew that they were going to move in with you in their old age? Would you feel closer to your brother if you had to support him when his wife ran out on him and his children? Maybe. But you would probably also feel resentful and frustrated. Reducing the burden of economic pressure on family relationships can improve the quality of emotional interactions and facilitate the kind of personal care that public assistance cannot provide. Public and private support can be complements rather than substitutes for each other.

The development of social insurance may have weakened incentives for family members to provide for their own, exacerbating the very problem it was designed to address. On the other hand, refusal to provide public assistance can leave helpless people, including children, destitute, and greater suffering doesn't automatically lead family or community members to fill in the gap. Social insurance programs emerged in response to problems created by a larger process of economic transformation. Cutting those programs won't solve the problems that led to them. For example, the growth of families maintained by women alone is just as dramatic in some countries that entirely lack social welfare programs—in Latin America and the Caribbean—as in our own.[5]

The crowding-out effects of various federal programs on the family seem pretty small. That doesn't mean we should stop worrying about them. Most of our solutions to problems lead eventually to more complex problems. Antibiotics dramatically improve our ability to fight infections. The more we use them, however, the greater the likelihood that more resistant strains of bacteria will evolve. We could just denounce the very concept of antibiotics, and ask God to cure our illnesses. Alternatively, we could use our God-given brains to develop and prescribe both antibiotics and social policies more wisely.

A third antiwelfare argument points to self-aggrandizing tendencies of government employees and politicians. Economists invented the term "rent seeking" to describe the efforts of interest groups to grab ever larger pieces of the economic pie. Rents are a flow of income that derive entirely from ownership, rather than from labor or entrepreneurship. It's never been clear to me how rents differ from profits, which can also be extracted in unproductive ways, even if they are sometimes the result of cleverness and midnight oil. But I certainly agree with the claim that groups of people often get together to pursue their selfish interests. I would put most politicians (and those who contribute to their campaigns) at the top of that list.

Making government smaller will not solve this problem. In fact, making government smaller is the clever rent-seeking strategy of an affluent group that doesn't want to share its good fortune with others. If you look at those parts of government they want to reduce, you will find that they involve transfers to people other than themselves. Pooling risks through social insurance is efficient because it shares the risks. But the easiest way to lower your own insurance (or tax) rate is to exclude risky (or unhealthy, or unlucky) people from the pool. If your health insurance provider banned everyone who was likely to have expensive problems (individuals over a certain age, those with family histories of cancer or heart disease, anyone with preexisting conditions such as HIV) think how cheap your policy could be. Of course, insurance would then be far more expensive for those who need it most.

Most campaigns to reduce social spending and to privatize programs such as Social Security declare that individuals should take more responsibility for themselves and embrace the virtues of self-reliance—as if the drama could be reduced to the Individual versus the Government. Often, however, affluent individuals form private groups that exclude anyone who might increase their costs or risks. They form country clubs, gated communities, private schools, and mutual funds with high minimum investments. Rent seeking continues in a different form, without any of the democratic safeguards that government can provide. Individuals outside the affluent group face even fewer opportunities for success.

Back to the bedtime story that lays all our woes on the doorstep of the welfare state. It's true that children can be spoiled by overindulgence. Public support can create perverse incentives and even partially undermine private support. Government bureaucracies are often unresponsive to the people they serve. These criticisms are reasonable. What's implausible, even nutty, is the claim that something called "the nanny state" created most of our social problems, and that cutting it back will solve them.

What Really Weakened the Family

It is often said that the growth of capitalism is about the growth of individualism. It shouldn't come as any big surprise that the growth of individualism weakened families—in some ways that were good and in some ways that were not so good. Part of the pressure came from technological change. As the scale of production grew and requirements for specialization increased, the family became less viable as a productive unit. At the same time, the growth of opportunities for employment outside the home pulled children out of the family economy, and offered them substantially greater independence.

More of them could make their own way, rather than simply wait to receive a dowry, an inheritance, or the right to work for the same master their father and mother had served. Wage employment was particularly important for women, giving them some alternatives to immediate marriage and motherhood. Even relatively poor jobs in early nineteenth-century textile factories gave young women more opportunities to make their own decisions than they had in the poor rural households they came from, where they were economically dependent on men. Most of us agree that the growth of individualism expanded personal freedom in some very healthy ways.

At the same time, however, capitalism and the growth of wage employment shook families up. They decreased the economic benefits of raising children, who became less likely to serve as a labor force for their own parents. The growing obsolescence of the family as a unit of production—and the accompanying rise of the business enterprise or corporation—drove a wedge between reproductive and productive work. Parents raised children who, when they grew up, went to work for someone else. Parents subsidized capitalists, producing workers that employers could hire without paying the actual cost of producing and training them. In addition, capitalists, unlike parents, had the power to hire and fire according to economic conditions. They were in the same relation to parents as men were to women—relatively unencumbered by family responsibilities. Thus, a system based on wage employment gradually began to supercede family-based enterprises.

It would be comforting if we could describe this whole process in technological terms, as though it were driven entirely by cost/benefit calculations. But history tells us that an enormous amount of collective conflict was involved. The early economic development of both North and South America led to the dispossession of the native populations and, in the American South and the Caribbean, to reliance on slavery as a means of mobilizing and exploiting labor. It is difficult to imagine any processes more disruptive of family life and community cohesion. The subjugation of such groups left their women vulnerable to rape and their children vulnerable to abandonment. A high incidence of births out of wedlock and high infant mortality rates were characteristic not only among slaves but also among the indigenous populations of Latin America who were incorporated into a system of forced labor and debt peonage.

Conservatives often argue that welfare programs bear responsibility for historical increases in the percentage of families maintained by women alone, as though it were feminine generosity that weakens families. But most welfare policies, including Social Security and Aid to Families with Dependent Children, originated in efforts to help individuals who had lost the support of family members—mothers who had been deserted or widowed, and the elderly who lacked sons and daughters willing or able to adequately support them.

A single mother might be able to make ends meet in an economy where her children could begin to work at an early age and where a network of kin and community could help her manage. Her position is more precarious in an economy in which children need to be sent to school and where kin and community are more diffuse. Demographic trends exacerbate the weakening of the family as an economic unit: declining fertility reduced the probability that an elderly person would have surviving children, while declining mortality increased the probability of surviving to old age.

Capitalist economies are prone to instabilities. Theoretically, the forces of supply and demand should help stabilize them and keep unemployment relatively low. But recessions, depressions, currency crises, and sometimes prolonged periods of inflation or unemployment are typical. Welfare state policies emerged partly as a response to such market failures. But they also emerged as a response to what we might call family failures—situations where networks of family and kin proved inadequate to the task of providing a social safety net.

The essential parallels between nation and family were first developed by a Swedish theorist of social democracy, Alva Myrdal.[6] She believed that nations could provide solutions for the weakening of family ties by developing health, education, a social safety net, and provisions for retirement. Myrdal was overly optimistic about public eagerness to assume such responsibilities, though Sweden and other European nations have gone much further in this direction than the United States. Myrdal also overestimated the efficiency of the welfare state, failing to recognize that it could be undermined by its own political and bureaucratic inertia. But her basic point is right: the welfare state is the family writ large.

The Daddy State

Until well into the twentieth century, the structure of political authority in the United States was male-dominated. The most obvious manifestation was women's lack of voting rights. But many other aspects of law and tradition reinforced the power of adult men. Regardless of what one thinks of the concept of a nanny state, it seems indisputable that, not too long ago, we all lived under the authority of a daddy state.

The Supreme Court, explaining why women should not be allowed to practice law, put it this way: "The paramount destiny and mission of woman are to fulfill the noble and benign offices of wife and mother. This is the law of the Creator."[7] In return, husbands had an obligation to support their families, and it has often been assumed that this support was reliable. Legally, however, support was defined quite narrowly as a minimum of subsistence—and even that responsibility was poorly enforced. Men who abandoned their wives and children were seldom pursued or prosecuted.

Traditional marriage offered women few rights in return for their obligations to care for family members. When nineteenth-century feminists suggested that wives should have a legal claim to one-half their husband's earnings in return for their own unpaid work, they were ridiculed. Even after women fought for and won rights to their own property and earnings, their legal claims on their husband's income remained limited.[8] Indeed, no such legal rights exist today. Married women who divorce gain rights to a share of joint property and, in some cases, alimony that represents a share of their husband's income. But within marriage a person who specializes in nonmarket work has no legal right to any more than the partner earning a wage or salary chooses to give them. So much for the ideal of partnership.

Divorce was uncommon until the mid-twentieth century, but economic desertion was not. Most abandoned mothers lived with kin, and therefore didn't show up in censuses as female-headed households. They became visible only when they gained enough economic independence to live on their own. Within marriage, fathers traditionally enjoyed absolute control over their children's lives (including their earnings) until they reached the age of twenty-one. Mothers begged, screamed, and fought for custody rights over their young children after separations and divorce. Opponents argued that wives would be more likely to leave home if they could take their children with them. Only toward the end of the nineteenth century did state courts begin to cede custody to mothers in cases of separation and divorce.

Historians argue that this shift reflected a growing appreciation of the best interests of the child. But it seems more than coincidental that this transition occurred just as children were beginning to be perceived as economic liabilities rather than as assets.[9] An increase in the importance of education was accompanied by a reduction in the productive contributions children could make to the household and laws restricting their participation in paid employment. Families had already begun making conscious efforts to limit births precisely because they recognized the growing costs of family commitments. Over the course of the nineteenth century, without any assistance from what we think of as modern contraceptives, the average number of children born per woman fell from over six to slightly more than three.

The subordination of women probably increased family stability. After all, it made families a pretty good deal for men. Women assumed primary responsibility for the tasks of care, making enormous contributions to family and community for which they were not individually rewarded. A woman's standard of living was largely determined by someone else's efforts and willingness to share. She was not paid for work performed. Few married women held paying jobs outside the home. Still, by the last decades of the nineteenth century, close to 40 percent of all unmarried women were working for wages.

Family Quarrels

As wage employment expanded, many feared that it would destroy the family. Because unmarried women had fewer dependents to support, and many could live at home, they could accept lower wages than married men. As they moved into paid work, they were accused of lowering wages for men. The economist John Ryan, as well as many of the skilled workers represented by trade unions such as the American Federation of Labor, argued that men should be guaranteed a wage sufficient to support their wives and children, a so-called "family wage." Grudgingly, they conceded that it might be necessary for unmarried women to work, but they insisted that married women should be excluded from paid employment.

Many employers implemented this policy of exclusion. Foremost among them were federal, state and local governments. Public schools, a major employer of women in the first decades of the twentieth century, required their female teachers to resign upon marriage. Such discriminatory policies were gradually undermined by employers' growing demand for labor. Furthermore, as fertility rates fell and cheap substitutes for many previously home-produced goods became available, housewives could not always occupy themselves productively at home.

Also significant were the collective efforts of women who demanded new rights in the workplace, the polity, and the home. But women never confined themselves to new rights for themselves. They also insisted on a more generous concept of social obligation and care for dependents. A motherly approach, they argued, would help the body politic.[10] Many men were horrified by the prospect. Around 1900, the famous English social Darwinist and philosopher, Herbert Spencer, warned that if women were given the vote, their soft hearts would cause the welfare state to run amok.[11] This sounds amazingly like the fuming of conservative critics of the nanny state today.

Other philosophers and writers, among them H.G. Wells and George Bernard Shaw, argued that mothers create a public good and deserve public support. Beatrice Webb, who helped lay the foundation for the British Labor party, explained the emergence of her philosophy in nanny-state terms: "We saw that to the Government alone could be entrusted the provision for future generations, to which neither producers nor consumers would attend as such. In short, we were led to the recognition of a new form of state, and one which may be called the 'house-keeping state,' as distinguished from the 'police state.'"[12]

Right before the outbreak of World War I, the case for public support for parenting was systematically explained by English feminist Eleanor Rathbone, who pointed out that capitalist economies, by paying workers on the basis of their individual product, provided no remuneration for the tasks of raising children. In a traditional family-based economy, reproductive work paid off in productive terms: as children matured they contributed to family output and consumption. The transition to an economy based on individual contributions to market production, however, was leaving mothers behind:

> If motherhood is a craft (as doubtless in a sense it is), it differs
> from every other craft known to many in that there is no money

remuneration for the mother's task, no guarantee of her maintenance while she performs it and (most important yet most ignored
of all) no consequential relationship recognized by society between the quantity and quality of her product and the quantity
and quality of the tools and materials which she has at her disposal. Children are the mother's product, food, clothing and other
necessaries her materials and tools; but a plumber's wife with one
puling infant has power to purchase more of these necessaries
than the plumber's labourer's wife, though she be the efficient
mother of a hungry family of six.[13]

Rathbone appealed to new standards of political economy that emphasized efficiency to suggest that the organization of parenthood was ar-
chaic as well as unfair. She ridiculed the notion of the "family wage,"
pointing out that paying a higher wage to men did not guarantee that
they would use that extra money for family support. Many of the men
who receive a "family wage," she pointed out, were unmarried and
childless.

Social provision for parenting would make it possible to support
those actually doing the child rearing. Initially, Rathbone's proposals
won few adherents, but after fighting two bloody wars, most of the
countries directly involved developed a poignant appreciation of the effort necessary to produce citizens and soldiers. After World War II,
Great Britain adopted Rathbone's proposals in the form of a modest
publically funded grant, or family allowance, per child. Other northwestern European countries, including France and Germany, also put
family allowance systems into place.

The American economist Paul Douglas, who later became a senator,
made a case for family allowances in the United States. But the concept
of public support for parenthood was less appealing in a country that
could easily attract immigrants—ready-made workers who were clam-
oring to embrace "freedom." Moreover, white Americans panicked
when they heard that fertility rates were higher among immigrants,
blacks, and Hispanics than among the "native stock." Racism increased
opposition to proposals that might have helped other people's children.

Even in the United States, however, the effort to push government policy in the direction of family support began quite early. Long before women won the right to vote, civic organizations campaigned energetically for family assistance programs.[14] The early twentieth-century movement for state old-age pensions was based on the assumption that the elderly deserved support in return for their parental labor. Many states developed programs that provided at least minimal support for mothers who had been widowed or deserted by their husbands. By 1921, forty states and two territories offered these "mothers' pensions."[15] Despite restricted eligibility and low benefit levels, they provided models for New Deal programs developed in the 1930s.

In 1921, women won the right to vote in federal elections, breaching the bastions of the Daddy State. One of the immediate consequences was the passage of the Sheppard-Towner Maternity and Infancy Protection Act, which was aimed at reducing maternal and infant mortality and enhancing reproductive health (though the clinics it funded were strictly prohibited from dispensing contraceptive devices or information). The Daddy State remained firmly in place. But men's monopolistic grip on government policy was loosening.

Subsidizing Homemakers

The Social Security Act of 1935 was the most important piece of social welfare legislation passed in the United States in the first half of the twentieth century. The Great Depression, which began in 1929 and lasted throughout the 1930s, created a painful awareness of the problems of sustained unemployment. Neither the labor market nor the financial market was working according to theory. Those who managed to keep their jobs found themselves burdened by family members who, through no fault of their own, had nothing to contribute to family income.

The Social Security Act reflected a consensus that neither the labor market nor the family could provide adequately for all dependents, especially the elderly. It provided insurance against unemployment and guaranteed a minimum level of support in old age for covered workers. It also provided life insurance in the form of survivor's benefits for the widows and orphans of covered workers. Finally, the Social Security Act put a program called Aid to Dependent Mothers into place (the precursor to Aid to Families with Dependent Children), providing public assistance to single mothers living in poverty and their families.

If Social Security represented something of a victory for the maternalist vision, it represented an even greater victory for benevolent paternalism. Many of its features were designed to reduce the financial burdens on male heads of household or—in the language of chapter 2—to diminish the penalty for men who accepted and fulfilled responsibilities toward family members. Married men who paid exactly the same taxes as single men enjoyed much greater benefits: support for their wives in old age, as well as insurance for their wives and children. In this sense, Social Security represented a partial, half-concealed victory for the concept of a family wage for men.

From among the turbulent efforts to cope with unemployment and poverty in the early 1930s, the elderly emerged as a powerful interest group, mobilizing in associations such as the Fraternal Order of the Eagles to demand more attention to their economic plight. The grassroots proposals of the period clearly reveal familial preoccupations. One national leader who emerged, a Dr. Townsend, called for a straightforward economic application of the biblical injunction to "honor thy father and mother" in the form of a monthly stipend of two hundred dollars for all men and women over age sixty-five. Funded by a sales tax, the Townsend Plan would have treated men and women, wage-earners and non-wage earners, whites and people of color, exactly alike. Significant numbers of people joined what were called "Townsend Clubs" to promote and lobby for this plan.[16]

Employers, as well as affluent taxpayers, winced at the thought, and argued for an entirely self-financing pension system instead, based on paycheck deductions. Such a system, however, would have done nothing to alleviate the problems of the current elderly population. Since it was too late for them to start paying in, they had no way to begin taking out. A political compromise emerged, one that required paycheck deductions but provided immediate support for a large number of retirees who, of course, had not paid into the system.

Sometimes Social Security is called "social insurance" and treated as completely distinct from "public assistance." But this distinction is misleading. Unlike private insurance or pension systems, where a clear relationship exists between what an individual puts in and what that individual later takes out, Social Security was based on a family model, a principle of intergenerational reciprocity. The elderly had helped support the young; it was now their turn to enjoy support. As in the traditional family, the young were helping to support the old. The burden was not too onerous because the size of the working-age population was large relative to the number of retirees. In 1945, there were 50 covered workers paying taxes into the system for each retiree drawing benefits.

From its inception, Social Security provided benefits for the wives of eligible workers as well as the workers themselves (husbands of eligible workers were not added until the 1970s). A married retiree receives an additional stipend for his spouse, making his monthly check far larger than it would have been if he were single. Furthermore, Social Security provides a form of life insurance for family members: if a covered worker dies before retirement, survivors' benefits are provided for his spouse and minor children. In this way, Social Security subsidizes the traditional breadwinner/homemaker family.

Note that it subsidizes a particular kind of family structure, rather than a particular kind of work. To illustrate, consider the following scenario: Mrs. Earn-a-Salary is a wife who works full-time outside the home, has no children, and avoids housework, never even cooking Thanksgiving dinner; Mrs. Stay-at-Home is a cheerful homemaker who works full-time at home, knits sweaters for her three children, and makes sandwiches for everyone's lunch boxes. Both women are married to men with the same earnings and employment history, so they will receive the same retirement benefits (Mrs. Earn-a-Salary can opt for benefits based either on her own earnings or on her rights as a spouse; since her husband probably earns more than she does, she is likely to opt for the latter). Let us assume that both women stay married for ten years, and will therefore remain eligible for benefits through their husbands even if they divorce (until 1965, divorced women lost eligibility).

These women are contributing to the economy in different ways. Both are working about the same number of hours overall and getting the same benefits, which seems reasonable. The main difference is that Mrs. Earn-a-Salary is paying Social Security taxes, and Mrs. Stay-at-Home is being subsidized. Now, switch parts of their story around a bit. What if Mrs. Earn-a-Salary not only works full-time outside the home, but raises three children, putting in a double day in order to take care of them? And what if Mrs. Stay-at-Home doesn't raise any children and doesn't do much work around the home, because she prefers going shopping? (Maybe, after ten years, her husband divorces her on these grounds.) But whether she is divorced or not, it seems odd that she receives the same benefits as Mrs. Earn-a-Salary.

The comparison brings home the point that the Social Security spousal benefit is not consistent with the principles of competitive markets, because it does not reward individuals for their own contributions. On the other hand, it doesn't actually reward the nonmarket work of raising children and caring for dependents. It simply subsidizes married couples in which one spouse stays out of paid employment, regardless of how many children they raise or how much nonmarket work is actually performed. The income tax provision that allows families a dependent deduction for a stay-at-home spouse has the same effect.

Contradictory Consequences

The specific features built into the Social Security system then reflected the profound tensions between the maternalist goal of public recognition and support for caring labor and the paternalist strategy for meeting this goal by keeping women at home and out of competition with men. It wasn't a bad compromise for its day, and it shored up the traditional breadwinner/homemaker family throughout the 1940s and 1950s. But powerful economic and political forces were challenging this traditional division of labor, and their effects gradually began to erode the very foundations of Social Security—intergenerational reciprocity, or the notion that, by supporting them in their old age, the young would repay the elderly for the costs of raising them.

From its inception, Social Security enjoyed enormous popularity. After all, it reduced poverty while reinforcing the sacred values of individual and familial responsibility. Originally, it covered only about one-half of the labor force. But coverage expanded almost continuously, in terms of both the number of workers covered and the amount of assistance offered. At the same time, the relative proportion of the elderly in the overall population was growing—a result of continuing fertility decline. By 1960, only five workers were paying into the system for every retiree taking money out.

Still, the program continued to expand. In the 1960s, a system of national health insurance for all those over age sixty-five was added (Medicare), and retirement benefits were indexed to the rate of inflation, thus protecting recipients against any loss of buying power. What made this expansion feasible? The weakening of the very breadwinner/homemaker model on which the system was based. Wives and mothers entered the labor force in increasing numbers in the 1960s. When they did, they began paying taxes into the Social Security system. Their benefits, however, remained largely unchanged.

When these women retired, they could choose between benefits based on their own employment history or their spousal benefit—what they would have received by virtue of being married to an eligible worker. Because women's earnings tended to be much lower than men's (and they still are), the spousal benefit was typically higher than their own—and so they took that. Therefore, most married women who paid taxes into Social Security received exactly the same benefits in their old age as a housewife who never paid any taxes in at all. It was more than a little ironic. The Social Security system discouraged married women from working for pay. But many of these women moved into paid employment anyway, which helped prop up Social Security finances.

This contradictory effect benefited the Social Security system itself. However, another unanticipated effect created serious problems.

Though Social Security initially strengthened feelings of solidarity between old and young, tensions began to grow as the relative size of the elderly population ballooned and the fiscal boost from married women's entrance into paid employment slowed down. Social Security itself—and federal policy in general—did little to offer financial support for parents. Thus, it contributed indirectly to a process of fertility decline that intensified conflicts of interest: fewer workers began paying higher taxes to support more elderly with higher expenses.

The reasons why Social Security initially strengthened intergenerational solidarity seem obvious. After all, it was based on an implicit contract between the old and the young. People in their late working years could see that the productivity of the younger generation was being shared with society as a whole. Because the retired elderly were receiving benefits of far greater value than the contributions they had made, they were probably more willing to pay taxes to support education and other public programs targeted at the young. Such attitudes were doubtless strengthened by the conclusion of World War II. A landmark piece of postwar legislation, the G.I. Bill offered public support for the college education of all veterans. (Unfortunately, few women could take advantage of it.) Federal programs also made it easier than ever before for families to own homes.

The prosperity of the 1950s and 1960s, however, did not lead to permanently higher birthrates. As pointed out earlier, the costs of raising and educating children were going up, and parents chose to concentrate their efforts and resources on a smaller number of offspring. Moreover, women now enjoyed a range of alternatives to full-time motherhood. New access to contraceptive information and technology made it easier to limit births. During the baby boom of the 1950s and early 1960s, the birthrate went back up to the level it had been at around 1920. Soon after, it resumed its downward trend.[17] The two-child family has since become the norm.

Advances in medical technology, on the other hand, combined with prosperity to significantly increase life expectancy of the old. In 1930, the population over age sixty-five represented 5.4 percent of the entire population. In 1990, it represented 12.5 percent. By the year 2050 it is projected to reach almost 20 percent.[18] Declining fertility offers initial economic benefits because it reduces the relative proportion of young dependents—children under age eighteen—in a population. It becomes costly, however, when that small cohort grows up to become taxpayers, and faces the prospect of supporting an older generation whose size reflects the higher birthrates of an earlier period.

Consider a purely family-based system of support in old age. The combined resources of five grown children can easily support one parent surviving past the age of sixty-five for, say, five years. The combined resources of two grown children cannot easily support two parents surviving past of the age of sixty-five for, say, fifteen years.[19] No system of intergenerational transfers can get around this demographic problem.

Social Security, however, actually made this problem worse in some respects. By "socializing" the principle of reciprocity between old and young, it offered much better insurance for the elderly than they could obtain from family members. But transfers from parents to children remained largely private, while transfers from young to old became public. Moreover, the principle of reciprocity was not really respected—the elderly were "repaid" by the young on the basis of their participation in wage employment and *not* on the basis of their actual contribution to rearing the next generation. Consider the above example of the family with two children who have two parents between the ages of sixty-five and eighty. Then add a childless elderly uncle in need of support. You can see why the younger generation might be showing signs of stress.

By redistributing money from young to old, regardless of whether the old had previously cared for the young, the Social Security system effectively redistributes resources from parents to non-parents. This is because benefits are based only on wages (and taxes paid out of them) or on marriage, with no consideration for the actual time and effort involved in raising children. A couple that raises three children receives the same retirement benefits as a childless couple, as long as the highest earner in both families had the same earnings history. Meanwhile, however, the parents have put tremendous time, money, and energy into raising the children who grow up to pay taxes to help support the older generation as a whole.

In the old breadwinner/homemaker world, this might not have mattered much, because most people were raising about the same number of kids and putting about the same effort into this task. But, increasingly, that is no longer the case. Since the 1960s, we've seen a small increase in the number of people who have no children at all, and a big increase in the percentage of families maintained by mothers alone. Few of these mothers are eligible for any spousal benefits through Social Security. When they do go to work for pay, their Social Security taxes are just as high as everyone else's.

After their paid work is over, they go home to take care of their kids, usually with very little financial or direct assistance from men. This activity of caring for kids is not considered work, even though it produces the next generation of taxpayers to keep Social Security solvent (and the next generation of workers, who will actually take on the physical and emotional tasks of caring for the elderly). A stingy divorced dad with a good employment record will receive far more generous benefits in old age than a dedicated mother who had to take time out from paid work to tend to her family. In this respect, the Daddy State lives on.

Let's go back to the tensions between maternalism and paternalism. The U.S. government could offer substantial direct support for the actual work of caring for dependents. Family allowance systems adopted in most northwestern European countries come close to doing this by offering an allowance for each child. Levels are too low to have much impact on fertility rates, but in conjunction with other public subsidies for health provision and child care, they succeed in reducing poverty rates among families with children, including those maintained by women alone.

In the United States, the greatest obstacles to such policies probably derive from racial/ethnic inequalities, which tend to undermine our sense of familial loyalty to fellow citizens. But resistance to maternalism also plays a role. Men don't want to pay for maternal services, especially when they can get them for free. And some women are justifiably worried that pay for parenting could be just one more way of encouraging women to specialize in a form of work that has historically put them at a disadvantage.

Piece of Cake

Conflicts of interest between men and women over who will pay the costs of care affect government policies in a number of ways. One of the best examples of women's challenge to the Daddy State concerns child support enforcement. Rates of both divorce and nonmarriage began increasing steeply in the 1960s as marriage rates declined sharply. Women had new options and, partly as a result, marriage ceased to be as comfortable an arrangement for men as it had once been. Much of the blame for the "decline of the family" was placed on women. But men were also eager to escape some of the traditional obligations of family life. Indeed, men have generally been quicker than women to jettison family responsibilities.

As Barbara Ehrenreich shows persuasively in *The Hearts of Men*, our cultural definitions of masculinity began to change in the 1950s. Before that time, marriage and fatherhood were seen as essential to the male transition to adulthood. Gradually, however, single men began to play a more idealized role. New men's magazines, such as *Playboy* and *Esquire*, celebrated unencumbered bachelorhood.

Strong communities and families had once exerted some pressure on men not to abandon pregnant women. Fathers and brothers who feared that they would become responsible for the care of children born out of wedlock acted as marriage enforcers with other men. But in the new big-city environment, men enjoyed the benefits of anonymity, and fathers and brothers lost both the incentive and the ability to act as marriage enforcers.

Another complicating factor was the advent of more effective access to contraception and safe, legal abortion. Many men welcomed a new cultural interpretation of pregnancy as a woman's decision, and therefore a mother's responsibility.[20] As women gained the right to choose, men gained the freedom to opt out of relationships. Increased economic and cultural independence for women certainly played a role in the transformation of the family. But if women had not struggled for that independence, they would have been even more susceptible to abandonment.

Until recently, government policy discouraged men from being responsible to families by failing to stipulate or enforce the child support obligations of non-custodial fathers. Throughout the 1960s and 1970s, policy makers refused to concede that child support was a social problem. They preferred to think of it as a private matter into which government should not intrude. But Congresswoman Pat Schroeder, among others, insisted that the Census Bureau conduct a survey to ascertain the amount of support that single, separated, and divorced mothers were actually receiving from the fathers of their children. The results, published in 1980, seized public attention. They showed that in 1978, only about 60 percent of all mothers living with a child under eighteen whose father was living elsewhere had child support agreements; only about half of these were receiving the full amount they were due.[21]

New administrative measures introduced in the 1990s included automatic wage withholding for new support awards. The emergence of effective DNA testing made it easier to determine fatherhood, and some states and counties developed highly effective means of enforcing child support agreements. Methods of determining the amount of child support to be paid also improved. But the difficulties of actually enforcing a child support order across state lines remained—and remain.[22] Public enforcement has focused on fathers of children living in poverty, on the grounds that doing so will save the taxpayers money. This kind of enforcement proceeds whether a mother wants it or not; indeed, it proceeds even if it causes her to live in fear of retaliation.

The desire to save taxpayers money contributed to a significant improvement in the percent of never-married mothers receiving child support, which rose from 5 percent in 1976 to 18 percent in 1997. Over the same period, however, never-married mothers increased as a proportion of all single mothers. This shift, combined with a virtually unchanging level of child support for separated and divorced moms, countervailed the improvement. Overall, the percentage of mothers receiving child support from non-custodial fathers has remained unchanged, about 31 percent.[23]

Some of these mothers didn't—and don't—wish to accept support from non-custodial fathers because they don't think that further contact will be good for them or their kids. One survey taken in 1989 showed that about 40 percent who didn't receive it said they didn't want it.[24] Some mothers were probably getting support "under the table." But even when we take these factors into account, the sheer numbers involved tell us that the problems remain serious.

Economist Elaine Sorenson estimates that if all single mothers had child support orders and received an average of $5,400 per year in child support, a total of $47 billion would be transferred each year. Compare that to the $17 billion that in fact changed hands in that way in 1997—and to the $16.5 billion that the federal government spends on cash transfers to poor families through the program people call welfare—Temporary Assistance to Needy Families.[25]

Opposition to aggressive child support enforcement—except where welfare recipients are concerned—is still widespread. First prize for the most imaginative metaphor comes from conservative Charles Murray, who explains that the father "has approximately the same causal responsibility [for getting a woman pregnant] as a slice of chocolate cake has in determining whether a woman gains weight."[26] Second prize goes to Stuart Miller, who, editorializing in the *Wall Street Journal*, labeled child support enforcement a "draconian transfer-of-wealth scheme."[27] He warns that fathers shouldn't be expected to pay when they are absent from the home and therefore deprived of their children's company. If children charged by the hour, would fathers be more likely to spend time with them? Another explanation is that fathers who don't pay avoid contact with their kids in order to minimize their feelings of guilt—the old "out of sight, out of mind" strategy.

Entrepreneurs, seizing a great opportunity, have begun offering to collect support from delinquent parents in return for a substantial share of the take.[28] Obviously, their only desirable customers are those with potential claims on relatively prosperous men. Among affluent families, the sums involved can be enormous. A Massachusetts man who fled to Florida to avoid paying his children an accumulated $200,000 in legally required support was recently nabbed, to a lot of attention from the press. Probably the biggest payoff to the increased enforcement effort is the emergence of new cultural sanctions against paternal desertion. One indicator is the increasing use of the term "deadbeat dad," which came into everyday parlance about the same time that the National Weather Service decided that hurricanes shouldn't always bear female names.

In the long run, changing the norms that stigmatize irresponsible fathers will probably exert even more influence than changing the laws. Women had to fight to change both, and their access to better paying jobs and greater political influence played a crucial role. Conservatives argue that empowering women weakens family obligations. The history of child support enforcement yields just the opposite diagnosis: women have not been powerful enough to enforce men's responsibilities. More than just money is at stake. Fathers in the United States spend remarkably little time actively caring for their children—less than three hours a week, on average.[29] The costs and risks of parenting continue to rest much more heavily on women than on men.

Nanny's Advice

Most discussions of the gender gap are far too abstract. I don't always expect men and women to behave differently, especially if they belong to the same nation, race, and class. Gender is only one dimension of a person's identity, and a pretty malleable one at that. But the gender gap shows up pretty clearly in political disputes. In 1996, 50 percent of all women saw themselves as Democrats, 29 percent as Republicans. Most men, on the other hand, preferred the Republican party. Women consistently expressed much greater concern about issues of social welfare. Education or health care was listed as a top priority by 37 percent of women but only 26 percent of men; conversely, one out of three male voters (but only one out of six female voters) ranked the budget deficit or taxes as a top priority.[30] One exit poll showed that 54 percent of women, compared with 43 percent of men, voted for Bill Clinton,

largely determining the outcome of the 1996 presidential election.[31] Results like these drove George W. Bush to portray himself as a "compassionate conservative" in the 2000 presidential campaign.

Much of this chapter has dwelled on the Social Security system, with
good reason. Social Security represents this nation's first major effort to
define and enforce our collective responsibility for the care of dependents. The effort has not been entirely successful. Eliminating Social
Security, however, would be a terrible idea. If we urged individuals to
take complete responsibility for themselves, saving and investing
money on their own for their old age, we would lose the benefits that
social insurance confers. More importantly, we would give the
working-age population less of an incentive to invest in the capabilities
of the younger generation. We would essentially be telling everyone to
go it alone.

Two long-term demographic trends have disrupted traditional links
between the family, the market, and the government: an increase in
women's participation in paid employment and a decline in the birth
rate. Yet both these trends have positive long-term implications. By
moving us toward a world of less specialization by men and by women,
they have created possibilities for a more democratic provision of care.

Most of us agree that more care for others would be better. But if we
can't agree on a good way of organizing it and a fair way of paying for
it, we're all tempted to skip out. We need to use our government to help
solve this coordination problem. Solving it will cost money and it will
require substantial redistribution of resources from men to women,
non-parents to parents, and rich to poor. Call it a nanny state if you
want. It sounds more like a family state to me.

CHILDREN AS PETS

I think I know why so many people seem to think that parents, especially mothers, should pay most of the costs of raising children. These people think of children as pets. Parents acquire them because they provide companionship and love. Therefore, they should either take full responsibility for them or drop them off at the pound. Some wind up with beautiful golden retrievers with cheerful, trainable temperaments. Others are stuck with ugly mutts. In any event, those who care for them are the ones who get the fun out of them; therefore, they should pay the costs. All dog owners should use Pooper Scoopers, observe leash laws, and not ask the taxpayers for subsidies.[1]

I love my pets. They include a beautiful white horse and a clever black dog, and I get a lot of pleasure from their company. But I would never argue that the time and money that I spend on them benefit anyone but me. Nor would I ask society to help pay for the expense of keeping them. My neighbors down the road are raising five kids as well as two dogs and four rabbits. Both parents work full-time, splitting shifts so that one adult is always home. They probably get even more pleasure from their menagerie than I do from mine. But there is another difference. The money, time, and love they devote to their kids will benefit the rest of us.

According to one recent estimate, a middle-income family raising a typical child spends about $1.45 million over a twenty-two-year period.[2] Both childless individuals and "deadbeat dads" can take that money and put it into investments that offer them a much higher private rate of return. Private retirement benefits as well as Social Security payments are based on market earnings, which are much higher for individuals who never took time away from paid employment to raise a family. Who is going to pay the taxes to finance those future benefits? Who are we going to hire to take care of us in our old age? The kids down the road, when they grow up.

Child-rearing provides important public benefits. That we provide relatively little public support for it—and what support we do provide comes in indirect and inconsistent ways—helps explain the anger that motivated the welfare reforms implemented in 1996. Many people said they disliked programs that gave people incentives "not to work." But that problem could be viewed in reverse: very few programs, apart from welfare, provided much support for family work, which is not rewarded in the labor market. Increasingly, it came to seem that mothers living in poverty were the only ones who could afford to take time out of paid employment to stay home with their kids.

This perception was inaccurate, based on a widespread misunderstanding of levels of public assistance as well as the high visibility of welfare programs relative to the tax benefits that more affluent families enjoy. Still, the stresses and strains on low- and middle-income families with children are pretty great. Indeed, most families currently living in poverty are there because the private costs of raising children are so high. If we provided more generous, universal support for families, as do most of the countries of northwestern Europe, we could dramatically reduce the percentage of children living in poverty. We could also produce happier, healthier, and more productive adults.

———◆———

Parents have joint primary responsibility for raising the child, and the nation shall support them in this. The nation shall provide appropriate assistance to parents in child-raising.

—United Nations Convention on the
Rights of the Child
(Ratified by all nations except Somalia and the U.S.)

———◆———

Children as Public Goods

To say that children are public goods is not to say that everyone should raise them or that we need a greater number of them. Rather, it is to say that once they are brought into this world, we all have something to gain from fully developing their capabilities. Parents should take responsibility for their own children. By the same token, the public should accept responsibility for recognizing, rewarding, and supplementing parental efforts. This principle is reflected in many of our existing social policies, but economists seldom examine the ways in which the costs of child-rearing are distributed.

Among other things, we allow families a dependent tax deduction and tax credits, offer public assistance for poor parents with young children, maintain a system of institutional and foster care for children whose parents cannot take care of them, and provide public education (a topic discussed in more detail in the next chapter). Economists Robert Haveman and Barbara Wolfe have calculated that government spending in 1992 accounted for about about one-third of total expenditures on children. Their calculation probably underestimates parental contributions, because it does not fully account for the cost of the time that parents devote to child care, which substantially lowers lifetime earnings.[3]

Government expenditures on education per student have increased over time, but public support for parents of young children has declined. Between 1948 and 1960, the value of the federal tax exemption for dependents was so high that few families with children even paid income taxes. The real value of the exemption, however, was undermined by inflation between 1960 and 1985. Economist Eugene Steuerle estimates that the tax rate of families with two children increased 43 percent over this period, while the average tax rate for families without children remained essentially unchanged.[4] Economist Ed Wolff argues that the relative well-being of parents has declined over the last three or four decades.[5]

In 1998, Congress added a tax credit of $500 per child sixteen or younger to the income tax code. While this is a move in the right direction, it does not counteract the previous decline.[6] If the value of the dependent tax exemption had remained at the same percentage of median family income at which it was originally set in the 1940s, it would amount to more than $7,000. In 1998, parents could subtract $2,700 for each dependent child under the age of eighteen from their taxable income, unless they enjoyed an extremely high income (over $189,950 in aggregate gross income for a married couple filing jointly). The amount saved in taxes depends on which tax bracket the family is in. For families with incomes below the poverty line, who pay zero income taxes, the benefits are nil. For families in the 31 percent tax bracket (with what the I.R.S. calls an adjusted gross income between $104,050 and $158,550 for a married couple filing jointly) the potential savings amount to as much as $852 a year in 1999. Add in the child tax credit, and a family in that bracket can receive $1,352 per child.

These tax savings amount to something similar to what northwestern European countries call a "family allowance." But there are three big differences. First, countries like France, Germany, and Sweden provide much higher benefits. Second, they provide a lump-sum benefit which is the same for children in all families, rather than a benefit whose value goes up along with the income tax bracket a family is in. Finally, these countries also provide substantial services such as nationally funded health care, child care, and paid family leave from work. In the United States, families with children pay the expenses for these services mostly out of their own pockets.

Income inequality among families translates into inequality among children. Analysis of household budgets shows that most families spend about the same percentage of their total consumption expenditures on their children—about 25–30 percent if they have one child and 35–50 percent if they have two children.[7] The distribution of private expenditures on children largely reflects the underlying distribution of income. The average income of the families in the richest 20 percent of families is more than twelve times that of the bottom quintile. Thus, about twelve times as much is available to the top fifth of children as to the bottom fifth.[8] Not surprisingly, most of the children in the bottom fifth live in families with incomes below the poverty line.

We do provide a "social safety net" in the form of programs targeted specifically at poor families with children. These programs include the program commonly termed "welfare," Temporary Assistance to Needy Families (TANF), previously called Aid to Families with Dependent Children (AFDC). Much attention has focused on the reforms introduced in 1996 which imposed both a work requirement and a time limit for assistance. That the real value of the cash benefits provided has declined substantially over the last fifteen years is seldom mentioned.

Poor families in which a parent is working for pay (and not receiving TANF) are eligible for the Earned Income Tax Credit. Unlike the other tax-linked family benefits described above, the EITC is refundable, so families enjoy the benefit even if it is greater than the income taxes they owe. Childless families can receive a small refund, but much larger benefits are provided for families with one or two children. No benefits are provided for children beyond the first two. In the United States, expenditures on EITC now exceed those on TANF. While the amounts provided do not guarantee that working families with children will enjoy incomes over the poverty line, they provide a significant boost for low-wage earners.

Income tax exemptions, the child tax credit, TANF and the EITC represent the main components of our public transfers in support of child-raising. One might suppose that they have a substantial equalizing effect, in keeping with principles of equal opportunity for children. Such is not the case. The amount of support received by poor families and their children doesn't add up to much more than that offered to affluent ones. Families in between get the least support of all.[9] Before looking at these numbers in more detail, it is useful to review how and why our policies of support for poor families have changed.

Down with the Queen

It was Ronald Reagan who formally introduced the icon of the "welfare queen" into our political discourse. He described her as a woman with eighty names, thirty addresses, and twelve Social Security cards who collected veteran's benefits on four imaginary deceased husbands. Her tax-free cash income alone, he explained, was over $150,000. When reporters tracked her down, they discovered an offender who had used two aliases in order to collect twenty-three public aid checks totaling $8,000.[10] No matter. The welfare queen was not cut out of cardboard. She was constructed of a magic metal that could attract every kind of fury. A political lightning rod, she was to the 1990s what the "Red menace" was to the 1950s—a unifying target of outrage.

The old system, AFDC, explained conservative Lawrence Mead, was too maternalist, too indulgent.[11] Feminine generosity, explained Rush Limbaugh, was the cause of male misbehavior: "Welfare is given with good intentions, but it has emasculated John Q. Stud. He has reverted to irresponsibility."[12] Naturally, in the world according to Rush, eliminating welfare would make him responsible again.

The rhetoric of the 1990s often described welfare as a "female problem"—a metaphor that became a gross conceit with one critic's characterization of welfare as the "umbilical cord through which the mainstream society sustains the isolated ghetto society."[13] According to journalist Mickey Kaus, snipping that cord would enable babies to begin to breathe on their own. Perhaps he also envisioned them feeding themselves and changing their own diapers. My experiences talking with many different audiences about welfare policy have persuaded me that very few people understand just how bad that policy has been or how it currently works.

I spent much of 1995 working with Randy Albelda and others on *The War on the Poor: A Defense Manual*, a book of facts and figures designed to counter some of the most common myths about welfare. As part of our efforts to promote the book, we did a number of shows on talk radio. These consisted of phone interviews on stations all across the country, with call-ins from their listeners. Ironically, this experience persuaded me that the facts I knew and could put in context were probably less important than the feelings I heard.

I knew I was in for a rough ride when the first caller described welfare as the "nectar of the gods." For a moment, I thought that he meant that welfare was some kind of cheap wine, but then I realized that he meant nourishment including the steak and lobster that, everyone knows, welfare recipients habitually pig out on. I was about to explain that the real value of benefits provided through AFDC and food stamps has fallen 20 percent over the last fifteen years when a grandmother started telling me about the welfare mothers who were ruining her bingo games. I had started to say something about how lotteries and other forms of gambling hurt the poor when she shut me up by asking if I had ever actually played bingo.

I felt like an accountant who had accidentally wandered into an express-your-anger workshop with no therapist in sight. Scott, the host of a Cincinnati show, told me he thought all welfare should be eliminated. I asked him if he knew that two-thirds of welfare recipients were kids. This really got his goat. "Every time I talk to a liberal," he complained, "they always start whining about the children." I was about to ask if he said this to his wife when she asked him to change a diaper, maybe once a week, but he had a caller on the line. A small-voiced woman who confessed that she was receiving public assistance. "But I'm not like those other mothers," she insisted, "I only have two kids, and I'm not going to have any more." I told her that she was typical. Two children are the average for welfare mothers, as for mothers as a whole. Scott laughed dismissively. "I just do not believe that," he responded, "and if government statistics say that, they're lying." He got his information about the poor from a friend who worked in a convenience store.

I cited the same statistic on the air with Jesse, a talk show host from Oregon who was debating me on a Cleveland show, and he called me a liar too. He added that all government statistics are part of a liberal conspiracy to keep poor people down. It was as if he needed to use welfare to explain all the bad behavior in the world, because otherwise he wouldn't know how to make it stop. He kept repeating the toll-free number of Brothers Organized for a New Destiny. He told our listeners that the worst thing about welfare is not that it causes women to over-mother but that it causes men to under-father. It undermines responsibility. If we could just get rid of it, men would step in and take charge again. Poverty, drugs, and crime would disappear.

I tried to think of something that listeners in Cleveland could relate to. Most, though certainly not all, welfare recipients in 1995 were either working or trying to find a job. About two-thirds of those on the rolls left within two years. However, they often ended up returning because the jobs they found paid poorly or petered out.

On the next show, on a Hartford station, I brought up the federal budget. I said that we spend more money on subsidies for the well-to-do than on programs for the poor. I would have given some specific examples of this nectar, but my host, "Sebastian in the Morning," thought I needed to see a shrink. The feeling was mutual.

Who Gets What

Poor people in this country lack the shield of glib self-confidence that well-educated, affluent citizens often use to deflect criticism of their own entitlements. Ask a group of young professionals how many of them receive federal housing assistance. Very few will raise their hands. Then ask how many deduct the interest they pay on their home mortgage from their income taxes. Many will get huffy at the very idea that this could be considered public assistance. Yet this tax deduction costs the federal government more than twice as much as is spent on low-income housing assistance and low-rent public housing.[14] There are no limits or restrictions on it—the deduction applies to summer homes in Aspen and beach compounds in Key West as well as homes for the middle class. It's worth about $5,000 a year, on average, to taxpayers making more than $200,000.

A look at family support policies yields similar results. The implicit family allowance paid in 1999 for a family in the 31 percent tax bracket amounted to $852 in tax savings per child plus a $500 tax credit, for a grand total of $1,352 per child. In 1996, the average monthly amount per TANF recipient amounted to only slightly more—$1,630 a year. Single mothers receiving TANF, moreover, were subject to strict income and wealth eligibility standards, time limits, and work requirements. None of these restrictions apply to affluent families enjoying the dependent tax exemption and child credit. Indeed, the affluent family described above could claim another $837 in tax savings if one parent avoided paid work and therefore qualified as a dependent.[15]

Poor families eligible for the Earned Income Tax Credit fare better. Among families receiving the maximum benefit, the additional benefits that accrue from the first child amount to $1,878 and for the second child, $1,446. In other words, EITC recipients with two children in 1998 could receive a slightly higher level of cash support per child (an average of $1,662) than either poor families on TANF or affluent families with $110,000 or more in taxable income. But since third and higher-order children receive no subsidy, EITC recipients raising larger families actually receive less per child than many affluent families of the same size.

What about in-kind benefits to poor families such as Medicaid and food stamps? Money spent on these programs adds up to a substantial amount. But if you count these in, you must also count tax expenditures that primarily benefit the affluent, such as the mortgage interest tax deduction described above, Medicare (which provides health benefits to citizens over age 65 regardless of income) and the tax exemption of employer contributions to health insurance and pensions from taxation.[16]

Federal support for child care can be compared more specifically. Like our implicit family allowance system, it takes two very different forms. Tax benefits are of primary relevance to families who are not poor. The child care tax credit amounts to 20–30 percent of child care expenses (depending on family income level) up to $2,400 for one child under thirteen, and up to $4,800 for two or more children if these expenses are incurred as a result of parental work for pay. Thus, it can offer as much as $720 per child. Since this credit is not refundable, it offers no tax benefit for most families unless they have at least $15,000 in income. No upper-income limit is imposed on this credit, and as high-income families are more likely to spend money on child care, they are the most likely to benefit.

A less well-known but more generous subsidy takes the form of "dependent care pre-tax accounts," which allow working parents with child care expenses to set aside up to $5,000 per year in an employer-sponsored account that is exempt from income and payroll taxes. Employers have an incentive to set up such accounts because their payroll taxes are reduced. Here again, the value depends on the tax rate, but a family in the top federal income tax bracket can garner a subsidy amounting to $1,980, not counting the effect of payroll taxes. In sum, the range of tax subsidies generates reimbursements ranging from $480 a year to a high of almost $2,000 (the benefit to a family in the highest tax bracket of a fully utilized dependent care tax account).

In the early 1990s, the cost of these tax expenditures far exceeded federal expenditures on programs aimed to serve low-income families. In 1993, the cost of the Child and Dependent Care Tax Credit alone was $2.5 billion, compared to $1.7 billion spent on child care for AFDC recipients, Transitional Child Care, At-Risk Child Care, and the Child Care and Development Block Grant.[17] Since that year, child care funding targeted at low-income families has been significantly increased and program delivery has been reorganized as part of the changes to the larger welfare system legislated in 1996. Still, the amount of total entitlement expenditures authorized for 1999, $2.2 billion, was still slightly below the overall cost of the Child and Dependent Care Tax Credit.[18]

Furthermore, most recent administrative effort has gone into providing child care for recipients of TANF as a way of encouraging transitions to paid employment. As a result, many of the working poor have found it difficult to find subsidized slots; families with an income above the poverty line but less than $40,000 a year remain the group least likely to receive assistance with child care costs.[19] As one expert puts it, "Concerns about the potential costs of that increased level of demand, along with concerns about the implications of future economic downturns, have made some states hesitant to expand their child care programs much beyond the welfare population."[20] Even states that allocated additional state funds, such as Massachusetts and New York, have long waiting lists for low-income families.

Another, more telling example of benefits to relatively affluent families lies in a comparison between the treatment of single parents receiving welfare and those covered under a universal program. A provision of the Social Security system known as Survivor's Insurance provides benefits for families who suffer from the death of an adult member. If you pay Social Security taxes and happen to be run over by a truck tomorrow, your spouse and children under eighteen will receive "survivor's benefits," a monthly check from the federal government.

The amounts of survivor assistance are generous. In 1997, the average annual benefit per child was $6,012. The average yearly benefit per widowed father or mother was $6,264. For a widowed father or mother with two children the total would have come to $18,288. Compare this number with the maximum TANF benefit in the typical state for a family of three: $4,548.[21] The family receiving survivor's insurance doesn't have to qualify as poor to receive this help. There is no requirement that the surviving spouse find a job. If you were one of those economists who think that people's actions are entirely determined by some calculation of benefits and costs, you might worry about the fact that a mother is much better off murdering her husband than leaving him, as long as she can get away with it (either way, she needs a really good lawyer).

Economist Gary Becker, who writes a regular column for *Business Week*, is referring to welfare when he says "It's bad for children to grow up in a family where all they know is that a check comes from the government every month. That's destructive of the child's self-respect and self-esteem."[22] Is it bad for children if their families get a check from survivor's insurance, or from a life insurance policy? Or, for that matter, from a trust fund set up by their grandparents? Do popular magazines of TV shows ever interview young middle-class widows or rich coupon clippers who are ashamed of receiving a monthly check?[23] The amount of federal money docketed for TANF in 1997 was $16.5 billion. State expenditures were about the same, for a total of $33 billion. The total amount spent on survivor's benefits was about $55 billion.[24]

Ironically, the only politician brave enough to call attention to this double standard is former senator Daniel Patrick Moynihan, who strongly criticized AFDC in the 1970s but strongly resisted TANF in the 1990s. He pointed out significant differences in the racial composition of children on programs that were considered welfare versus those considered "social insurance," and emphasized that welfare had become "stigmatized as a program for people who did not work in a world where other people did."[25] In the end, it comes down to how we define insurance, as well as how we define work.

In the early 1990s William Weld put his inherited millions to effective use in a campaign to become governor of Massachusetts. When he established time limits on public assistance, he explained that his motives were the very best. "It's bad for children," he explained, "to live with a parent who does nothing but hang around the house."[26] As though parents who stay home with their children are only hanging around! I wonder if Governor Weld's mother ever worked for pay. I wonder if she ever collected Social Security, despite being so unproductive a member of society.

The Big Stick

The so-called welfare reform bill of 1996 revoked a guarantee of assistance to poor families with children that had been in place for sixty years, giving the states considerable freedom to design their own policies. The bill set a limit of five years on the amount of time a family can be on welfare and mandated new work requirements, changing the name of the program from Aid to Families with Dependent Children (AFDC) to Temporary Assistance to Needy Families (TANF). It also reduced eligibility and benefits for a wide variety of other programs, including food stamps.

Some parts of the 1996 reforms made sense, such as the emphasis on getting mothers into self-supporting jobs. But the package that Congress approved was designed to punish those who accepted responsibility for the care of others. Its passage publicly declared that raising children is not work. We had gone from a set of rules that discouraged good behavior to a big stick that presumed that individuals would behave badly unless threatened with sanctions.

Aid to Families with Dependent Children provided a stipend — albeit a small one — for poor single mothers who wanted to stay home with their children. The working poor and borderline poor—as well as the more affluent—grew to resent this. Between 1975 and 1995, the hourly earnings of most workers in the U.S. stagnated or declined. Family income increased significantly over this period only because an increasing number of mothers of young children entered paid employment. The concept of appropriate work for women changed from one in which they specialized in family care to one in which they juggled the responsibilities of family and paid employment.

Mothers themselves were probably better off being less specialized. Staying home with their children, they were not developing many marketable skills. What would happen to them when their children were grown? They were unlikely to qualify for much support from Social Security, or to accumulate any savings for old age. It's not even such a great idea for children over the age of two to spend the entire day with a parent, if the alternative is a few hours of well-designed, high-quality education.

David Ellwood, one of the early architects of Clintonian welfare reform, argued passionately that a paid work requirement would actually help poor families.[27] So, there was an element of tough love here, as in, "It's for their own good." But training is supposed to be about positive incentives as well as negative ones. Most liberals and conservatives agree on why welfare recipients found it difficult to move into steady employment in the 1980s. It was economically irrational for them to do so. The jobs for which they qualified were poorly paid. Going to work imposed new costs, including transportation and child care. Once they left AFDC, they lost health insurance coverage through Medicaid. And finally, the most perverse aspect of the system: for every dollar of reported earnings, recipients lost a dollar of the benefits they received. In other words, they were subject to an implicit tax rate of 100 percent.[28]

Working out the implications of this system is a great exercise for the students in my introductory microeconomics class, who initially cringe before technical terminology. Here's how to drive the meaning of implicit tax home. Imagine that you are back in the ninth grade and your parents are giving you a weekly allowance. It's enough to buy some basics, but not enough to buy the sneakers of your dreams. So you decide to get a job, and you find one in a local fast-food restaurant, where you are paid the minimum wage. You tell your parents, thinking they'll be proud of your hustle. They are proud, but they also see an opportunity to increase their own disposable income. They tell you that they are going to reduce your allowance by the exact amount of your earnings. For every dollar you earn, a dollar of your allowance will disappear. That is an implicit tax of 100 percent.

In class discussion, students are outraged by the notion that parents would do such a thing. "That is so unfair," one of them will say, "that is like discouraging work." "So," I ask, "what would you do in this situation. Would you take the job, or not?" They think about this for a while, then explain. "Well, it would depend. How big is the allowance?" I asked them how much they think the average welfare recipient receives per month in cash assistance. The answers range from $500 to $1,500 a month.

In 1995, the first year I went through this exercise, the average benefit per AFDC recipient (including children) was less than $200 a month plus food stamps worth another $70. The real value of these benefits, adjusted for inflation, was 20 percent lower than it was in 1970. The value of the real minimum wage was also much lower than in 1970. Even taking advantage of the Earned Income Tax Credit, and working full-time year round, a welfare recipient would not have earned enough to bring her family over the poverty line, much less pay for health insurance. By almost any calculation, a single mother with two children was better off on welfare than working at a job that paid minimum wage.[29] The high implicit tax rate pushed her to choose between these two alternatives, rather than to combine work with welfare.

One of the big puzzles of poverty research in the early 1990s was that the expenses that families on welfare reported were much greater than their income. In cities like Boston and Chicago, the monthly AFDC benefit was not sufficient to pay rent even in the crummiest of neighborhoods. Economists couldn't figure it out. Enter sociologist Kathryn Edin, who understood that the culture of poverty, like any culture, looked different from the inside. She spent time getting to know individual mothers on AFDC, making it clear that she cared about them. She took her own children to play with theirs. What she learned was that a lot of these women were working very hard.[30] They were figuring out all sorts of ways to earn money on the side, running hair salons in their kitchens, babysitting each others' children, even running a numbers game. Not all of them were cheating in such appealing ways. Some of them were selling drugs or sex. But Edin's intensive studies showed that they were anything but lazy.

They were doing what most people do who get paid under the table in cash for work. Except welfare recipients were trying even harder to hide their earnings, because they were subject to an implicit tax rate of over 100 percent, instead of the 30 percent rate that most taxpayers face. You would think that a bunch of Republicans worried about tax incentives would have made much of this problem. Instead, they focused on the "big stick."

First, the work requirement. Though the details were left up to the states, the 1996 legislation required recipients to get a job or, if they failed, to perform community service jobs. Exemptions were offered for some families—those with very young children, those who were disabled, etc. But states that failed to move a certain percentage of their recipients into work by a target date would be penalized. Since most recipients were already working, what this requirement amounted to was a demand that they work harder and longer. In some cities and states, the long hours required in community service meant that welfare recipients were working for an implicit wage (the value of their monthly benefits divided by the hours of community service performed) of less than $2 an hour, a violation of federal minimum-wage law. What a convenient substitute for unionized public employees who had been earning more than twice as much![31] Fortunately, political pressure has forced many states to back off on the number of hours required. With unusually low unemployment rates in the 1990s, jobs were not hard to find. When the unemployment rate goes back up, however, the time limits will still be in effect.

Theoretically, the post-1996 social order brandishes the big stick at absentee fathers as well as mothers, but it doesn't seem like poor mothers have benefitted much. A uniform, top-down requirement of child-support enforcement took the following form: "Honey, you don't have a choice. Name the father or you won't be eligible for assistance." Almost all the child support subsequently collected from the father goes to reduce the amount of public assistance received.[32] The aim is to save the taxpayer's money, not to improve the child's standard of living. Mothers and children benefit financially only after they leave public assistance. Then they are allowed to receive the child support directly.

Since they do benefit in the long run, you might wonder why they have to be threatened in order to name the father. The reason is simple. Acknowledgment of paternity brings men privileges as well as obligations. When a man's name appears on the birth certificate he can assert the right to visit the child, and, under some conditions, demand custody. For a poor mother who feels she has already made one mistake, that can be a problem.[33] A significant share of all women on welfare have experienced domestic violence. Conceding this point, legislators have included a paternity-disclosure exemption for mothers who can prove that they are physically at risk from their child's father. Local officials have some discretion about how they apply this exemption; some may require more "proof" than others. A father who does not want to acknowledge paternity can give the mother a black eye in order to help her get an exemption. In this situation, she might even give herself a black eye.

Between August of 1996 and December 1999, the welfare rolls fell by more than 40 percent. In public forums, the big stick took most of the credit. But statistical analyses indicate that the declining unemployment rate played a critical role. Other carrots, or positive incentives, were at work, among them the provision of subsidized child care and the expansion of the Earned Income Tax Credit that reduces the implicit tax rate on low-income working parents by giving them substantial tax refunds. States like Minnesota, which offered decent support for women leaving welfare, achieved much better results than states like Texas, which did not. Moreover, on the national level, success in reducing the welfare rolls was much greater than success in lowering the poverty rate for children, which remained higher than it had been in 1975.

Burdens of Proof

Our legal system operates the way it does because we decided that it is worse to punish an innocent person than to let a guilty one go free. This principle has some significant implications for the way we think about welfare. What TANF does, essentially, is shift the burden of proof. Previously, a poor person was eligible for relief unless it could be shown that he or she had done something wrong. Now it goes the other way around. A poor person who can show that he or she has followed all the rules may, just may, be able to get relief.

Whether or not you think this is a good change depends on whether you think individuals should have a right to public assistance, and under what conditions you think they should lose that right. TANF does a better job than AFDC at punishing the guilty. It kicks the ass of the underclass, the socially irresponsible, the behaviorally impaired, the lazy bums.[34] The problem is, it also punishes the innocent, a category that is not limited to those who are under eighteen. A single mother who has enrolled in a community college and is making progress toward her degree is notified that she no longer qualifies for assistance. She will lose her benefits unless she finds a paying job or shows up for community service. A mother under eighteen whose father has sexually abused her is told she will be cut off unless she moves back home (she doesn't have any other adults that she can live with). A single man in his fifties who is laid off from his job but doesn't qualify for unemployment benefits is told that he cannot receive food stamps for more than three months in any given year. An elderly couple, legal immigrants who have worked hard and paid their taxes for many years, are told that they are no longer eligible for assistance even though they are infirm.

Innocence is a metaphysical concept. We don't have a bar code for it, so it's difficult to inventory. If you study the personal histories of most poor people in some detail you will find that once upon a time they did something dishonest, lazy or mean. Most middle- and upper-class people have, too. So let's use a different term and define good behavior as a combination of honesty, a willingness to work, and a willingness to care for others. People who receive an above average total "good behavior score" are in the top half of the good behavior distribution, and we will call them relatively well-behaved.

Now the question is, what percentage of those receiving public assistance fall into this category? Are welfare recipients any less honest, on average, than other folks? Many of them lie about their income but so do most taxpayers. In 1998, the federal government lost an estimated $195 billion from tax evasion and inaccurate reporting, an amount greater than *total* federal and state spending on AFDC for the last five years.[35] Are adult welfare recipients any more likely to commit crimes than other people? This seems unlikely, since most of them are women, who are much less likely than men to commit felony crimes. (Note: it costs about ten times as much to incarcerate someone as to put them on welfare.)

Next, consider welfare recipients' willingness to work. (Let us agree, for the millionth time, that raising kids *is* work.) Willingness to take a paying job is hard to measure, since most of these individuals have faced significant disincentives to paid work, as well as severe constraints on their ability to find and keep decent jobs. Studies have shown that about 68 percent of those who received AFDC left the program within two years, though some half of those found it necessary to return at a later date. About one third gave up and became dependent on assistance, but we don't know whether this is a problem with their motivation or a result of low skill levels.[36]

What about the "willingness to care for others" component of good behavior? Individuals are not even eligible for assistance unless they are taking care of a child under the age of eighteen, and the fact that they have assumed this responsibility largely explains their vulnerability to poverty. Almost all mothers would be better off economically if they handed their children over to the state for care in group or foster homes. Then they would be able to find paying jobs without worrying about child care. In fact, when some mothers run up against the time limit on TANF, they are forced to do just that.

In a speech he made in 1980, before he became a supreme court justice, Clarence Thomas criticized his sister for living off of AFDC. "She gets mad when the mailman is late with her welfare check," he exclaimed. "That's how dependent she is." What Thomas never explained was that his sister, in addition to raising four children without any assistance from their father, worked two jobs to support her family. Emma Martin applied for AFDC only after an aging aunt, who had been helping take care of her children, suffered a stroke. At that point, she found she couldn't work for pay and care for five dependents on her own.[37] Her brother Clarence declined to provide enough help to fill the gap. So much for the moral high ground.

As Newt Gingrich led the charge to reduce welfare spending in 1994, he was asked what would happen to the children of parents who failed to meet the new time limits and restrictions. With his customary charm, he proposed that they be deposited in orphanages. As Charles Murray had previously explained with relish, "those who find the word 'orphanages' objectionable may think of them as twenty-four-hour-a-day preschools."[38] Much of the ensuing debate pitted movie fans of Father Flanagan, played by Spencer Tracy in *Boys' Town*, against advocates for Oliver Twist, the abused orphan-hero of Charles Dickens's famous novel.

Certainly, there are many things about child development that we don't understand. But one thing we do know is that a strong, stable relationship with a primary caregiver is the single most important determinant of healthy child development.[39] It seems a bit ironic that men otherwise critical of government intervention are so sure that it can do a better job raising children than mothers can. Full-time institutional care for children in the U.S. is limited precisely because its often unhappy consequences are widely recognized. In 1997, only about 500,000 children lived in institutional and foster care combined, compared to about ten million children receiving TANF.[40] Foster care is notoriously problematic. At least twenty-one states are either under court order to meet federal standards regarding health and safety or have been sued for failing to meet those standards.[41]

Poverty and Kids

The summer of my sixteenth birthday, my mother found me a job working as a teacher's aide in a Head Start-style program for underprivileged kids. One of my students, a six-year-old named Ernie Rodriguez, smelled terrible—so bad that the other kids made fun of him. He looked pretty clean, but on closer inspection we discovered the source of the smell—thick yellow-green stuff oozing out of both his ears. I talked to his mother, who didn't speak any English, didn't have a car, was not on welfare, and had no medical insurance. I called up our family doctor, Frank Martin, and asked him if he would see Ernie for free.

Dr. Martin, good friends with my uncle Tom, also a physician, was a wonderful old-fashioned kind of family doctor like Marcus Welby. He took a look at Ernie and rounded up enough free samples of antibiotics to clear up the infection. Next, he suggested that I take Ernie to see a specialist in ear surgery who worked in my uncle's office. The specialist informed me that both of Ernie's eardrums were ruptured, leaving his inner ears vulnerable to infections. The infections, he said, would probably recur and gradually erode the bones of the inner ear. The end result would be complete and irreversible loss of hearing. The only remedy would be surgical repair of the eardrums, which involved skin grafts. The cost would be $3,000.

The surgeon wasn't the least bit apologetic about his refusal to operate on Ernie for any less. It took Uncle Tom a couple of weeks to figure out a solution. He knew a competent and amenable surgeon who would be on rotation at the county hospital. I took Ernie to the emergency room when he was there, and he agreed to write up one of the ruptured eardrums for surgery and the requisite hospital stay. Fixing both ears, he said, would be pushing it. Afterwards, with one ear bandaged, the kid looked like a lopsided Mickey Mouse.

That year I ran a small after-school program in a local neighborhood center that Ernie and his brothers faithfully attended. What unnerved me was the fact that they were always hungry. They spent hours hunting for pecans in vacant lots, sometimes eating green ones that made them sick. They cared more about the cookies and milk I usually brought them than about the projects I organized. It was a relief, the following summer, to leave for college. But I took the image of Ernie and his brothers with me to class, along with memories of my fathers' employers, the McFarlins.

Almost one in five kids in the United States lives in a family with an income below the poverty level. For African American and Hispanic kids, the figures are double that—over 40 percent. These rates have declined with the recent economic boom, but compared to European countries, our child poverty rates are off the scales. Among African Americans in this country, infant mortality rates are twice as high as among whites. Largely because of income inequality, the average life expectancy in the U.S. is lower than that of France, Sweden, Canada, and Japan.[42]

Early childhood education, child care, and parental training shape the capabilities of the younger generation. Children who grow up in poverty seem slower to develop their cognitive and emotional skills. Some of the reasons are obvious. Like Ernie Rodriguez, who introduced me to emergency room care, they may have serious health problems. Or they may live in violent, stressful environments that have traumatizing effects. And they may lack the attention and stimulation they need to develop their abilities.

Social scientists have collected a surprising amount of data exploring the relationship between income, neighborhoods, family structure, and a long list of outcomes, including I.Q. scores, school performance, and tests of psychological competence and well-being. It's difficult to separate the effect of income from other factors, but sustained poverty among young children clearly has negative effects.[43]

Some parents (both rich and poor) don't do a particularly good job with their kids, and their shortcomings reduce the impact of any additional income they might receive. We are still left with the question of where their shortcomings come from. This leads us back to some consideration of the conditions under which they grew up, and their parents in turn grew up, and so forth, ad infinitum. It's not an inexorable cycle, but a probabilistic one. Clearly, some individuals escape it. They successfully swim against the current and jump over any obstacles in their way. We can admire them, the same way we might admire those salmon who are big enough, strong enough, and determined enough to make it up the fish ladder and over the dam. But like the biologists who tally the fish who never reach the upstream waters, we can at least analyze the strength of the current and the design of the ladder.

Many social scientists who are, like me, critical of the larger structure of our economy, hate this "cycle of disadvantage" stuff because it calls attention to the behavior of the little fish rather than the existence of the dam that makes the ladder necessary in the first place. It "deflects attention from the unyielding inequities of institutions, the machinations of power and privilege, and unpopular redistribution plans."[44] But it seems to me that if we concentrate hard enough, we can worry about all these things at the same time. It's our responsibility to develop children's capabilities as best we can, whether or not this will end poverty or radically change the world.

Many liberals argue that we can improve outcomes for children. They point to a variety of social programs that have generated good results. Conservatives argue that we can't, either because poor children are inherently less intelligent or because poor parents are irredeemably incompetent. They seem to debate the question in empirical terms, as though everyone agrees that if we could break the cycle of disadvantage, we should. But, as usual, it's what people want that shapes their sense of possibilities. The crucial questions are not whether we can break it, but rather how hard we are willing to try—and who, exactly, would pay.

Consider one program developed during the "war on poverty" that hasn't been accused of encouraging bad behavior—Head Start. First of all, it was misnamed: Catch Up would have been more accurate, since the intent was to help children from poor families who were way behind the starting line when they reached first grade. Head Start was carefully designed to help parents help their children and to foster emotional and social, as well as cognitive, skills. Its effects, and those of related efforts, have been extensively studied over a long period. They reveal small, significant improvements in children's academic performance and increases in the probability of successfully graduating from high school.[45]

Since its inception Head Start has been a public relations success, serving young children who are "picturesque in their innocence."[46] However, between 1970 and 1985, the real value of federal spending per Head Start recipient declined significantly, and the program never served more than one-fifth of eligible children.[47] Presidents Bush and Clinton both pledged to increase federal funding so that all eligible children would be served. Both helped win funding increases, but neither came close to meeting their stated goal. In 1997, approximately 40 percent of all eligible children were enrolled in Head Start.[48]

The program would fall seriously short even if it were 100 percent funded. Because it is only a part-day, part-year program for children ages four and five, mothers must make other child care arrangements if they hope to find paying jobs. Eligibility is almost entirely restricted to families with incomes below the poverty line, leaving most of the working poor without access to free, high-quality preschool education. Some states, like Georgia, are moving toward greater public provision of these services, but their progress is slow and uneven.

Why does this early childhood education, this "most popular" of anti-poverty programs languish? Poor children's contributions to electoral campaigns have probably been on the slim side, and I doubt that any of them have spent the night in the Lincoln Bedroom. A more serious problem is that relatively few poor people vote. Maybe they don't know enough about what they could accomplish at the polls. Then again, maybe other people know too much.

Vive La France

Young Americans used to travel to France to study art, write poetry, or play jazz. Nowadays, they ought to go there to start families. In the United States, pregnant women who work for large firms (about half of the total) have the right to a job-protected leave of twelve weeks—if they can afford it. The leave is unpaid. In France, any woman with at least ten months of prior work experience can take a leave of sixteen weeks, paid at 84 percent of her salary (up to a ceiling). New parents who have been working for a current employer for at least a year have the right to an extended unpaid parental leave or a reduction in work hours (with a proportionate reduction in pay) until their child is three years old.[49]

In addition, France provides a variety of payments to parents that are far more generous than the modest deduction for dependents that the I.R.S. allows here. French single mothers receive regular payments until their children reach the age of three, at which time they are expected to return to full-time work. All families, regardless of income, enjoy a family allowance for children beyond their first. The French are trying to encourage families to have more than one child. This is an aspect of their policy I don't agree with, but I note that it doesn't strongly affect the birth rate. French families have, on average, two kids, slightly fewer than families in the United States. What public support for child rearing does well is reduce child poverty rates—which in France are about 6 percent, compared to our 17 percent.[50]

French family policies, combined with their national health insurance system, also have a dramatic effect on children's health. As soon as a woman learns she is pregnant, she registers with the local health system. If she wants to receive maternity benefits, she must meet a regular schedule of prenatal checkups, and, after the birth, a series of hospital visits for her infant, which include vaccinations. The local clinic exists as a kind of intermediary between the family and the hospital, a place where parents can drop in for advice or assistance. Special efforts are made to look after immigrant families who might not have a good command of French or who may not know how to get access to state services. Clinic workers see themselves as advocates.

In 1999 I set out on a study tour of French child care centers with about fifteen other people, mostly journalists and politicians, people who seem to learn about the world by actually asking real people questions. We visited three different "maternal schools," which provide early childhood education. All children who have been potty-trained (a skill usually acquired by children between 2½ and 3 years old) are eligible. Attendance at French schools is not mandatory until the first grade, which begins at age 6. The maternal schools, however, are extraordinarily popular. Close to 100 percent of French 3–5-year-olds attend them, whether or not their parents are working for pay.

Kids can stay for fewer than the normal six hours a day, or more if needed, making use of "wrap-around" care services at a low cost. Kids in France don't go to school at all on Wednesdays (a legacy of a previous era, when these days were reserved for religious instruction) but on those days schools provide supervised leisure services and field trips. And children usually attend on Saturday mornings.

Visiting the schools, I understood their popularity. The teachers are well trained. They have more than the equivalent of a U.S. college degree. They are paid the same as elementary and secondary school teachers and treated as professionals. As government employees, they are assured good benefits and job security. Not surprisingly, their turnover rates are low. They are passionate about their pedagogy. "Our job is not to make children learn," one explained, "but to teach them to love learning." Regular bouts of exercise, hot meals at lunch, naps for the younger children, and art projects are interspersed with such tasks as learning the alphabet, the days of the week, and the months of the year.

Class size is fairly large, averaging about twenty-five students. But the teachers have aides, hired by the municipality, to help them. One teacher we watched seemed a bit strict in her efforts to keep things orderly; most were quite relaxed, allowing kids who weren't interested in the lesson, or who were just not feeling social to go off into a corner and play on their own. Children's artwork was everywhere, including, among the usual lovable and silly stuff, copies of paintings by famous French artists. One four-year-old I talked to confided the secret of Matisse. "He is very joyous," she said.

The most beautiful school we visited, in a Paris suburb called Vanves, was built on what they called a "daisy pattern." Each classroom was shaped like a petal around a central hub, a large indoor play area full of gym equipment. Each had a door to the outside, as well as to the hub. Parents could bring their children directly to the room and stay a while if they wished. The mayor joined us for lunch at the school dining room. While the first course of artichoke hearts, leek, and tomato salad was being served to everyone, he had to make a speech. He asked the children, "Do you know who is visiting us today?" They shouted out, "*Les Americains.*" Then he asked, "and what do you think of when you think of Americans?" They suddenly became quite shy, but one finally piped up "*MacDo!*" This is what the French call McDonald's.

Another school on the tour was in a low-income neighborhood called Villejuif. It had just applied for the special consideration and extra resources given to "economic priority zones," or low-income neighborhoods. The children there were more ethnically diverse, with a large number of boys named Mohammed. There, the mayor explained earnestly how crucial maternal schools are to the integration of immigrant children into French society. He served us some excellent Sancerre wine . at lunch, waxed eloquent on the history of friendship between the U.S. and France, and ended his speech with the warning that "the whole world was not soluble in Coca-Cola." At least that's what I, given my imperfect command of French, believe he said.

Our delegation kept asking how much the maternal schools cost. The answer turned out to be quite simple: about the same per student as the cost of elementary education. What most amazed our group was the virtually unanimous pride the French expressed in these facilities. We kept asking, "But what do you say to critics who . . . ?" The answer was always, "We don't have critics." Everyone in France supports maternal schools. There are wide divisions among political parties, which range from communist to proto-fascist. But on the subject of maternal schools, there seems to be no disagreement. Perhaps because of their history, their experiences with two world wars, and their previous ethnic homogeneity, the French maintain an extraordinary sense of national solidarity. "Our children," they say, "are our greatest resource." I tried, in my fractured French, to explain to the mayor of Villejuif how different things were in the United States. He poured me more wine and told me that we should make another revolution.

France is not a perfect model. The unemployment rate is distressingly high, especially among youth. The French finance their social programs with a heavy per-worker tax on employers, exacerbating this problem. The French do little to encourage absentee fathers to take more direct responsibility for kids. The easy availability of child care (provided mostly by women) may actually reduce the pressure on fathers to become more involved.

French food is delicious, but not always healthy. We don't need to mimic the French. We just need to learn from them.

Family Generosity

There are plenty of good examples of countries that provide decent support for children and families: they include most of the countries in northwestern Europe. Their family structures look similar to our own, in terms of the percentage of births out of wedlock. Their teen pregnancy rates are generally lower than ours. The reason that countries like France, Sweden, and Germany better protect children from poverty is simple. They provide more public assistance, and what they provide goes way beyond what we call welfare.

Indeed, remarkably few of their public policies are actually targeted at poor children. The reason is pretty simple: countries with strong family support policies don't have many poor children. Generous programs of public assistance for families raising children represent official recognition of the value of parental efforts. They represent a form of social reciprocity, payback for the economically important work of raising the next generation. They embody respect for the value of nonmarket work.

Providing "universal" support is not enough. As comparisons between tax breaks, public assistance, and Social Security show, we actually have something resembling a universal system of support for families in this country—it just happens to be inadequate, inconsistent, and so confusing that many families don't even know what they are getting or what they might be eligible for. The anger directed at welfare recipients in the 1990s did not all come from the assumption that poor families were getting something for nothing. Much of it came from the perception that other families raising children were getting very little public support for an enterprise crucial to the future of our society.

ROBIN HOOD SCHOOL

What the best and wisest parent wants for his own child, that must the community want for all its children. Any other ideal for our schools is narrow and unlovely; acted upon, it destroys our education.

— JOHN DEWEY,
The School and Society

I attended unusually good public schools in San Antonio, Texas, and I still remember the day Miss Hill, my third grade teacher, praised my compound sentences. A few years ago, I got an upscale brochure from my alma mater asking for a donation to the Alamo Heights School Foundation. They were upset about changes in the school finance system in Texas that redistributed funds from rich districts to poor—a so-called Robin Hood plan. The brochure explained that private donations to the foundation, unlike tax revenues, would be used exclusively for the Alamo Heights system. "We don't want people to get the wrong idea about what we're doing," explained the foundation's president. "We're not trying to get ahead of other people; we're just trying to make up for what was taken from us."[1] I guess a lot depends on who "we" are, and what we think belongs to "us." Anyway, I didn't exactly whip out my checkbook. What can you expect from someone who was elected "most revolutionary" graduate of the class of 1969? (It was a new category; I don't imagine that it lasted many years.)

It's not easy to figure out exactly who pays the costs—or who gets the benefits—from public education. The development of human capabilities is a complicated undertaking that generates important benefits not just for the individual student, but for society as a whole. Education is also a very expensive undertaking, which helps explain why even those who directly benefit would prefer that someone else pay the costs. As with other public goods, the distribution of the costs is strongly affected by political power and economic position.

In the nineteenth century, factory owners who needed skilled workers took the initiative in developing and expanding public schools. As businesses became more mobile, however, they learned to offload these costs, using the threat of relocation and plant closings to demand abatements of the property taxes that have traditionally been a primary source of school funding. In the 1980s, for instance, General Motors led a corporate tax revolt in Michigan and demanded a waiver of property taxes in Tennessee in return for locating a new Saturn factory there. Such abatements, along with rising residential real estate values, reduced the corporate share of local property taxes in the U.S. from about 45 percent in 1957 to about 16 percent in 1990.[2]

Affluent families are generally happy to pay high taxes for good schools—as long as their own children are the primary beneficiaries. As we have reduced the legal barriers to greater racial, ethnic, and class integration in our schools, we have witnessed a resurgence of efforts to construct economic barriers.[3] The increased resources being funneled to private schools, along with enthusiasm for the privatization of existing public schools through vouchers, reflect efforts to avoid paying for "other people's kids." Because the education of children who have grown up in poverty is particularly costly, this problem is closely related to the one discussed in the previous chapter.

This chapter is about the quality of schooling that most kids get: how quality is produced, what it costs, and why it is so unevenly distributed. Families and communities are co-educators, along with schools, and problems in one arena can spill over into another. As a service of care, education is characterized by many of the measurement problems described in earlier chapters. Teaching Johnny to read is easier than teaching Johnny to love reading. Standardized exams capture some dimensions of student achievement. What they don't capture—and may actually undermine—is student motivation. Still, broad measures of success, as well as test scores, show that poor neighborhoods tend to have poor quality schools.

A growing awareness of this pattern has sparked legal challenges and grassroots struggles for equalization of per-student funding, yielding positive results in a number of states such as Texas and Kentucky. Conservatives generally prefer an alternative strategy, a decentralized voucher system that would allow public funds to flow to private schools. But while such a system would increase choices for some, it would almost certainly also lower educational quality for those who are left behind. Our current system of public funding for higher education, with its reliance on financial aid, resembles a voucher system. Yet the quality of our colleges and universities remains extremely uneven, and access for students from low-income families remains quite limited.

Inputs and Outputs

Some people argue that school funding doesn't really matter much— though if this were true it would be hard to explain why rich districts are so opposed to giving some away. A lot of publicity has been given to the lack of a strong statistical relationship between per-student expenditures and educational outcomes. In the United States as a whole, per capita educational spending has increased dramatically in real terms over the past thirty years, while average SAT test scores have declined. Some schools that spend a lot of money per student are less successful than other schools that don't.[4] Statistics can't tell us much about what causes what.

Statistical analysis finds a negative relationship between the amount of money a person spends on medical expenses and their health. Do we conclude that doctors make people sicker? No. Obviously, when people are sick, they appropriately spend more money on their health.

Statistical analysis finds a negative relationship between the amount of time parents spend helping their children with homework and children's grades in school. Do we conclude that parents' efforts have a negative effect? No. We observe that parents are more likely to help their children with homework *in response to* the low grades they are getting. Children who find their homework easy are obviously more likely to do it on their own.

Similarly, if students are having a hard time, we need to devote more resources to helping them. This doesn't mean we shouldn't look at the relationship between inputs and outputs, or shouldn't try to design more efficient schools. It does mean that we shouldn't expect a simple correlation between expenditures per student and standardized test scores. I ask my students in Introduction to Political Economy to research the amount of money spent per student in their high schools and relate that to average scores on the SATs. Most of them are fascinated by the large differences in the amount of money spent on members of the same economics class. And they are surprised that the differences in performance are neither predictable nor great.

We talk about seven different reasons for these results.

1. Test scores, the most common indicators of performance, do not adequately capture what children actually learn in school.
2. Expenditures on students aren't necessarily devoted to education. A large portion of school budgets goes toward buildings, equipment, social services, and counseling. In high-crime neighborhoods, security costs alone (which often include metal detectors) can be enormous.
3. Educational expenditures per student are unevenly distributed, and their effects depend on the composition of the student population. For instance, children with disabilities and those from non-English-speaking households require more resources than other children.
4. The effect of educational expenditures is nonlinear. Only after a certain threshold is reached do additional expenditures show any discernible effect. That threshold may be higher for students from poor families.
5. The efficacy of educational expenditures is strongly affected by factors outside of the school environment, including the home, the community, and the mass media. Most children now spend far more time watching television and playing computer games than they used to, activities that may help explain overall declines in reading ability.

6. Peer groups have important effects on both the desire and the ability to learn. Who students go to school with is probably even more important than what schools they go to.

7. The effect of school expenditures depends on how effectively the school is managed, how good the teachers are, and how much spirit the students have.

My students respond vehemently to the issue of standardized tests. They feel branded by their SAT scores. Some people simply test better than others, they say, defensively. The ones who score high often sound sheepish about their success, as though they suspect they are getting away with something.

The great virtue of standardized test scores is that they make it easy to rank applicants. Admissions offices rely on them partly because high schools vary so much in quality that grade point averages are often not good indicators of achievement, a problem obviously related to the differences in educational quality described above. For that reason, SATs are not designed to test for knowledge—high school curricula vary too much for that. Rather, they are designed to test for cognitive skills—verbal, mathematical, and analytical reasoning. In this, they are at least partially successful. But what the test scores utterly fail to capture are the individual qualities of motivation, inspiration, and discipline that are central to the learning process.

The amount of information in the world that bombards each of us is growing at an exponential rate. Classroom curricula offer carefully chosen samples of that information, much of which is rapidly becoming obsolete. I lectured enthusiastically in 1990 on many ideas that turned out to be flat wrong in 2000, including the notion that a 4 percent unemployment rate would inevitably cause inflation and my prediction that the stock market would head south that year. You can measure my success at imparting these specifics far more easily than you can measure my success at teaching my students to mobilize the information they need to make their own assessments of the economic future.

Traditional human capital theory describes young people as investors who calculate the rate of return on an additional unit of human capital and convert an input of education into an output of skill, with varying degrees of efficiency. If this were the way the world worked, my job would be as easy as selling stocks and bonds. Collecting and clearly conveying information is crucial (and surprisingly difficult). But the invisible heart of teaching is showing students how to love learning so much that they will keep on doing it for the rest of their lives.

Evaluating teachers solely by how well their students perform on standardized tests ignores the complexity of the learning process. It also insults the professional standards of care that teachers try to develop in themselves and in their colleagues. Some economists argue that teachers' unions are simply a strategy for increasing job security and earnings.[5] Without intending to, unions probably do protect some shirkers. Teachers, like other people, can sometimes fool themselves and others into thinking they are doing a good job when they are not. But the negative effects of this deception are small compared to what would happen if teachers were unable to defend their own professional values—that is, if they were hired, fired, and paid according to their students' test scores. Some people might agree to teach under such conditions, but they wouldn't be people who cared much about their students.

———————◆———————

Merit is various, not unidimensional. Intelligence tests, and also education itself, can't be counted on to find every form of merit. They don't find wisdom, or originality, or humor, or toughness, or empathy, or common sense, or independence, or determination, let alone moral worth.

—NICHOLAS LEMANN,
The Big Test: The Secret History of the American Meritocracy

———————◆———————

Remember the Alamo

The debate over school funding equalization in Texas reminds me of a joke I heard in high school about thirty-five years ago. There's an Englishman, a Frenchman, a Texan, and a Mexican—plus a pilot—on a four-engine cargo plane flying an emergency mission. One of the engines conks out, and the pilot warns that the plane will crash unless the load is lightened. He asks for a volunteer to parachute from the plane. The Englishman murmurs "God save the queen" and steps out the door. A few minutes later, a second engine conks out. Another sacrifice is required. The Frenchman leaps out with a gallant "Vive la France." A third engine goes up in flames and the pilot screams, "Act fast, boys, somebody else has got to jump." The Texan yells "Remember the Alamo!" and pushes the Mexican out the door.

Many books have been written, television series filmed, and courses taught, on the civil rights movement. Still, I find that most of my students don't know much about it. In my Introduction to Political Economy, I show a section of *Eyes on the Prize*, the television documentary about school desegregation in Boston. Even though many of my students grew up there, they are embarrassed and amazed. After Judge Garrity ruled that the schools must be desegregated, the school board did everything in its power to resist. Many members of the white community urged violence against the black children who were being bused to predominantly white schools. A riot outside one high school threatened the lives of a group of black students who were only able to sneak out the back door after several volunteers agreed to drive some decoy buses to the front. Busing was not successful in eliminating segregation. Some say that it simply prompted white flight from the public schools. Still, that struggle challenged and weakened racism. It helped create new generations of college students who were strongly and unequivocally opposed to any public expression of racist views.

People look back on the era of the civil rights movement as if it is over. The landmark Supreme Court ruling that struck down the principle of "separate but equal" education in 1954, *Brown v. Board of Education*, however, did little more than set the stage and send a powerful signal. Although school segregation is no longer enforceable by law, it is reproduced by economic inequalities that are, in their turn, reproduced by unequal access to good education. This circular process has been challenged by a series of state court rulings. More than half the states are now engaged in a serious consideration of school funding equalization, and many have already begun redistributing funds. The Texas struggle is going to put a case called *Edgewood* into the history books right alongside *Brown*.[6] In both cases, teenagers got things started.

In 1953, a bunch of African American students walked out of a Kansas classroom, protesting the poor quality of their education. Their parents were initially peeved, but soon rallied around a challenge to legal segregation that inaugurated the modern civil rights movement. In 1968, Chicano students filed out of classrooms in the Edgewood district of San Antonio. Again, parents were initially skeptical. But they soon demanded a meeting with teachers and administrators to ask why the roof was caving in and bats were roosting in the attic. They learned that money was short not because the local tax rate was too low, but because the district didn't have much taxable wealth.

The Edgewood Concerned Parents Association held meetings and hired a lawyer. A sheet metal worker named Demetrio Rodriguez was first to sign the complaint. There's no way he could have known he was signing up for a lifetime fight, but he probably would have signed anyway.[7] Like Rosa Parks, he was not the kind of person who would move to the back of the bus.

From the very start, plaintiffs in the *Rodriguez* case made comparisons with my alma mater, Alamo Heights. Even though residents of the poorer district had one of the highest tax rates in the area, they could spend only 56 percent per student of what the prestigious school on the north side spent. Alamo Heights was an affluent community, but even its property wealth per student was greatly exceeded by districts in other parts of Texas that had more oil wells than kids.[8]

Adequacy, as well as equity, was at issue. Even average levels of per-student expenditure in the state were well below national levels. Students in the poorest schools weren't getting much of an education. Drop-out rates were high, and few students went on to college. In 1968, that meant a greater likelihood of being drafted and sent to fight in southeast Asia. I started protesting the Vietnam War shortly after I enrolled at the University of Texas, but not a single family member or friend of mine at the time ever served in Vietnam. While researching the school funding issue, I met someone who graduated from Edge-wood the same year I graduated from Alamo Heights. Manuel said that more students from Edgewood than any other high school in town ended up in the army, and he told me a story about his own experience.

His cousin had been killed in Vietnam while his brother was still fighting there, so he turned down a scholarship to Columbia University in order to enlist. Then his brother came home on leave and told him he was a fool. Manuel wouldn't change his mind, so his brother brought some friends over to help persuade him. Manuel still wouldn't budge, but he got so tired of arguing he finally said, "Well if I can fight you and win, I can go to Vietnam and survive." The challenge was accepted, and the brothers fought. Manuel definitely didn't win, and there they were on the front lawn when the sun came up, crying and hugging each other. So this Edgewood graduate ended up at San Antonio College, and later joined the group that pursued the school funding lawsuit.

Demetrio Rodriguez and his family and friends were gravely disappointed when, in 1973, the federal Supreme Court ruled five to four that equal access to education is not a fundamental right under the Constitution. Two years later, the same justices ruled in the *Milliken* case that white suburban districts did not need to participate in desegregation programs within their cities. The Alamo Heights School district encompasses the suburban townships of Alamo Heights, Terrell Hills, and Olmos Park. These, needless to say, are not legally part of the city of San Antonio. Desegregation rules did not apply to them. The inequality festered.

In 1984, the Mexican American Legal Defense and Educational Fund (MALDEF) filed a new suit in state court, noting that the Texas constitution asserts that a "general diffusion of knowledge" is "essential to rights and liberties of the people." On October 2, 1989, Rodriguez and Edgewood won the legal battle. The Texas Supreme Court ruled nine to zero that "glaring disparities" in spending between wealthy and poor districts violated a constitutional requirement that the state support and maintain an efficient educational system.[9] The court observed that Mexican Americans comprised 30 percent of total statewide enrollment, but 95 percent of enrollment in the poorest districts.[10]

Football is a big deal in Texas, but the Alamo Heights Mules never did too well when I was among them. I remember parents chuckling and saying the school was just too white to win at football. I don't know how Edgewood did, but in 1989 their widely photographed stadium scoreboard temporarily ignored football to proclaim "We won. Edgewood 9, State 0." The Governor went into a nervous huddle but failed to act. The court justices warned him that if the legislature didn't take action, the court itself would play Robin Hood.

Wealthy districts screamed at the fiscal pain. They had to stand by as much of "their" revenue was redistributed to others. This was the loss Alamo Heights was trying to recoup through private fund-raising from alumni. Many legal maneuvers later, a compromise plan was approved. As a result, the budgets of the poorest school districts in Texas increased significantly in the 1990s.[11] At Edgewood, the roof was fixed and teachers' salaries got a small boost. The bats were evicted. Demetrio Rodriguez was pleased, even though he didn't think the redistribution went far enough. More than twenty-five years had passed since the original suit was filed. All his children had long since graduated from high school. Two of his grandchildren, however, were attending elementary school in the Edgewood district.

Taxing Truths

The lines of most school districts were drawn long before overt segregation was outlawed. Families were willing to tax themselves more heavily if they were sure the benefits would be enjoyed by their own children and those of their friends. They drew district lines that excluded groups they considered undesirable, and they established good schools. The earliest deeds to houses and land in the Boston suburbs forbade sale to any "Negro or native of Ireland." In pre-1950s San Antonio, most northside deeds included restrictive racial covenants that explicitly excluded Mexican Americans.[12]

Property values within affluent districts increased because many people wanted to buy homes there in order to take advantage of good schools. As property values rose, a lower tax rate was adequate to raise

the same amount of revenue, making the neighborhood even more attractive. Exactly the opposite process took place in communities whose
residents were barred from good neighborhoods and excluded from political power. Because they didn't have much wealth, they had to set
high tax rates in order to fund good schools. But if they set high tax
rates, they discouraged businesses and prospective home owners from
locating in their community. Their collective property wealth remained
low, and so too, therefore, did their educational spending.

Today, most educated parents understand exactly how this works,
and they do a lot of asking around about schools before they decide to
buy a house. In the Alamo Heights Foundation brochure, a local realtor
explains the threat that school funding equalization poses even to those
residents who don't have children: "Property values are directly related
to the excellence of education in the Alamo Heights School District. To
maintain that excellence the foundation needs the support of our community now more than ever." The average taxable value of property in
Alamo Heights in 1991 was $461,884; in Edgewood, it was $35,288.[13]
Reliance on local funding for schools goes a long way toward explaining why U.S. neighborhoods are segregated by class and ethnicity, and
why that segregation has changed little over the past twenty years.[14]

My father, a man whose immense patience survived forty years of
verbal wrangling with his pointy-headed daughter, used to say, "Well,
let those Rodriguezes work hard and save until they can move into
Alamo Heights. There's nothing stopping them from doing that, now."
Certainly, the demographics of the Alamo Heights school district have
changed a great deal since I went to school there. But it's still not easy to
find low-rent housing in Alamo Heights—or to live there if your job is
on the west side of town. At Edgewood, an overwhelming majority of
students come from low-income Latino families. Instructional spending
per student there averaged about 75 percent of that at Alamo Heights
throughout the 1980s, and test scores were significantly lower (compar-
ing Latino students, as well as all students, at the two schools).[15]

Several Alamo Heightsters I talked to said, "Equalization is a good
idea, but not if it involves taking money away from rich districts and
giving it to poor ones." Guess what. There's no other way to accom-

plish equalization. If you want equal opportunity for children, you have to pay for it. In 1991, a group of student council representatives from Alamo Heights got together with their counterparts from Edgewood and wrote a letter to the governor. They didn't like the way they were being played off against each other. "The most important factor to both communities," they wrote, "is that all students get the best education possible."[16] They're right. But the older generation doesn't see it that way.

The bottom line is that wealthy districts don't want to lose control over revenues they consider theirs. Many conservatives argue that parents' rights to spend their tax dollars locally should supersede children's rights to equal educational opportunity. Robert Barro, who teaches economics at Harvard University and often writes for the *Wall Street Journal*, came to town a few years ago to debate my colleague Samuel Bowles on the general topic of inequality. Barro declared that it was in American tradition for parents to give their own children every possible advantage. Bowles's response was low key: "Wait a minute," he said, "we have already put some restrictions on what parents can do for their children. We don't think they should be able to buy them jobs or buy them protection from the rules of law. Why should they be able to buy them a head start in what is supposed to be a competitive race?" Why, indeed?

Back in his September 1990 decision, Judge Scott McCown argued that equity required more than simply guaranteeing all students an adequate education. He used a parable to illustrate his point. Imagine a father with two sons, John and Javier. What if that father provided John with food, clothing, shelter, a car, tennis lessons, and pocket money, and provided Javier only with minimal food and clothing? Would we conclude that he had treated both fairly?[17]

The president of the Alamo Heights Foundation, Warren Wilkinson, was not worried about Javier. He just didn't want John to get dragged down. He said, "If we have money we're not willing to accept mediocrity," and then explained that equalization is a "demotivator" because kids feel demoralized when money is taken away from them and given to somebody else. "What's the point of trying hard," they ask, "if I'm just going to get equalized?"

But redistribution doesn't take away money that kids have earned. It just limits the extent to which taxpayers can support one set of kids more than another. People lose their motivation when some kids can't get a decent education no matter how hard they study. Equal opportunity in education is not a violation of family rights; it's an expression of family values. Judge McCown put it this way:

> The other thing that I have heard people say is "our taxes"—why do we have to send "our taxes" to educate other people's children? Well, there are two problems with that. First, it's not "our taxes." We expect people who have no children to pay taxes, and businesses their taxes. I guess the thing that upsets me the most is to hear people talk about "our children"—they miss the whole point of the Constitution. They are all *our* children.[18]

State by state, lawsuit by lawsuit, advocates for school finance reform have made headway. As of 1999, sixteen states had shifted their funding formulas in a more egalitarian direction.[19] Fears were expressed that pressures to redistribute, combined with resistance to tax increases, would lead to "leveling down"—saving money by taking money away from the more affluent districts. That's what happened in California. Once among the best in the country, by the 1990s California's equalized system ranked thirtieth among all states in per-pupil spending.[20] But other states, with effort, avoided this outcome. In most cases, equalization has been associated with an *increase* in per-pupil spending.[21]

State-level reforms will never completely solve the problem because huge differences persist among states. We could and should follow the European example of providing national funding for education, as well as setting national standards. But the enormous resistance to increased funding for poor schools has coalesced around the accusation that schools don't spend their money as effectively as they might. The simplest solution, for believers in the invisible hand, is to forget about funding reform and force schools to compete more aggressively in a competitive marketplace.

Shopping Around

Here's how the argument for competitive forces works. Instead of funding public schools directly, we could give parents vouchers worth a certain amount of money. These they could spend on whatever school they like. If students, as educational consumers, could vote with their feet, the increased competition would eliminate poor schools—in much the same way that McDonald's, Burger King, and Wendy's drove all those inefficient family-owned cafés and diners out of business. This argument is not convincing for someone who works in higher education, where public universities are already like fast-food enterprises and private liberal arts colleges are like classy little restaurants that require a reservation days in advance.

Shaking up bureaucracy is generally a good idea. A dose of competition, carefully monitored, with a guaranteed minimum standard of quality for all students, could have healthy effects. Unfortunately, that's not what most advocates of school vouchers have in mind. They describe choice as a panacea and assume that market forces can have only good effects. They also misunderstand the reasons why public schools are not as cost-effective as they could be.

Private schools often get better results in terms of test scores per dollar spent. But the greater cost-effectiveness of private schools has more to do with selectivity than with efficiency. Unlike public schools, they don't have to admit anyone they don't want—they can screen out the disabled, the contentious, the poorly motivated, and the untalented. A reporter from the *Miami Herald*, exploring a Florida proposal to provide vouchers to students at public schools that were not performing well, called dozens of private schools to ask if they would be willing to accept these students. The answer was usually "no."[22]

Parents who send their children to private schools—especially low-income parents, for whom even a low level of tuition represents a significant sacrifice—are often highly motivated parent-educators. They pay special attention to their children's education, attention that tends to improve children's performance. Students who attend good private schools come from very different kinds of families from those who attend bad public schools. A study of Florida schools found that the best predictor of differences in school performance was the percentage of students with incomes under the poverty line.[23] Surprise.

It's easy to create more opportunities for parents to help their children by moving them to a better school. It's harder to figure out what to do about the students left behind in poorly funded and/or poorly managed public institutions. It's not the kids' fault that their parents lack the motivation, the car, or even just the time necessary to transport them to a better school. Educational reform should not penalize children simply because their parents are poor or make poor choices.

"Choice" programs tempt parents to give up on the prospects of any improvement in their local public schools. This is not a completely irrational response, as indicated by Demetrio Rodriguez's long wait. Unfortunately, it is also a cooptive strategy, one that helps defuse the pressure to increase educational quality for all students. Parents who are well-educated enough to recognize that Johnny will have a hard time learning to read at School A can take him to School B. No more complaints from those parents about School A. That's the school attended by children whose parents are not as vigilant.

Markets can enforce discipline, but they can also encourage opportunism. Wisconsin has taken the lead in developing and extending a voucher system. Bob Peterson, the 1995–96 "elementary teacher of the year" in that state, describes the ill effects on his public school, where he personally caulked his classroom windows to help keep out the cold. Vouchers, he wrote, "make it possible for the Wisconsin legislature to pretend it is doing something about reforming the Milwaukee public schools while it ignores them."[24]

Many states have encouraged the development of charter schools, start-ups that are absolved of some traditional bureaucratic strictures in order to encourage more diversity and competition within the public sector. Some, like Massachusetts, have done a decent job regulating them. Others, like Arizona and Michigan, have been extremely lax.

Awarded a certain amount of public money for every student who they register, profit-seeking owners have an incentive to cut costs as much as possible (the technical term for this is a "fly-by-night operation"). Some plunk students down with automated worksheets in front of a computer; others give credit hours for working at fast-food restaurants. With particularly creative malfeasance, a Michigan school opened up in a neighborhood with an extremely high dropout rate, offered students fifty-dollar bonuses for registering, then collected head money from the state for an entire year for students who, not surprisingly, never showed up for classes.[25] Now, that's cost effective.

Studies of the effects of magnet schools, charter schools, and other programs designed to give parents more alternatives for their children show that these programs often increase economic segregation.[26] In recent years, the Supreme Court has rejected many efforts to explicitly remedy racial and ethnic segregation. Partly as a result of white flight to the suburbs, U.S. cities are, on average, no more racially integrated than they were twenty years ago. Minorities have more freedom to move into white neighborhoods, but affluent whites have more incentives to move into rich economically segregated neighborhoods.[27]

Still, educational reform is not a lost cause. Many good models exist. The state of Kentucky combined a commitment to higher and more equitable funding for schools with teacher training and saw students' performance steadily improve.[28] Overall, the Texas system is now thriving (due to Demetrio Rodriguez, I would argue, and not to George W. Bush). Still, naysayers argue that nothing public can succeed, and they have the money to help prove it. In 1998, the CEO Foundation offered to provide $5 million annually for vouchers for ten years to fund private education for students in the Edgewood school district.

The program's goal, clearly, is to show that private schools can do a better job than public schools.[29] The CEO vouchers were set at four thousand dollars apiece, about a thousand dollars less than per-pupil expenditures at Edgewood. Of course, Texas exempts private schools from the state's accountability system; nor has the foundation set standards for recipients of their vouchers.[30] Private schools can decide not to accept all students who have vouchers. Not a very good experiment, by scientific standards—a better strategy would be to randomly assign students to the two types of schools.

It's hard to quarrel with charitable donations. Still, you have to wonder why the foundation chose Edgewood, the symbol of educational equity, to test its theories. The disruptive effects of shifting enrollments will make it harder for the district to take advantage of the increased state funding that Demetrio Rodriguez's supporters fought for so long. Vouchers themselves are not inherently bad. Increased choice and competition could be healthy, if equality of educational access were guaranteed and quality standards were enforced at both private and public schools. Most voucher supporters don't worry about such details. One of my students is more honest. He argues that the whole idea is to weed out those students whose parents are not sufficiently affluent or pushy. "Our economic system cannot accommodate equal education," he writes. "The country needs garbage men, mailmen, waitresses, and hamburger flippers. There are only so many jobs available for college students."

Reasons for State Universities

I work in a quasi-care industry known as higher education. I say quasi-care because I know only a small proportion of my students' names. One of my primary teaching responsibilities has been for a large introductory economics lecture. Like most such classes at the University of Massachusetts, it's usually oversubscribed, which means there are more students than seats. Last time I taught in Morrill 329N. Most of the foldup desks didn't work, and fifteen of the auditorium-style seats had lost their seat-back cushions, exposing a long, curved rim of sharp metal. I could imagine someone absentmindedly sitting down, settling in, and then letting out a yelp before wiping the blood from the back of his neck. When I realized that about 15 percent of my students were routinely flunking the course, I looked up overall completion rates. Of students who entered the University of Massachusetts in 1991, only 58 percent of the men and 65 percent of the women had graduated within six years.[31] We have no idea what happened to the others.

I asked a class of economics majors, juniors and seniors who classified as survivors, to tell me why they thought dropout rates were so high. In addition to complaints about financial stress, they described the personal difficulties of operating in an impersonal environment: "The freshman year classes are always too crowded and unorganized. People feel discouraged." They didn't absolve themselves of responsibility; rather, they explained that responsibility was hard to sustain. "Students are dropping out because they are partying too much. People are not motivated to go to classes because they are so big, and the teacher doesn't know any of the students."

I appeal to my students' self-interest, showing them a graph of what has happened to average wages over the past twenty-five years. In terms of real purchasing power, they are still lower than they were in the 1970s. College graduates are the only ones who have seen marked improvement. A high school degree buys even less in today's labor market than it used to. Pass this course, I tell them. Graduate from this university. Succeed. Behind my pep talk, I conceal my worries about the uneven quality of the education these students have received, as well as the lack of personal attention they receive here.

Support for public higher education in the state of Massachusetts has never been great. Throughout the first half of the 1990s, that smiling, freckle-faced, independently wealthy Republican governor Weld vetoed legislative efforts to get us more money. Most of the powerful politicos in Boston went to Harvard, Boston University, or Boston College, not to a state university in the western boondocks. In a desperate effort to increase our popularity with the state legislature, our chancellor reallocated money away from academic programs and lobbied for a bigger football stadium that would qualify us for Division 1A football.

My students know they need diplomas to prosper in today's labor market. A lot of them have opted for the University of Massachusetts because it's a relatively good deal. But the cost of tuition and fees, room and board for in-state undergrads (in inflation-adjusted dollars) roughly doubled between the 1980s and the 1990s.[32] Financial aid increased, too, but not enough to compensate.

Right about the time of the big price hike, the chairman of the economics department at Boston University wrote an opinion piece for the *Boston Business Journal* helpfully entitled "No Reason for State Universities."[33] With the confidence of an expert conveying state-of-the art knowledge to college freshmen, he asserted that governments should not help finance higher education. No one really benefits except college students themselves, and why should we help them? At most, we should enable them to borrow money to pay for college themselves.

I don't buy this argument. Society as a whole benefits from a better-educated, more highly skilled work force, one that can protect itself from computer viruses and surf the World Wide Web. The government will be collecting a percentage of my students' paychecks through Social Security to help support me in my old age. Furthermore, higher education helps keep kids out of trouble until they calm down. As Ross Perot has pointed out, the cost of maintaining an inmate in the state prison at Huntsville, Texas, exceeds the cost of attending Harvard (to which the classic Texan response is, "Send those Huntsville prisoners to Boston!").[34] More importantly, higher education is an end in itself. Everyone deserves it, regardless of his or her occupational aspirations.

Yet public subsidies for higher education are declining. Since 1980 the average cost of tuition and fees in the U.S. has increased far more than the supply of financial aid.[35] Combine this rise in cost with the lower probability that children from low-income families will graduate from high school and the result is inherited inequality. In 1979, only 8 percent of students from the poorest quarter of families had received a college degree by age twenty-four. That percentage was unchanged in 1994. Over the same time period, the percentage of children from families in the richest quarter earning college degrees increased from 31 percent to 79 percent.[36] Liberal college professors are not the only ones who have noticed this trend. Lehman Brothers, a brokerage firm that touts new investment opportunities for private schools, proclaims: "The spiraling cost of a private education and the reduced purchasing power of financial assistance have priced much of the lower and middle classes out of the market for post-secondary education."[37] Lehman

Brothers argues that private schools are the solution. But the educational institutions that compete with public universities are private nonprofits that operate as charities even though they charge a hefty price. The subsidy to students at private schools averages out to about the same as the subsidy to students at public schools—around $8,200 a year.[38] The major difference is that private schools finance their subsidies through charitable gifts that are invested in stocks, bonds, and real estate, rather than through state appropriations. The more expensive the school, the higher the subsidy.

More than half of Massachusetts scholarship aid goes to students attending private colleges and universities. This means that the legislature is beefing up private education even as it maintains its public system on a strict subsistence diet.[39] Taxpayers further subsidize private schools by exempting their real estate, wealth, and income from taxation. The estimated value of Harvard University's endowment in April 1999 was about $13 billion. Assuming a 10 percent annual rate of return on its investments, Harvard enjoys about $1.3 billion in tax-free income. If the state taxed that income at 30 percent—about the same rate affluent individuals pay on their income—it would raise about $390 million—more than enough to pay the entire UMass operating budget. And that's not even counting the value of the property tax exemption on the real estate that Harvard owns in the Boston area.

For a number of years, starting in the late 1960s, many elite private schools offered, as a kind of noblesse oblige, "need-blind" admissions, admitting students purely on the basis of merit and then providing them with the necessary financial aid. In the 1990s, however, competitive pressures among schools largely undermined this commitment. I first became aware of this when nearby Mount Holyoke College proposed phasing out its need-blind policy and replacing it with a cleverly worded "need-sensitive" policy. In the spring of 1997, twenty students occupied the admissions and treasurer's building, while a hundred students rallied outside, despite the rain, chanting "Education is a right not just for the rich and white."[40]

In 1984, when I first came to this university as a faculty member, there were few African American, Hispanic, American Indian, Alaskan

Native, or Asian American students. At the time, they represented only about 7 percent of all undergrads.[41] In addition to high tuition costs, they were deterred by our location in the western part of the state, a long way from Boston and other urban areas, where the minority populations of this state are concentrated. However, the university made a commitment to affirmative action and increased its need-based financial aid. By 1997, diversity had substantially increased, and the group that called itself ALANA (for African, Latino, Asian, and Native American) represented 16 percent of all undergrads.

But the rapid influx of these students was not accompanied by much additional support for them. In the spring of 1997, about one hundred activists walked into the Goodell administration building and refused to leave until the chancellor agreed to negotiate with them. Their main concern was the lack of support for minority and low-income students on campus. They demanded more resources, not just for recruitment but also for retention—for advising, counseling, and tutoring services that could help reduce the dropout rate.

Rallying around issues of economic access, as well as ethnic diversity, the organizers included first-generation college students in their list of groups who needed more support. They asked faculty members to cancel classes so that students could come support them. I'm not quite that loose, but I headed over to Goodell right after my introductory economics lecture, heartened to see what a multiethnic group of students, unified by concerns about class as well as race inequality, could accomplish. A local reporter noted that "Student after student told grim stories of financial desperation, of having their enrollment canceled because they couldn't come up with the last $1,000 or $2,000 of their tuition, or working two jobs after a full-time course load to pay rent and buy food."[42] Administrators, who were basically sympathetic, made enough promises to talk the students out of the building. In the end, though, it's not a problem that we can solve on our one campus.

We need more public aid for higher education. Sitting in the Blue Wall Café, I read a flyer left over from the protest that detailed the demands. An angry student had penciled on it: "Where do you think this money will come from? It doesn't grow on trees." I wanted to find that student, to argue over coffee that the money could come from the greater capabilities that education helps develop. But he or she had already disappeared into the crowd.

———————◆———————

For the most part, we see the larger forces at work right now in American higher education as forces that will tend to increase the gaps between the "haves" and the "have-nots" among institutions and between the more and the less needy among college students. These forces include a withering of support for higher education and an intensification of the competition among institutions.

—MICHAEL MCPHERSON AND MORTON SCHAPIRO,
The Student Aid Game

———————◆———————

Equal Opportunity

Some of my friends warn me that equal opportunity is a tired old slogan. I tell them we are the ones who are old and tired. The slogan still rocks, and it embodies what we value most in competition—giving people incentive to try their best. Over the last thirty years, Americans have thrown some weight behind this principle by outlawing discrimination against individuals based on race, gender, or age. Yet many people seem to define equal opportunity as simply the absence of unfair discrimination—as though equality were a buoyant cork that, left to itself, would always surface.

Equal opportunity means something far more complicated for children than for adults. It cannot be assumed. It must be constructed piece by piece, by fostering human capabilities for emotional and cognitive achievement. These capabilities are complicated and expensive to develop, because they require care—personalized, customized, sustained, and committed attention. However difficult it may be to measure the inputs and the outputs, we know that human capabilities are enormously productive and intrinsically valuable. Within our national boundaries, we have ruled out the inheritance of all political privileges except citizenship itself. Yet we have done little to limit inheritance of economic privilege. Adults, as well as children, should be aggrieved by this; but it is children who suffer most. The more valuable that asset we call "human capital" becomes, the more important it is that everyone enjoy a fair chance to develop it.

Public school bureaucracies have plenty of problems that have nothing to do with funding. But it's unlikely that the voucher programs that many conservatives advocate will solve those problems. In fact, they will probably make them worse. What we could and should do is combine improvements in school accountability with a renewed commitment to both academic quality and equality in funding all levels of our educational system. Then, we might actually be able to guarantee all the teenagers in this country a shot at a college degree.

Equality of opportunity does not imply that we should level down, imposing some strict standard of perfect equality that could easily be reached by cutting spending at all schools. It means that we should level up and spend enough on all our schools to develop fully our collective capabilities. The Sheriff of Nottingham is not going to like it. Too bad.

THE GOLDEN EGGS

Taxation is the price we pay for civilization.

—JOHN KENNETH GALBRAITH

Social programs that support family values are costly. Public support for such programs must be financed by taxes. Relentless efforts to lower taxes and to reduce the bite they take from the income of affluent families make it difficult to implement progressive change. Conservatives argue that steep taxes on wealth and income penalize hard work, risk-taking, and saving—the very forces that foster economic growth. Their favorite maxim is "Don't kill the goose that lays the golden eggs."

I've never understood this goose business. It seems as though a bird that lays golden eggs would find it difficult to reproduce itself over time. When King Midas got his wish that everything he touched would be transmuted into gold he accidentally turned his own daughter into a lifeless statue. My main complaint about taxes is that we have to spend more time figuring how to fill in our 1040 forms than thinking about what we actually pay for. In this chapter, I defend the principle of taxing the rich more heavily than other folks, and argue that progressive taxes can increase happiness, fairness, and efficiency.

What Money Can't Buy

As a child, I observed that money created a lot of unhappiness among the second generation of McFarlins, E. B.'s sons. My father was fond of

R. B. McFarlin, even though he was an alcoholic who would sometimes go off on a binge, leaving town without telling anyone where he was headed. My father would simply wait until the next bank statement arrived, study the check stubs, figure out what town R. B. was in (usually Las Vegas or Miami), get on a plane, rent a car, and cruise around looking for the kinds of bars that R. B. liked to drown in. When he found him, he could usually talk him into coming home.

R. B. pretty much went off the deep end after his wife Lucy died of cancer; alcohol was the primary cause of his own death. John McFarlin, the other son, never had R. B.'s warmth, and though he functioned better in the real world, he was for years on medication for manic depression. John McFarlin entertained himself by collecting expensive artifacts, including Chinese jades and French Impressionist paintings. For a while, he invested in miniature horses, as well as in the stock market.

Teenage horse-lover that I was, I kept pestering my father to take me out to the estate and show me the herd. He finally agreed to an expedition that included my young nieces and nephews. When we arrived at the barn, I thought I discovered the reason for my dad's reluctance. Brass name plates on the box stalls indicated that all the little horses were named after the office staff. The secretary and receptionist, Joy and Ruby, were represented by two brood mares. The little stud was named after my father, Jay. Enjoying the company of his grandchildren, however, my father was not the least bit embarrassed by the dubious honor.

The Transformation of Money into Happiness

In his classic 1973 essay, "Does Money Buy Happiness?" Richard Easterlin brought together the results of several surveys.[1] They were remarkably consistent in showing that within all societies, individuals in higher income brackets reported themselves as happier than those in lower brackets. Across societies, however, income didn't seem to make any difference. People in rich countries didn't report being any happier, on average, than people in poor countries. Easterlin speculated that the more we get, the more we want. We are, as a species, insatiable. If true, this is depressing.

Reading Easterlin's article made me unhappy. Then I discovered an article by Robert Lane written twenty years later that revisited the question. Lane argues persuasively that Easterlin's data were flawed; he summarizes survey evidence that money does not seem to buy happiness. If you ask people how happy they are, positive responses are associated with a happy family life, good friends, and enjoyable work. Once they have reached what they consider a comfortable level of income, they don't care greatly about getting more. There is only one exception to the rule that money doesn't matter much: the poor are generally less happy than people who are not poor.[2]

Lane goes on to ask why people often say they want more money even though, when they get it, they are not made happier. He points out that people are not good at explaining why they feel sad, so they often resort to a conventional explanation: I don't have enough money. One additional factor is that money is a primary indicator of status in our society. If we get more, we hope to feel better about ourselves. And we may, for a while. Then we move into a new income category, hang out with a different group of people, and realize that we're not any better off, relative to them, than we were before. Lane's findings run counter to standard economic theory, which tells us that money does buy happiness, that individuals maximize their utility (which is another word for happiness). Therefore, if they want something, it must be because they know it will make them happier. Greater income is supposed to increase the range of choices and lead to greater welfare.

Rational Economic Man

Economists have a fancy name for the principle that more is better: "nonsatiation." When I lived in New York City, I used to hang out at a bar for Texans in exile. Called the Lone Star Café, it was on the corner of Fifth Avenue and Thirteenth Street. A giant iguana sculpture on the roof glared out over a banner that proclaimed, "Too Much Is Not Enough." There is one principle of standard economic theory that supports Lane's argument: the principle of declining marginal utility. The short version goes as follows: all else being equal, if you consume more and more of the same thing, you enjoy it less and less—and you may actually get sick of it.

Obviously, it is possible to talk people into wanting things they never wanted before. A large sector of the U.S. economy is devoted to this task. Also, getting some things makes you want them more. Cigarettes work that way, even though they are poisonous. Alcohol works that way, especially if you are an alcoholic. Heroin and cocaine will make you forget you ever wanted anything else. A lot of other things are addictive in more subtle and confusing ways. Most people get a kind of rush, a feeling of exhilaration, from buying a big-ticket item. When the feeling wears off, they may discover that they don't even use the thing. They find themselves feeling low again, wanting to buy something else just to perk themselves up. This seems to be especially true if they hate their jobs. Of course, it's easy to hate a job that is nothing more than a means for earning money to buy things.

Most people fear losing something that they already have much more than they fear never getting something they always wanted. Downward mobility hurts a lot more than just staying in the same place. We've all heard people with high-paying jobs say that they're sick and tired of the rat race, but they can't drop out of it because they "couldn't live" on a lower salary (even though most people do). I admire the Voluntary Simplicity movement, which encourages people to "downshift" and trade some of their income and earnings for more time with family and friends. One thing I loved about my father was that he never wanted too much, even though the people whom he worked for always did.

———————◆———————

Dr. Lionel Gift, distinguished professor of economics, was, as everyone including Dr. Gift himself agreed, a deeply principled man. His first principle was that all men, not excluding himself, had an insatiable desire for consumer goods, and that it was no

coincidence that what all men had an insatiable desire for was
known as "goods," for goods were good, which was why all men
had an insatiable desire for them.

—JANE SMILEY,
Moo

◆

If You're So Smart, Why Aren't You Rich?

I've been trying to reconstruct the history of the McFarlin fortune.
Myrtle McFarlin outlived her husband and reached the age of ninety, at
which point a reporter for the *San Antonio Express-News* wrote a chatty
profile of her. According to the article, Myrtle grew up on a ranch in
Mundy, Texas. A lot of town names in Texas are anglicized versions of
Spanish words, and this one is close to the word *mundo*, which means
"world." Her father was from Ireland, and in her own words, "He came
to Texas on a white horse, making his own trail."

When she first married E. B. they started out on a ranch. Later he
went to work in a hardware store, then went into the oil business with
his uncle, Mr. Chapman, in Tulsa. E. B. always claimed that he started
out at the bottom, as a roughneck, and worked his way up. My father
pointed out that this was an exaggeration, since E. B. spent only about a
week at each of the more menial jobs. According to Myrtle, E. B. was
just lucky. "He'd strike oil in a spot condemned by geologists." The
original company was called "McMan," combining the names of Mc-
Farlin and Chapman.

On May 29, 1930, the *Tulsa Daily World* published a front-page article describing the sale of the McMan Company to Standard Oil of In-
diana, in exchange for stock worth between $15 and $20 million dollars.
If that sum had remained invested and yielded 10 percent a year it
would have grown to over $2 billion by the year 2000. Not terribly im-
pressive by today's standards. According to the Bill Gates Wealth Clock
(www.webho.com/WealthClock), the richest man in the world on May
19, 2000 was worth $73.6 billion. The McFarlin money, wisely spent,
quite possibly could have ended illiteracy in my home town. The

United Nations Development Office estimates that Gates's fortune could provide basic education, health care, adequate food, and safe water for the entire human population of our planet.[3]

One pundit observed that if Bill Gates saw a hundred-dollar bill lying on the ground he'd be foolish to waste time by picking it up: his pay per second exceeds that sum. My nephew told me about a computer exposition where Bill Gates compared the computer industry with the auto industry and said: "If GM had kept up with technology like the computer industry has, we would all be driving twenty-five-dollar cars that get a thousand miles to the gallon." In response to Mr. Gates's comments, General Motors issued the following press release: "If GM had developed technology like Microsoft, we would all be driving cars with the following characteristics: 1) For no reason whatsoever your car would crash twice daily; 2) Every time they repainted the lines on the road, you would have to buy a new car; 3) Occasionally, executing a maneuver, such as a left turn, would cause your car to shut down and refuse to restart, in which case you would have to reinstall the engine."

I'm no Microsoft fan. But at least Bill Gates helped create something of value to society. How about the rest of the *Forbes* 400? In 1997, 42 percent of them had inherited enough wealth to rank among the richest Americans without doing a thing. More than two-thirds started with some inherited wealth.[4] That's the typical pattern, though we do have a little more upward mobility than we used to. Back in 1985, about 45 percent of the super rich inherited most of their money, and another 15 percent had a significant inheritance to help them get started.

Did E. B. McFarlin earn his fortune? Although he came into the business at an early age, it was already pretty well underway. But the question is more metaphysical than chronological. What does it mean to say that a person "earns" something? That they deserve what they get? At one extreme, it could mean that they didn't lie, cheat, or steal to get it. At the other extreme, it could mean that nobody else, under the same circumstances, would have done as well. When someone wins the lottery, we don't normally say that they earned it. How people think about the relationship between money and luck turns out to be critically important to politics. Those who believe that luck plays an important role in individual wealth accumulation are far more likely to favor redistributive policies.[5]

But luck cuts both ways, politically. If luck is randomly distributed, some day it could be there for you and me. Politicians have discovered that lotteries are a great way to raise revenue. Low-income families, in particular, pay out a lot of money to play. Either they don't know what a bad investment a lottery ticket is, or they don't care, because it's the only investment they can afford. In any case, the resulting revenue makes it possible to lower taxes on property and income, thus benefiting the affluent, who generally know a good political investment when they see one. An even more attractive feature of lotteries is the way they celebrate luck as an agreeable principle for allocating income. Being born with a silver spoon in your mouth is like winning the birth lottery. Let's not begrudge the winners because any of us could be among them. Yeah, sure. One of the differences between people who play the lottery and people who don't is that the former think the lottery is a metaphor for the real world. Standing in line in the grocery store and watching people buy "Megabucks" tickets, I want to ask them to philosophize. In my imaginary scenario, the checkout clerk, who knows I'm a professor, teases me. "I wish they'd raffle off $70,000-a-year jobs with summers off," she says. "Wait a minute," I reply. "I worked real hard to get my job." "Yeah, sure," she shoots back, "but some people are born eggheads." From her point of view, I have been just as lucky as old E. B., but in a different way.

It's difficult to distinguish between luck and effort, between what we've been given and what we've earned. Conservative economists often say that redistributive policies, like progressive taxes, penalize the rich for their skills and hard work. This is true only if the rich have succeeded entirely as a result of their own capabilities and efforts. To the extent that their success results from luck, gifts from others, or from a higher power, the disincentives work the other way: failure to energetically tax them lets them rest on their luck and their laurels. It also discourages the less fortunate, whose skills and hard work receive far less generous rewards.

---◆---

The inequalities of poverty which arise from unequal industry, frugality, perseverance, talents, and to a certain extent even opportunities, are inseparable from the principle of private property, and if we accept the principle, we must bear with these consequences of it; but I see nothing objectionable in fixing a limit to what any one may acquire by the mere favour of others, without any exercise of his faculties, and in requiring that if he desires any further accession of fortune, he shall work for it.

—JOHN STUART MILL,
Principles of Political Economy, Book II

---◆---

What Money Can Buy

Economists will give you all sorts of reasons not to even think about redistributing income. First, you can't compare one person's happiness with another's. A rich man might have a greater capacity to enjoy money than a poor man, in which case income redistribution would decrease, rather than increase total economic bliss. This is not completely implausible. It takes practice to spend money happily: performance probably improves with education and experience. On the other hand, in time, poor people could probably get the hang of it.

If you've ever been down and out, you may have gathered some empirical evidence to support the hypothesis that money spent to satisfy basic needs of food, health, and shelter creates more satisfaction per dollar than money spent on caviar, downhill skiing, or vacation homes. But economics textbooks warn us not to generalize. Their definition of potential improvement in social welfare is restricted to cases in which you can make one person better off without making another person worse off. This criterion is named after Vilfredo Pareto, the economist who stated it most precisely.

Pareto's principle is best understood in terms of a pie. If you can make a pie bigger then all the pie lovers benefit. However, if you hold the size of the pie fixed, there's no way you can make someone's slice bigger without making someone else's slice smaller. Pareto argued that no one should draw any conclusions about redistribution because of the difficulty of ascertaining whether the psychic gain to one person exceeds the psychic loss to the other person. In other words, trimming a bit from a rich man's dessert to feed a starving child is not "Pareto optimal." There is always the possibility that a rich man felt greater pain than the starving child felt gain.

It was the English economist Stanley Jevons back in 1895 who insisted that comparisons of happiness were futile. "Every mind," he wrote, "is thus inscrutable to every other mind and no common denominator of feeling seems possible."[6] I wish I could go back in time, take Stanley out on the town and convince him that bodies, if not minds, have a lot in common. People sitting next to each other, even if they are strangers, can generally sense one another's pain. There's nothing inscrutable about it. The problem is, on this planet, rich people and poor people seldom sit next to one another.

Economists, journalists, teachers, and writers are generally well educated, and, as a result, prone to economic segregation. My friends sometimes kid me about my McFarlin and Rodriguez stories, hinting that my political views are simply the product of a strange and twisted childhood. But when I ask them about their early experiences with wealth and poverty, they often have little to report: most were well insulated from both extremes. I don't think their introduction to economic realities was any more accurate than mine.

Because they assume that you can't believe what people say and that everybody wants more anyway, economists seldom ask what people think about wealth and poverty. But artists do, sometimes. I have a book of splendid photographs by Jim Goldberg. It consists of informal portraits of very rich and very poor people whom he got to know personally. Each is inscribed with a comment by someone in the picture, explaining his or her reaction to it.[7]

These people often rationalize their place in the economy by emphasizing that money doesn't buy happiness. In one photograph, a man in a black silk dinner jacket is standing next to a piano in an extremely classy living room. Behind him stands his butler in a white coat and black tie.

The man in the dinner jacket writes, "Though it would seem so, there is no difference between myself and the man behind me. He is happy working here, as I am living here. Ownership provides control but also many obligations." I wonder what the butler was thinking.

Often, Goldberg's poor people adopt a resigned tone, perhaps because it hurts too much to want something you don't think you will ever get. A short Latina woman wearing an apron stands next to her mistress in a well-appointed kitchen. "In Guatemala I was my own boss; I was middle class, I was a nurse. At the beggining [sic] I was sad to be a housekeeper, now I am used to it. When your illness has no cure, why worry?"

Young people tend to have great, almost exaggerated expectations. On her portrait, a young girl wrote, "I look ugly and serius [sic]. I wish I had money. Then I can look and be who I want to be." At a certain point in life, young people begin to blame themselves. In a class where I draw a detailed picture of the distribution of wealth and income in the United States, I give an exam that requires students to locate their family within that picture. The first time I did this, one student became agitated, protesting that this question was out of bounds, an invasion of her privacy.

Since then, I've been careful to advise students that they need not divulge their family's actual position—they can fantasize, as long as they effectively demonstrate their knowledge of the facts. Still, I usually get what sound like truthful answers, heartfelt, often apologetic that their families don't quite measure up. "If my family *were* in the top 10 percent of the income distribution," several essays conclude, "I wouldn't be at the University of Massachusetts. Of course, if I were smart, I would have gotten a scholarship to Amherst, Smith, Hampshire, or some other private college."

Years ago, in a wonderful book called *The Hidden Injuries of Class*, Jonathan Cobb and Richard Sennett described how lack of economic success lowered self-esteem. Their point was not that everyone should blame the system instead of taking responsibility for themselves, but that individuals often blame themselves for outcomes beyond their control. People don't always get what they deserve, and vice versa.

What seems odd is how little opportunity we all get to talk about this. Compared to all the therapeutic energy spent encouraging people to process their relationships with parents, lovers, pets and other codependents, little attention is paid to money, wages, or work. We understand the meaning of sexual, but not of economic, abuse. People aren't expected to feel guilty if they inherit privilege or angry if they don't. This says something about who runs our therapeutic culture—not, it seems, individuals who grew up in poverty.

Maybe people don't get unhappy about something unless you suggest they should, in which case it's better not to bring this up. Maybe ignorance is economic bliss. But I have a feeling that's more true for the rich than for the poor. Groups that raise money to fight world hunger sometimes invite potential donors to a banquet, seat them, and announce a simulation game. One randomly chosen guest out of every five is served a delicious gourmet meal; two out of five are served plain brown rice; the remaining two are served nothing at all. It's important that those with differing quantities and qualities of food on their plate be seated next to each other so that they can watch, smell, hear, generally sense the effects of an arbitrary and unfair distribution.

Our senses are more empathetic than our minds. Sometimes it seems as though our minds take measures to protect us from dangerous sympathies. How rational you are, economic man, simply to avoid circumstances where your sympathies might come into play.[8] The following principles apply: make friends only with those in your own income bracket or above; steer clear of neighborhoods where you might see people in dire need; avoid vacationing in countries where people are miserably poor, or, if you do wind up there, stick to well-policed resort areas; make your charitable contributions to tax-deductible causes by mail.

These principles are seldom articulated. It would be surprising if they were because their purpose is to minimize moral dissonance. Marvin Minsky, expert in the area of cognitive psychology, would call these principles "censors": they prevent uncomfortable facts from being publicized to the conscious mind. But Minsky argues that the mind is not a single entity but a metaphorical "society" in which different elements contend for attention and influence.[9] We may have internal "critics" as well as "censors." I like to think of inner Gandhis, pestering the Paretos of the mind.

Tax Payback Year

In 2000, May 3 was Tax Freedom Day. If Average Joe sent all his earnings from January 1 to May 10 to Uncle Sam, he could keep everything he earned for the rest of the year. In other words, people pay, on average, about a third of their income in taxes. It's a big chunk. I used to wonder why people fussed so much about taxes and so little about profits. From the point of view of economic theory, both categories represent a kind of surplus over and above the actual cost of producing things. When I started playing with the numbers, I realized that the total value of federal, state, and local tax revenues in the United States is more than five times the amount of corporate profits before taxes.

Taxes are almost everywhere, far more visible than other kinds of mark-ups. Deductions from paychecks and additions to bills—they get you coming and going, as my father used to say. In my town, I even pay taxes on my horse and my dog. We see some of the things we get in return for taxes, such as roads, schools, and snowplows, but we don't see what they actually cost. The only dollar amount that's relatively easy for us to figure out—because the Social Security administration will provide us with it—is our projected retirement benefit. But worries about financing future benefits make even that seem less than a sure thing.

In short, it's easy to assume that the costs of paying taxes exceed the benefits. Libertarians and conservatives encourage this assumption. Notice that the whole concept of Tax Freedom Day rests on ignoring what people get in return for taxes. Let's say you have two kids who are going to public schools. You should deduct what it would cost you to send those kids to unsubsidized private schools from your tax bill. Let's say you are paying into Social Security, which provides you not only with old age and medical insurance, but also with a pension for your spouse and dependent children should you die. If you didn't have that, you would probably spend money on similar private insurance. You should also tally up the costs of hiring a private police force, fire department, emergency medical services, and road crew, not to mention your neighborhood cruise missile and anti-terrorist facility.

Both taxes and benefits are distributed in complicated ways over the life cycle. Look back at your own personal history. The day you were born you began providing your parents with a modest tax deduction, and within six years you probably began taking advantage of publicly financed education. Let's assume you earn a college degree before you start earning a paycheck. How many years of paying taxes will it take before you have reached your "tax payback year"? Assume that per capita public expenditures on education are about $6,000 a year for sixteen years (college costs are higher but subsidized less, so it averages to about the same). If you had borrowed that money you would have to pay interest on it, so it would amount to considerably more than the absolute amount of $96,000. In fact, at a modest interest rate of 5 percent, you would owe about $13,140 just to pay back the costs of the $6,000 spent on your first grade. Depending on how much you earned after you graduated, you might clear your debt for first grade with the income taxes that you paid that year.

If you kept going with this payback schedule (repaying your debt for second grade the next year, and so on) then fifteen years later, after paying $210,000 in taxes (ignoring any further benefits you might enjoy from the government), you will become a "net" taxpayer, that is, one who contributes money to the system. However, a good portion of the taxes you pay will be returned to you in old age through Social Security and Medicare. Depending on how long you live, you may or may not end up putting in more than you took out. Of course, Social Security may go bankrupt. But the mutual fund you invest in might also tank. Even the bank that you keep your savings in could fail, except that (thank goodness!) it's insured by the federal government.

These calculations omit consideration of another, larger loan. Individuals born into U.S. citizenship automatically enjoy the use of many

dimensions of national wealth. That wealth includes tangible infrastructure like the interstate highway system, public libraries, natural resources, and national parks. It also includes the intangible infrastructure
of culture, knowledge, and technology bequeathed to us by our prede-
cessors. Since we all benefit from such forms of common property, it
seems reasonable to expect us to maintain and expand them.

Citizenship is like membership in a club. You are required to pay
dues, called taxes, in return for the benefits of membership. It's fairly
difficult to opt out of this club—though if you're rich enough, you can
emigrate to almost any country that you want. For most people, the
only option is to try to change the club's rules through democratic participation. Libertarians just want out. From their point of view, taxation
is theft, and Tax Freedom Day is the annual escape from prison. The
Web site of the Libertarian Party declares that it is the third largest political party in the U.S. The party platform warns, "Since we believe
that all persons are entitled to keep the fruits of their labor, we oppose
all government activity that consists of the forcible collection of money
or goods from individuals in violation of their individual rights."[11] In
other words, the party holds that individuals have rights but no obligations.

Tax Wealth

*The parent who leaves his son enormous wealth generally deadens the
talents and energies of the son, and leads him to lead a less useful and
less worthy life than he otherwise would.*

—ANDREW CARNEGIE,
The Gospel of Wealth

As the progressive lobbying group Citizens for Tax Justice points out,
you'd think that the same conservatives who fought to slash welfare
would insist that we should tax inherited wealth. After all, if $300 a
month can undermine someone's incentive to work, imagine the terrible
effect of interest and dividends worth a hundred times as much. I agree

that incentives are important. Hard work, risk-taking, and saving should be rewarded (though I reserve the right to argue over the size of those rewards). But a prosperous childhood, excellent schooling, and inherited wealth are not rewards for anything productive: they are often privileges of birth.

Equality of opportunity is acceptable, conservatives sometimes say, but equality of outcome punishes those who work hardest and smartest. But once you take families into account, it's difficult to separate the two. Grossly unequal outcomes for one generation result in grossly unequal opportunities for the next. Conservatives like Bruce Bartlett, of the National Center for Policy Analysis, argue that the right to dispense unearned resources to one's own children is a necessary component of the original incentive to create those resources.[12] I don't think so.

Even if this were the case, we would still need to balance the goal of freedom for one generation with the goal of equality of opportunity for the next one. Taxing large transfers of unearned income like gifts and inheritances is a good idea. Teddy Roosevelt agreed, Franklin Roosevelt agreed, even Herbert Hoover agreed. All of them helped put steeply progressive estate taxes into place in this country. Only the very wealthy were subject. By 1941, about 7 percent of all estates were taxed, and the top rate (on estates of $20 million and over) was about 70 percent.

In 1981, as part of the Reagan Revolution, the top rate was cut to 50 percent. But the tax rates are less important than the exemptions, which currently protect the first $675,000 of wealth (or twice that if half goes to a surviving spouse) from taxation. The exemption will rise to $1 million by the year 2006. Some members of Congress want to phase out the estate tax altogether. And that's not because they are being deluged with pathetic handwritten letters from young couples unable to pay the taxes on dad's farm that would allow them to stay in business.

Less than 5 percent of those who die in this country leave estates from which this tax is actually deducted.[13] "Soft and blobby"—that's how Henry Aaron of the Brookings Institute describes the estate tax. Exemptions, deductions, the potential to give money away before death, trust funds, and charitable foundations all minimize its impact.

Even in 1969, when the top rate was 70 percent, the actual tax paid on estates in that category was only about 27 percent. In the 1980s the loopholes gaped so wide that those in the know began calling it "the stupidity tax": most people who paid it simply hadn't bothered to figure out how to avoid it.[14] If we were to tax gifts and inheritances as heavily as Japan does, we could raise about $50 billion a year to spend on programs like universal preschool.[15]

Congress would be moving toward this goal, if only a significant number of voters gave a darn about this issue, right? Wrong. In 1998, a large majority (63 percent) of Americans polled agreed that money and wealth should be more evenly distributed. As the Gallup Organization put it, "This belief in the need for at least some income and wealth distribution has been a stable fixture of American public opinion over the past fourteen years."[16] I fantasize about an advertisement, a parody of a series of soft-drink ads. In mine, Ray Charles sits at the piano and sings, "Them that's got shall get, them that's not shall lose. So the Bible says and it still is news. . . ." At the end, Ray looks up with that great smile and says, "Tax the real thing." An ad like that in prime time could make a difference. The question is, who will pay for it?

Progressive Incentives

The history of taxing rich people's income at a higher rate than others' is a history of the ups and downs of national solidarity. Whenever the country needed to pull together against some external enemy, the rich reduced their resistance to taxation. The first progressive income tax was levied during the Civil War, when the Union imposed a 3 percent tax on incomes between $600 and $10,000 and a 5 percent tax on incomes over $10,000. After the war ended, it was dismantled. When World War I came along, Congress imposed a 50 percent surtax on incomes over $1 million, and raised the top estate tax rate to 25 percent.[17] Top rates declined steadily after that war, too.

Then came the Nazis, and the Japanese attack on Pearl Harbor. Franklin Roosevelt, declaring that all Americans should devote their excess income to the war effort, argued that no citizen should have an income after taxes greater than $25,000 a year. Prices have increased more than sixfold since then; the equivalent amount in 1999 would be about $150,000. Congress disagreed with Roosevelt, but increased the top income tax rate to 82 percent in 1941, and later invented a Victory Tax that set a 93 percent tax rate on incomes over $200,000. The postwar era enjoyed steady economic growth, accompanied by inflation that gradually increased the dollar amounts that people were earning, along with prices in general. This meant that people kept moving into higher tax brackets, a process that accelerated, along with inflation, in the 1970s.

Then, in 1981, the Reagan Revolution meant the largest tax cut in history. Rates were cut 23 percent across the board. People at the very top, however, benefited most, as the maximum rate was slashed to 50 percent. In 1986, it was cut further, to 28 percent, then raised, during the Clinton administration, to 39.6 percent. The Clinton administration also increased the Earned Income Tax Credit, which provides large tax credits to low-income families with children. The result, today, is an income tax system that is mildly progressive.

Still, most of the other taxes we pay are regressive, taking away a larger share of income from people who have less to start with. Social Security taxes apply only to about the first $60,000 in earnings, so a person earning $120,000 pays the same amount as someone earning $60,000. Also, the sales tax that many states and some cities use to raise revenue is a fixed percentage of money spent purchasing some items. Lower-income people spend a larger share of their money on taxable items like clothing, gasoline, alcohol, and cigarettes. Therefore, a larger proportion of their income gets sucked into sales taxes.

Overall, the U.S. tax system is roughly proportional. That is, most people pay about the same percentage of their income in taxes. Still, many conservatives want to eliminate the remaining progressive aspects of the income tax. They argue that it is simply unfair to apply different rates to different people. If everybody paid the same rate, then the rich would still pay more in taxes, since they are paying the same rate on a larger sum. This reasoning sounds fine if you believe in the every-man-for-himself principle. That principle ignores the collective responsibilities that are part of both family and social life.

Critics of the progressive income tax argue that it reduces the amount of time and effort that individuals will devote to earning taxable income and that this is a bad thing. But the empirical evidence suggests that taxes don't have much effect on men's hours of paid work, and they affect women's labor supply primarily by reducing the benefits of working for pay relative to working at home. Managers, doctors, lawyers, and academics tend to put in very long hours not because they want additional pay but either because their jobs require it or because they find great satisfaction in what they do.

But what if a hefty increase in the marginal income tax rate led to a decrease in hours devoted to paid employment? This wouldn't necessarily be a bad thing, if it led to increases in work devoted to family and community—work that is not taxed. Let's say a highly paid lawyer who wants to avoid moving into a higher income tax bracket decides to work four days a week instead of five. If he spends that time watching soap operas, the economy may suffer. If he spends it learning how to use some new software, cooking a nice meal for his family, and coaching his daughter's soccer team, the economy will benefit, though not in ways that show up in conventional statistics. Progressive income taxes reduce the "opportunity cost" (or the income sacrificed) when high earners devote time to family and their community rather than purely business or professional concerns. Sure, maybe they'd rather just donate money. But money is not always a substitute for time, especially where personal relationships are concerned.

This is not an argument for ignoring the ways that taxes affect incentives. It's an argument for realizing that incentives are more complicated than opponents of progressive taxation would have us believe. We should reward hard work. But we should also notice that not all forms of important work offer a monetary reward. By taxing earnings at a progressive rate, we reduce the temptation for highly paid individuals to neglect their family and community responsibilities.

Middle-Class Analysis

I'm reluctant to talk about gifts that I've received, for fear of making friends or colleagues a bit resentful. I notice that other people are also reticent about their windfalls: when they luck out they don't always telegraph the good news. But many people enjoy windfalls: I observe many of my blue-collar neighbors, as well as my white-collar colleagues, buying houses and cars they could not afford on the basis on their salaries alone. These family perks of ours are small compared to what the truly rich enjoy, but the principle is the same. And the percentage of individuals over age twenty-one who anticipate some significant gift or bequest from their parents is high.

According to one estimate, the total worth of estates at death, which averaged about $84 billion in 1995, was expected to reach about $143 billion in 2000.[18] Who is going to get it? The next generation, from families now earning over $50,000 a year. These are people who call themselves middle class: the managers, programmers, doctors, lawyers, professors, opinion makers, and trend setters who make deprecating remarks about the truly rich, especially those who misbehave. To jail with Ivan Boesky, Michael Milken, Leona Helmsley. Shame on those who say out loud that greed is good. The middle class is different. Hardworking, responsible citizens putting in more than forty hours a week, they feel they deserve whatever unearned windfalls come their way.

So, who, exactly, is a member of the middle class? Nearly all my students at the University of Massachusetts raise their hands when I ask if they belong to it. So I ask them to write down on an index card how much money a family would have to receive annually to make it into (and out of) the middle class. Some students are reluctant to take a guess; some waffle with "it depends"; most of them say that people in the middle class have jobs but need to work hard and are always afraid of falling into poverty. Most of them say that a family needs at least $50,000 or more to make it into this happy and virtuous category. There's more disagreement on the top end, with "upper class" income generally set between $120,000 and $200,000 a year.

What is the right answer? If there are three groups of roughly equal size, we can rank all families by income and ascertain the top income of the bottom third and the top income of the second, or middle third. Every year, the *Statistical Abstract of the U.S.* publishes a table that enables a rough approximation. It is called "Money Income of Families—Percent Distribution of Income Level." In 1997, families with incomes of $50,000 or more (my students' most frequent definition of the middle class) represented the top 37 percent of all families. Families earning $25,000 a year or less comprised the bottom 34 percent.[19] The group that is really in the middle, defined in these simple terms, consists of families earning between $25,000 and $50,000—the ones my students think of as "low-income."

We shouldn't rely too heavily on these numbers: the real economic welfare of families is determined by a number of factors, including their wealth, the value of the nonmarket work they do (housework and child care), and the number of dependents they are supporting. But my point is that when my students guess at a simple annual family income number, they guess way too high. There are a couple of reasons for this. First, it's difficult to actually see how much money families live on. Most of us don't know how other people get by, and we make generalizations based on our friends and neighbors. In my experience, relatively few kids from families earning under $25,000 make it into my university. Second, many people feel uncomfortable thinking of themselves as members of the "upper class," a term that still conveys a faint sense of unearned privilege. Much better to be a middle-class family earning an upper-class income.

The upper third seldom says out loud that all the people below them are undeserving. But most of its members absentmindedly nodded their heads when conservatives like George Gilder and Charles Murray began arguing that public assistance to poor families with children was actually doing more harm than good, by creating "perverse incentives." The poor were getting something for nothing; they were caught in a spider's web of dependency. In 1996, we changed all that: now poor people are required to work for pay.

The principle seems to be that no one should get something for nothing—unless they inherit it. The average bequests that families in the top third can expect are small compared to what Bill Gates's children or the Wal-Mart Waltons will enjoy. But they provide a psychological basis for a quiet coalition between the slightly affluent and the downright rich. Nothing like a nagging sense of guilt to bring people together. What better way to assuage it than to blame the poor for their own problems?

It is time for me to confess that I am an heiress, a recipient of several small fortunes.

The Mexican woman who cared for my father, his sister, and his brothers as children also cared for me when I was a baby. She was known to all of us as Tía, meaning "Aunt." We never knew much of her family, except that she'd had a husband who had run out on her. When I was about five, Tía retired from the rigors of child care to live with my grandmother and care for her. But she often came to visit me, the youngest of the grandchildren.

I remember her as a very old woman with a beautiful, deeply wrinkled face, a light-brown counterpart to my powder-white grandmother, bigger and stronger but with the same calm and dignified demeanor. She always called me *Reina*, Queen. At one point, I was taken to a studio to have my picture taken with her. Why was this picture taken? My father doesn't remember, and my birth mother died many years ago. I still have part of the photograph, the part that shows me as a blond, curly haired child. Tía cut herself out of it, because she said she looked too old. In the picture, only her hand remains, disembodied, resting on my shoulder.

She must have been my primary caregiver, because I learned to speak Spanish before I spoke English. My vocabulary was never as large as that of a true native speaker, but new words came easily to me. The last time I saw Tía I sat in her lap in the breakfast room and we both giggled at some joke I no longer remember. When she died, she bequeathed all her possessions and life savings to me. I was eight years old. My father invested the money, about $2,000, in Texaco stock. It was an opportune time, and the proceeds later paid for the better part of my graduate education in economics.

I stuck to state universities because I wanted to support myself, but my parents helped me buy a car and, later, a house. About ten years ago, my father inherited some money (a kind of gift in lieu of the pension they had never provided) from the last of the second generation of McFarlins. He gave me enough money to buy a new Honda Civic and a Gateway 486 computer. So you could say that old Mr. Mac, in the end, was pretty good to me. Every once in a while, I toast a jar of mayonnaise to his memory. Last year, I received another windfall, a five-year fellowship from the MacArthur Foundation. I decided to use it to support the kind of research on which this book is based.

Equity versus Efficiency

Many economists believe there is a trade-off between equality and efficiency.[20] That is, the only way to get more of one is to accept less of the other. This principle is enshrined in most elementary economics textbooks, and it helps justify their lack of attention to issues of economic justice. It's easy to think of situations where such a trade-off comes into play. In competitive sports, we reward winners with prestige, and often with money, in an effort to elicit from them greater dedication and better performance. Perfect equality of outcomes—the extreme example usually featured in textbook discussions of this issue—often does reduce incentives.

But this doesn't mean that the greater the inequality, the greater the effort. Professional basketball players earn salaries in the millions. How much do you think the game would improve if their salaries rose to the billions? Effort is determined not just by the size of the reward but also by the probability of getting that reward. Most people don't play very hard unless they think they have some chance of winning. That's why games are not much fun to watch unless the competitors are fairly evenly matched.

Here's a more direct example. In my introductory microeconomics classes, about 15 percent of my students get As, and about 15 percent fail the class. I could announce that everyone will receive the same grade, no matter what their performance: A. I would expect a pretty significant reduction in their effort, and therefore in the efficiency of the whole learning process. Alternatively, I could announce that students in the bottom 50 percent of the class will fail, and only the top 5 percent will get an A. Would I get more effort? Some individuals—those on the edge of those extreme alternatives—would probably hustle. But a lot of others would either drop out or give up.

Not enough competitive pressure may result in students slacking off. But too much encourages them to become obsessed with test performance (an output that is easily measured) at the expense of developing their capabilities for learning.

The bottom line is that equality and efficiency aren't always at odds.[21] Up to a certain point, inequality of outcomes may increase efficiency, but past a certain point, it may well lower it. There may be some optimal level of inequality that maximizes overall social efficiency—a level that probably varies according to cultural, political, and economic circumstance. We ought to try to figure out where it lies, instead of simply assuming that more equality will be costly. In doing this, we should think about the long-term effects. As Arthur Okun pointed out some years ago, there is something disturbing about a set of institutions that allows "big winners to feed their pets better than the losers can feed their children."[22]

A growing economic literature suggests that the easiest way to improve the link between effort and reward is to give individuals control over their own economic environment.[23] Reforms that distribute land to those who actually do the farming often increase agricultural output. A farmer who owns his or her own land works harder and smarter than one forced to sharecrop and pay a landlord 50 percent of the yield. A family that owns its own home is far more likely to take care of it (and the surrounding neighborhood) than one that is simply renting for a year. Why do large corporations like to pay their chief executives with stock options, as well as with salaries? For the obvious reason that it gives them a stake in the performance of the firm. For similar reasons, employee ownership often increases worker productivity.

One of my favorite stories about the University of Texas economics department concerns Cowboy Bob Montgomery, a professor who was called before a group of state politicians in the 1950s, at the height of McCarthyism, to face accusations that he was a communist. Legend has it that Cowboy Bob had a pink suit tailor-made for the occasion. "Just tell us one thing," one of his inquisitors asked. "Do you believe in private property?" "Senator," he replied, "I believe in private property so much that I think everyone in the state of Texas ought to have some."

Between the Devil
and the Deep Blue Sea

Whatever efforts we make to champion family values at home or in our home country must be placed in the larger context. This requires both critical analysis of the global economy and efforts to rethink, even to redesign, our economic institutions.

Debates over globalization reveal familiar tensions between individual achievement and care for others. Increased international exchange is leading to significant improvements in standards of living in some areas. On the other hand, it is weakening democratic governance of the market and intensifying some dimensions of inequality.

Democratic governance itself is more complicated than it seems. The models that we have seem woefully inadequate. The venerable tradition of debating capitalism vs. communism offers some important suggestions for developing economic alternatives. Unfortunately, it doesn't provide a simple prescription for ways of organizing and rewarding care for others—only a few important clues.

CORPORNATION

I have long dreamed of buying an island owned by no nation and of establishing the World Headquarters of the Dow Company on the truly neutral ground of such an island, beholden to no nation or society.

— CARL GERSTAKER,
Dow Chemical Executive

Imaginary scenario: A multinational corporation, tired of the frustrations of negotiating over taxation and regulation with host governments, buys a small, uninhabited Caribbean island. Perhaps it is a guano island, previously used only for collecting bird poop for fertilizer. Its new owners write a constitution and announce the formation of a country called CorporNation. Anyone who is a citizen of the new country will automatically receive a highly paid job (minimum salary $50,000 per year). The following restrictions apply to citizenship: Individuals must have advanced educational credentials, be physically and emotionally healthy, have no children, and be under the age of fifty. They need not physically emigrate, but can work from their home country over the Internet. However, they will instantly lose CorporNation citizenship and their job should they require retraining, become ill, acquire dependents, or reach the age of fifty.

In short, CorporNation takes advantage of the human capabilities of its citizens/workers without paying for their production or their maintenance when they become ill or old. It can attract the best childless and carefree workers in the world by offering relatively high wages, and do so without threatening the company's own profitability. CorporNation is likely to enjoy unprecedented success in global competition, at least until other corporations adopt the same strategy. (Perhaps some will operate from space stations or previously uninhabited planets, rather than islands.) In the long run, however, the new corporate states will run into problems similar to those created by slash-and-burn farming or overfishing. They are exploiting a natural resource without replenishing it. Their strategy is not sustainable.

This chapter concerns the perverse incentives created by unrestricted global competition. It describes what countries, employers, and even parents have to gain by minimizing the costs of care—making somebody else pay for creating and maintaining other people's productive capabilities. John Gray, Professor of Politics at the London School of Economics, summarizes the problem this way: bad capitalisms drive out good ones. Employers who assume their fair share of social costs by following the rules imposed upon them by democratic governance will operate at a disadvantage. They risk being competed out of existence.[1]

The new global order seems to offer us two equally unattractive choices: we can go back to a patriarchal society in which women are forced to assume the burden of care for others because their other opportunities are severely restricted. Or, we can move ahead to a world in which individuals are on their own and nobody provides care unless it is paid for in carefully calibrated low-cost units. Reasonable alternatives to these extremes are hard to imagine and even more difficult to implement. But they are worth fighting for.

Ready-made Workers

Bits and pieces of the CorporNation scenario are already in place in a number of countries. In 1965, the United States shifted its immigration system from one based on national quotas to one based on occupation and skill. Canada rates immigrants who have no family members within the country on a point system. A perfect score is 100, with up to 12 points based on education, 10 points depending on age, 10 points based on knowledge of English and French, and 15 on Canada's specific occupational needs. Canadian citizenship can also be purchased. Anyone with sufficient money to invest in Canada, a sum ranging from $250,000 to $500,000 that must be locked into a government-registered fund for three years, is automatically admitted. (To Canada's credit, however, they also have more generous immigration policies for political refugees than do most countries.)[2]

Immigrants are a tremendous boon to advanced economies, because they are literally free. No tax money was spent paying for their production, their maintenance, or their education. From the point of view of developing countries, the migration of highly educated professionals represents a major brain drain. India has supplied the United States with many engineers and doctors. According to economist Laura Tyson, immigrants account for at least one-third of the scientific and engineering workforce in Silicon Valley, and occupy senior executive positions in at least one-quarter of its new technology companies.[3] The Philippines exports many nurses. Migrants send some remittances back to their family members, but the amounts tend to be relatively small unless they plan on returning themselves.

The great advantage of temporary immigrants is their compatibility with last-minute methods of inventory control. If you don't need them, you don't order them. If you accidentally get too many, they can be returned. In the United States, foreign workers are brought in to meet the demand for seasonal labor to harvest fruits and vegetables. Germany sends its contract or "guest" workers back to their home countries when unemployment goes up. In Malaysia, economic crises led to the immediate deportation of non-native workers. Another reason that temporary immigrants are cost-effective is that they can be denied social benefits. Within the United States, the state of California refuses to provide any social services for illegal immigrants, although they do little to punish employers who hire them. Most Persian Gulf countries provide free medical care to their own citizens, but not to the many Asian workers recruited for one-year contracts of employment. In fact, large employers and employment agencies called *khafeels* wield enormous power over migrant workers. In Saudi Arabia, employers pay workers according to the income level in the worker's country of origin. Thus, a Thai can earn five times as much as a Bangladeshi for doing the same job.[4]

In the United States, we used to think of third world countries as sources of low-skilled labor. Over the last twenty-five years, however, many of these countries have improved their educational systems. India and China now produce far more college graduates than we do, many of whom are fluent in English. The opportunities for U.S. firms are obvious, although they are just beginning to take advantage of them. Texas Instruments employs fifty Indian programmers in Bangalore. Aztec International, a data processing company nominally located in Kansas, sends most of its actual work to the Philippines.[5] Why not let other countries pay the costs of educating a top-notch labor force? Teachers, as well as production workers, come cheaper overseas.

In democratic countries, citizens have some say over immigration policies. But they have no say at all over what we might call "virtual" immigration. The growth of cyberspace is increasing global competition for service jobs. You don't have to bring workers into the country to get them on-line. American Airlines sends much of its accounting and ticketing processing to Barbados, while Swissair prefers Bombay. New York Life sends its insurance claim forms to Ireland.[6]

These service jobs are not particularly highly skilled. But high tech is next. A little guidebook published by *Business Week*, called *Preparing Your Business for the Global Economy*, glorifies the information superhighway.[7]

> Perhaps the best known joint venture of an American high-tech company and an Asian facility with superlative talent is the Silicon Graphics Inc. operation in Bangalore, India. Software designers there earn $300 a month—middle-class wages in India, though well below the poverty level in the U.S. They develop, among others, programs that produce three-dimensional images for diagnosing brain disorders. In Singapore, where wages are similar to those in India, native engineers design future generations of personal digital assistants for Hewlett-Packard Co.[8]

Computer geeks, beware. Students, choose your majors wisely. So far, law and accounting firms haven't yet figured out yet how to "outsource." It's only the really productive occupations that are at risk.

Disposability

Cost-cutting is nothing new. As a theme in economic history, the tension between the short term and the long run is like the tension between passionate romance and stable marriage in literature. What is new and disturbing is a rather sudden tilt in the balance, a significant increase in the opportunities that large corporations have to pursue their uninhibited instincts. A characteristic feature of the export-oriented industrialization that has blossomed in many areas of Latin America and Asia is the employment of young women. Firms like them not only for their nimble fingers and cooperative attitudes, but also for the convenience of firing them as they grow older, more experienced, or more demanding. "I call electronics our evergreen industry," explains the leader of the Malaysian Electrical Workers Union. "It's been here for twenty years but the workers never age."[9]

In many countries, youth and beauty, as well as the absence of childcare responsibilities, are the primary criteria for female employment. L'Oréal Cosmetics placed the following help wanted ad in *Beijing Youth Daily* in 1998: "Promotion rep., female, under twenty-eight years old, above 1.65 meters tall, white skin, skinny, healthy."[10] In Indonesia, recruiting banners at Toko Electronics ask for "female production workers, age sixteen to thirty years, not married, should be able to read and write." Minolta Camera has more restrictive standards: it refuses to employ women workers younger than seventeen or older than twenty-seven.[11]

In countries where women frequently bear children out of wedlock, a proscription against marriage is obviously not sufficient to keep employers from having to pay for services such as the paid maternity leaves nominally required by law. Human Rights Watch has documented many cases of Mexican *maquiladora* plants requiring female job applicants to provide certificates verifying that they are not pregnant,

and firing women when they become pregnant. After a six-month review in 1998 that confirmed these findings, the U.S. Department of Labor noted that discrimination against pregnant workers violates
Mexico's own labor laws.[12] Abuses are common in other countries, as
well. The National Labor Committee has charged the *maquila* factories
in the Cholomoa region of Honduras with injecting young women with
the contraceptive Depo-Provera and handing out packages of contraceptive pills without medical supervision.

The companies' motives are obvious. Mexican law requires firms to
provide twelve weeks of paid maternity leave and the option of an additional sixty days at 50 percent salary.[13] The idea, of course, is that employers should help pay for the production of the labor power they
utilize. Instead, employers minimize their costs by penalizing maternity
among their workers. To eliminate this disincentive, countries need to
provide public support for child-rearing (as do Sweden, France, Germany, and other European countries) rather than require individual employers to shoulder the costs.

Importing Nannies

Not only multinational corporations are tempted to minimize the costs
of care. In fact, it's hard to imagine a more telling example than the efforts many affluent parents in the U.S. make to find the cheapest possible high-quality child care. To illustrate this point I've developed a
little vignette, based on a cartoon by Norman Dog. I pretend to be looking in a mirror, fussing with my hair, applying lipstick, when I look up
suddenly, as though I've just heard or remembered something.

"Oh, bye-bye, darling," I say, throwing a kiss to the child at the door
of the room. "Have a wonderful time growing up in Mexico . . .
What's that? You don't want to go? But Sweetkins, Mummy and Daddy
have decided that it's no longer cost-effective to raise you in this country. We must be efficient, you know. It's a global economy!" In reality,
U.S. parents don't need to send their children to other countries to be
raised: they can bring nannies here from more "cost-effective" countries.

Illegal immigrants are generally willing to work for low wages and eager to follow orders. Furthermore, young women who don't have the time or money to develop a personal life of their own may well pour their emotional resources into caring for their wards. In 1993, the honest young mother of new-born triplets looking for a nanny confided to a *New York Times* reporter: "I want someone who cannot leave the country, who doesn't know anyone in New York, who basically does not have a life."[14] An additional advantage is that you don't have to pay Social Security taxes for illegal immigrants, much less provide them with pensions or health insurance. They *want* to be paid in cash. For obvious reasons, the government does not collect information on the number of illegal nannies in the country. Talking to friends of mine who are highly paid professionals suggests to me that under-the-table nannies can be found easily in Los Angeles, Houston, San Antonio, and New York—an amenity of multicultural cities.[15]

Why not settle for a less-educated American worker? Obstacles loom on both the supply side and the demand side. Most less-educated American workers are women of color who don't want to return to the forms of domestic service that their forebears were condemned to. Besides, most of them are hip to the fact that child care is a lousy career track. At the same time, affluent families prefer not to put women they consider culturally "disadvantaged" in charge of their children. They have been far more eager to hire young European women through the government-sponsored au pair program that, in the 1990s, became a de facto child care service.

The French term *au pair* literally means "as two people" and implies work as a kind of mother's helper. Most of those who signed up to participate considered it a cultural exchange program. Upon arriving at their new home-away-from-home, however, some of the young women discovered that they were expected to assume virtually full-time child care responsibilities. Many European countries don't allow au pairs to work more than twenty-five hours a week; U.S. regulations allow forty-five. Moreover, there are very few standards for eligibility for applicants and no minimum wage. Earnings of less than $140 a week are typical.

The potential for abuse became so obvious in the 1990s that an inter-agency government panel reviewed the au pair program and recommended that it be placed under the supervision of either the Department of Labor or the Immigration and Naturalization Service. Congress declined to make the change, bowing—in the words of one journalist—to "constituents' demands for cheap child care."[16] Shortly afterward, the au pair program lost its luster when the death of an infant in Boston was attributed to a young English au pair named Louise Woodward. Suddenly, the idea of regulating the program—requiring, for instance, that any person paid to take care of an infant should be over the age of twenty-one—became more appealing. Largely as a result of the Woodward case, the number of au pairs brought to the U.S. each year has fallen substantially.

A movement is now afoot to create a special temporary visa or permanent-resident category for immigrant nannies. If we can relax our restrictions to bring in agricultural workers to help harvest sugar and oranges, why can't we do the same to help raise our children? It would be incredibly cost-effective. "There are a vast number of women who have had and raised many children who'd be delighted to come to the U.S. and care for children," explains one Washington immigration lawyer.[17] Another activist with the National Organization for Women (NOW) emphasizes how sexist it is to define child-care workers as "unskilled." She's right, and I have no doubt that a major nanny import program would make life much easier for moms in the $80,000-plus salary category—many of whom are loyal members of NOW.

Nanny Imports, Inc., however, suffers from the same limitation as CorporNation. It purchases short-term efficiency at the cost of long-term sustainability. An increase in the supply of women who want to provide one-on-one child care and domestic service will definitely lower the price. But while it may take a long time, that cheap supply will eventually run out. And in the meantime, we might question the desirability of creating a new caste of care workers whose specialization is determined by gender, ethnicity, and nationality, like the Bangladeshis working in Saudi Arabia. Affluent mothers can reduce their child-care costs by increasing the supply of low-cost nannies. If they do so successfully, they will become less likely to participate in broader efforts to redistribute more equitably the costs of care.

The Next Stage

For some service industries that involve face-to-face contact, like child care, we have to bring the workers to the jobs. But for manufacturing and for an increasing percentage of service jobs, it's cheaper to take the jobs to the workers. This is what capital mobility is all about. Money has been moving around the world just as long as workers have, maybe longer. What's new is the increased ease of that movement. The 1980s and 1990s witnessed significant increases not only in the flux of imports and exports but also in global investment, a process that is essentially unaffected by tariff barriers. International treaties, such as the General Agreement on Tariffs and Trade (GATT) and the North American Free Trade Agreement (NAFTA), are reducing barriers to trade. The proposed Multinational Agreement on Investment (MAI) would make it illegal for a country to impose any restrictions on the movement of investment capital across its borders.

Very few restrictions exist today, and the growth of mutual funds for investments in so-called emerging markets has made it possible for even small investors to allocate their capital—and place their bets—on companies overseas. Economists energetically disagree over how many manufacturing jobs in the United States have actually been lost as a result, but you don't need to be a weatherman to see which way the wind blows. The mere threat of job loss has enormous impact, discouraging both unionization and demands for higher wages. Companies can throw up their hands and say, "We have to compete in the global market. If conditions here don't allow us to do that, we can and will relocate."

This phenomenon has been newly dubbed the "footloose corporation." *Business Week* puts it this way: "Though few companies are totally untethered from their home countries, the trend towards a form of 'stateless' corporation is unmistakable."[18] By one estimate, multinational corporations now account for about one-third of world output and two-thirds of world trade. Their combined output is approximately as large as that of the United States economy as a whole.[19] This is more than mere internationalization. This represents a deep reorganization of the very process of production.

Statelessness is not imminent. The nation-state remains the basic unit of military force and the crucial arbiter of access to the natural resources that fuel economic growth. A variety of state policies, from regulation to support for research and development, affect the competitiveness of firms headquartered in their territory. Cultural loyalties remain significant, embedded as they are in the very ways that firms do business. The state protects property rights, a role that may become increasingly important, given the growth of the digital economy involving electronic encoding of information and entertainment that can be easily pirated. As the federal antitrust ruling against Microsoft shows, the state remains a crucial umpire on the corporate playing field. Geographer Peter Dicken warns against anticipating its imminent demise: "The state is dead," he writes, and, "long live the state!"[20]

Now you see it, now you don't. Whether the state is becoming bigger or smaller, stronger or weaker, is far less important than how the role of the state is changing. It seems to be changing in ways that increase the power of footloose corporations and decrease the power of "footbound" workers and consumers. The new international order allows corporations to elude regulation. Got laws giving workers a right to organize and protection against discrimination? Hey, we'll go someplace they don't. Got rules against pollution? You'll be sorry, because there are plenty of countries that don't. Got requirements for occupational health and safety? See you later.

Wait a minute, you object. Consumers can stick by their principles if they are willing to pay the costs. But that's not so easy. Consider the proposed Child Labor Deterrence Act of 1995, which would have banned the importation to the United States of products manufactured using the labor of children under the age of fourteen. Unfortunately, it violated the rules of the World Trade Organization (WTO), which do not allow for discrimination among commodities or countries on the basis of differences in the mode of production. The United States, needless to say, is a member of the WTO.[21] Some companies—like Reebok, which warrants that its soccer balls are not made through child labor—respond to consumer pressure. A hefty majority of Americans say they won't buy products made under unsafe or unfair working conditions.[22] But how will they know? Some things are labeled, some are not, and who knows whether labels are accurate?

Remember the campaign to boycott tuna that had been caught using nets that also killed large numbers of dolphins? It appealed to U.S. consumers, particularly dolphin-loving kids whose moms fixed them tuna salad sandwiches. Some large corporations like StarKist imposed restrictions on their suppliers. Flipper and his kin began enjoying some protection and made a bit of a comeback. But when the United States banned imports of Mexican tuna because that country had not taken steps to regulate fishing practices to reduce dolphin mortality, Mexico appealed to the WTO and won. Consumers in this country don't have the right to collectively enforce their environmental preferences, and most cans of tunafish do not stipulate whether or not they contain Mexican tuna. Next time you order *tekka maki* at a sushi bar, try asking the chef what country the tuna came from. Ten to one, he won't know.

In addition to weakening the state's ability to regulate corporations, the new international order weakens the state's ability to tax them. They can threaten to relocate, or they can simply change their accounting procedures so that their multinational operations make profits in countries with low or no taxes, and incur losses in countries with high taxes. Only if these strategies fail are they forced to relocate. In contesting the claim that globalization encourages nation-states to engage in a "race to the bottom," the *Economist* points out that social spending has remained fairly constant over the last twenty years in most advanced industrial countries. What the *Economist* doesn't mention is that the burden of paying for these programs has been shifted to wage earners as corporate income taxes have been slashed and rates on high-income earners have been reduced. In the United States, since 1960, the contribution of corporate taxes relative to total federal tax revenues in this country has fallen by more than half.[23]

At the beginning of the twentieth century, Edward Bernstein and other European social democrats argued that Karl Marx was far too obsessed with the need for socialist revolution. Capitalism, they insisted, could be reformed. Once tamed by the electoral power of the working class, capitalists would be forced to share the benefits of their highly productive industries. The latter half of the twentieth century seemed to prove them right. Germany and France, as well as Scandinavia, became models of social democracy, providing health care, education, and a basic social safety net for their citizens. Even in the United States, where racial and ethnic inequalities remained particularly intense, economic expansion created something of a trickle-down. With the demise of the state socialist economies of Eastern Europe in the 1980s, the debate seemed over. An ebullient new confidence in capitalism led to a rapture of political consensus.

Now we are entering a new stage. By pitting one nation against another, global corporations can minimize the impact of democratic governance. William Greider puts it this way: "In military terms, the free-running market has mounted a pincer movement against the modern welfare state and is advancing to disable it."[24] Karl Marx always argued that in the long run the dictates of profit maximization would make capitalism untamable. Perhaps he and his followers simply failed to realize how long that run would be.

Some economists despise the term "globalization" because it highlights changes in terms of spatial rather than social organization, deflecting our attention from capitalism as a system based on competitive efforts to maximize profits. Perhaps globalization is simply the highest—or, some would say, the lowest—stage of capitalism. It would be presumptuous to call it the final stage. But it is almost certainly the next stage.

The Low-Down Laid-Off Downsizing Blues

In the fall of 1996, my local newspaper carried some moving photographs of workers at a plant in nearby Easthampton, Massachusetts, who had just lost their jobs. The EKCO Corporation announced that they were closing the Kellogg Brush Company and moving its production to Ciudad Obregón, Mexico, a town with its own promotional site on the World Wide Web. I decided to put the photographs together with some facts, figures, and a link to the Mexican site, and create an educational Web site on plant closings that would illustrate the process of globalization.

The announcement came on October 10, 1996. Two hundred and twenty employees were told they would soon lose their jobs. Downsizing has become routine in the town of Easthampton. Some fifty years ago, it was a center of the textile industry, specializing in elastic products. Now it can only be described as a decaying mill town. The community did all it could to prevent the job loss. The chairman of the town's Economic Development Commission met with EKCO to discuss tax incentives and cuts in water and sewer fees. State representatives, congressmen, and senators explored possibilities for public assistance. The employees' union placed an advertisement in the local paper making it clear that they would offer the company concessions.

The EKCO representatives were polite but firm. Their costs were up and their profits down, along with their stock prices. They had been operating a small manufacturing facility in Cuidad Obregón quite successfully since 1990. One EKCO manager summarized the reasons behind their decision as follows: "It's a very cost-competitive environment. The decision was made purely on a cost analysis basis, whether that's labor, overhead, efficiency, or synergy of consolidation." A union activist said the same thing in plain English: "Basically, what's happening in the blue-collar industries is they're saying, why pay $7 or $8 an hour when you can pay $2 an hour in Mexico?" His numbers were off. The minimum wage in Mexico is more like $3 a day.

Mexico is an attractive business location for other reasons, too. As established earlier, firms can refuse to hire or decide to fire workers who become pregnant. Already minimal environmental regulations were reduced after 1995 in order to attract more investment. New maquiladoras constructed on land already zoned for industrial use don't even have to come up with an environmental assessment. Nearby residents have no

idea what to expect in terms of pollution and contamination.[25] Taxes on
business are low, because Mexican workers are willing to live in communities without running water, plumbing, or electricity. The Mexican
government provides state-funded training firms for prospective employees. It also waives duties on all imported equipment and materials
used to manufacture goods sold outside of Mexico.

Was NAFTA to blame for EKCO's decision to leave Easthampton?
Not directly. U.S. firms were already moving to Mexico, especially to
the regions designated as free trade zones. EKCO invested there before
NAFTA was passed. Indirectly, however, the treaty probably contributed to EKCO's decision. Intensified international competition resulting from the reduction of trade barriers has increased the pressure to cut
costs.

Ironically, in February 1997, EKCO decided not to move more production to Mexico after all. Instead, they decided that they would transfer their Easthampton operations to their Hamilton, Ohio, plant. The
Ohio state government offered them financial incentives that included a
70 percent job-creation tax credit for eight years; a manufacturing and
equipment tax credit with an estimated value of $270,000; a $1.1 million
low-interest loan; a $100,000 Business Development grant; and a job-
training grant of up to $150,000. Sometimes, the threat of moving pro-
vides greater benefits than the move itself. And, if Ohio runs out of
money, Mexico will still be there.

Have you ever heard Rush Limbaugh ask, "Why is it that when a
corporation fires workers, it is never speculated that the workers might
have deserved it?" Al Franken, former writer for *Saturday Night Live*
and author of *Rush Limbaugh Is a Big Fat Idiot*, has a great rejoinder:
"I've had the same thought about airplane crashes."[26] Downsizing has
become a routine aspect of the employment landscape, picking up speed
even in 1998, a year of otherwise surprising economic resilience. With
an unemployment rate of below 4 percent, the impact is substantially
buffered. It's not so hard to find another job. But many of the downsized, especially those over age forty-five, suffer an irretrievable loss in
their standard of living. Looking at the full-time workers laid off from

permanent jobs (i.e., jobs held at least three years) between 1995 and 1997, here was the picture in early 1998: 38 percent had taken jobs at lower pay; 15 percent had started working part-time or at home; 13 percent had dropped out of the labor force, and about 10 percent remained unemployed.[27]

In 1996, Michael Moore published a book called *Downsize This*. I bought the audio version, and was listening to it on tape while I drove around Easthampton taking pictures of abandoned factory buildings. Moore's voice sounds gravelly and nasal at the same time, and you can tell that he's good at talking to people. He describes his conversations with the businessmen who sometimes sit next to him on planes. They often tell him that companies can't make too much profit, and that their responsibility to their shareholders is to make as much money as possible. Moore starts talking about the cocaine industry, and how profitable it is. Fewer people die from cocaine overdoses than from car accidents. So why doesn't General Motors go into the cocaine business? "I'll tell you why," says Moore. "Because cocaine destroys people and communities. That's why we have laws that punish people for selling cocaine." He goes on to point out that closing factories also destroys people and communities. We can regulate this process. We can outlaw forms of profit maximization that have harmful effects.

In the early 1980s, I became interested in the effect of advance notice on plant closings in Maine. I was teaching at Bowdoin College at the time, and a couple of students approached me asking to do an independent study. Maine, which had been hit hard by deindustrialization, had a law on the books requiring all corporations employing more than fifty workers to give sixty days advance notice of a plant closing. We decided to figure out exactly how many plants had closed. The two students, Julia Leighton and Melissa Roderick, turned out to be tenacious researchers, and they did most of the work. Since the information was not readily available in published documents, they worked from newspaper accounts and electric company records (most factories use large quantities of electricity, so when a big account gets canceled, a factory has likely closed). Every detail had to be confirmed by phone.

One of the students came from a rich family: her father was a well-known corporate CEO. She had a confident, take-charge manner. When she called business offices, she got results. In fact, several managers who returned her calls got the impression that I was her secretary.

The other student came from Fall River, Massachusetts, where both her parents were involved in local Democratic Party politics. She had a working-class accent that she put to good use calling union offices for necessary information. While conducting this research, we discovered that relatively few Maine companies that closed had in fact observed the advance notice requirement since no one was actively enforcing it. We also discovered (surprise!) that when companies gave advance notice of a closing, the resulting unemployment was lower. Workers had more time to adjust, make plans, find other jobs. Relatively few (only 13 percent) of the firms that closed between 1973 and 1982 had gone bankrupt.

We were invited to a meeting in the state capital to discuss a possible strengthening of the plant closing regulation, one that would require firms to offer severance pay. The unions brought in busloads of unemployed workers. I remember that the meeting room had no windows, red paisley wallpaper, and an elaborate chandelier. One legislator who slept through my testimony woke up with a start, deciding that it was time to put me in my place. "Young lady," he asked, "do you think you can get blood from a turnip?" I was taken aback, but a laid-off shoe worker in the audience remembered what I had reported about bankruptcy rates and piped up: "She's just shown that the companies that shut down were not turnips!" It was the only laugh workers got that day: the severance-pay provision never had a chance.

A couple of years later, Congress began to consider a national requirement for advance notice modeled on the Maine precedent. I was flown down to Washington to testify.[28] Eventually, a bill was passed: the Worker Adjustment and Retraining Act of 1988. Economists are still debating whether it really helped lower the unemployment resulting from large plant closings.

Federal law also mandates assistance and retraining for downsized workers who can show that their job loss resulted from international competition. By most accounts, however, this law doesn't do much.

A Letter from Home

Of the many articles heralding globalization in the pages of the *Wall Street Journal*, my favorite, called "Capitalism Isn't Broken," openly acknowledges the downside. "There is no way to eliminate the private pain that comes from the adjustment. We all wish it were different, but without the private pain, most people will not change." They go on to calmly predict that real wages for all workers in the West are unlikely to increase much, and some will fall dramatically—by as much as 50 percent—in the decades to come.[29]

Short-term costs are so inconvenient. Unfortunately, it's not readers of *The Wall Street Journal* who will pay them. Russell Baker, the usually mild-mannered columnist, was driven to bitter sarcasm by a corporate manager who appeared on Jim Lehrer's *News Hour* and explained how he had fired a third of his workforce, then given himself a multimillion-dollar raise. Baker titled his *New York Times* column "The Market God" and described the sacrifices apparently required to placate him:

> Why is it that people who praise "downsizing" for its salubrious effect on the economy are invariably people in no danger of being "downsized" themselves? It is because nothing sharpens a man's vision of what's good for the country better than a well-paid job, unless it is the assurance that he will not be among those who must be fired for the common good. A man in this position can see with amazing clarity why mass firings are vital to the nation's welfare. Such a man can see why it is foolishly sentimental to snivel and whine and deplore the plight of these regrettably "downsized" workers.[30]

Consider the similarities between a parent who devotes time and energy to enhancing his or her children's capabilities and a country that devotes a large portion of its national budget to social welfare. In the short run, both are at a competitive disadvantage in the market, because they are devoting fewer resources to goods and services that can be directly sold. A college professor who is also an involved mother is probably not going to produce as many journal articles as one who's not raising kids. A lawyer who is an involved father is not going to generate as many billable hours as a bachelor competitor. A manager who is a mother is unlikely to spend twelve hours a day at the office.

Families with kids are like little welfare states. They prioritize something other than their market earnings, and the adult earners tax themselves heavily in terms of both money and time to fulfill obligations to their dependents. My favorite parody of downsizing is a short piece by Robert Sullivan that appeared in the *New Yorker*. Called "A Letter from Dad," it features a father who seats his family members around the kitchen table to explain that the family must be downsized.[31] Shifting the son to part-time, he points out, would reduce food and milk overhead ("I think even your mother will admit that at seventeen you're not as cute as you used to be.") The position of mother-in-law has simply not panned out, and will be permanently discontinued. The CEO, however, is giving himself a raise.

The increasing mobility of capital will undermine the obligations of citizenship, just as it has undermined the obligations of family life. Why should multinational firms that can go elsewhere remain within countries that tax them to support the production of human capabilities? They will remain for a while, out of force of habit and quaint old-fashioned loyalties. But the current rules of competition suggest that the ones who jump first to take advantage of new opportunities, like CorporNation, will win any race that is defined in terms of maximizing the short-term gains.

———————◆———————

To globalize the economy by erasure of national boundaries through free trade, free capital mobility, and free, or at least uncontrolled migration, is to wound fatally the major unit of community capable of carrying out any policies for the common good.

—HERMAN DALY

———————◆———————

Jihad versus McWorld

Fathers are to the family as capitalists are to the nation-state: the agents with the greatest power. If you're confident that both are naturally benevolent, you needn't worry about either. This is the confidence that true believers in the market—people who sometimes describe themselves as libertarians—tend to embrace. Social conservatives, however, are worried about globalization. If you believe in the need to enforce a father's obligations to his children, you might also want to enforce a capitalist's obligations to his fellow citizens. Free trade, like free love, poses a threat to the established order.

Ross Perot, whose candidacy for president in 1992 helped ensure Bill Clinton's victory, campaigned vociferously against the North American Free Trade Agreement on the grounds that it would hurt American workers. The most memorable phrase he used was "the giant sucking sound of jobs moving south." In 1996, Pat Buchanan scared Republicans by railing against immigration and plant closings. "Where does one's loyalty lie?" he asked. "That is the issue raised by the onset of the Global Economy and the rise of the transnational elite. To whom, to what, do we owe allegiance and love?"[32] He later groaned, "We are ceasing to be a band of brothers."[33]

On this point, Buchanan is right. The rise of multinational corporations creates an international managerial class that has no roots in any specific geographic or cultural community. This new class also weakens the traditional brotherhood by lowering the cultural barriers to women's participation in management. The conservative response is to circle the wagons. Throw up trade barriers. Restrict immigration. Change the slogan from "every man for himself" to "every nation for itself." The prescription is appealing in its simplicity, a return to the ideals of Ike Eisenhower and the *Father Knows Best* world of the 1950s.

Not surprisingly, social conservatism also includes a call for women to return to their traditional roles. In June 1998, the convention of Southern Baptists, the largest Protestant denomination in the United States, declared that a wife should "submit herself graciously" to her husband's "leadership."[34] But there's more going on here than a power play by a group of white padres who would like to see their authority restored. Much depends on people's perceptions of their alternatives. Globalization, modernization, the growth of individualism—whatever you call it, it threatens to create a world that lacks all sense of community. It could be a world in which individuals are free of any social obligation whatsoever, a world largely without compassion, a world in which everything is bought and sold. By comparison, patriotism and patriarchy don't look quite so bad.

Benjamin Barber captures the dilemma in a book called *Jihad vs. McWorld: How Globalism and Tribalism Are Reshaping the World*. It describes a kind of global polarization. "McWorld" represents an "unobstructed set of exchange relationships among individual consumers and individual producers," a nightmarish theme park of undifferentiated malls and fast-food restaurants called McWorld.[35] Barber doesn't dwell on the implications for care, but it's easy to extrapolate from his analysis. Pick up your Egg McMuffin at the daycare center when you drop off your kids. Hit the freeway, use your cell phone to check on your parents at the nursing home. Clock into your cubicle at work. And, finally, pick up an antidepressant on the way home, along with your Big Mac, at the drive-through window.

The worldwide resurgence of religious fundamentalism testifies to anxiety about the destabilization of the traditional patriarchal relationships that have ensured a relatively cheap supply of caregivers. Some of this anxiety reflects political interests based on nation, race, class, and gender. But it also reflects a deeper response to McWorld. A consistent demand of religious fundamentalism worldwide is the reestablishment of rules that would restrict women's rights to avoid caregiving. The policies implemented by the Taliban in Afghanistan are the most extreme. They ban female employment outside the home. Young girls are allowed only enough education to read the Koran. In Saudi Arabia, women are not allowed to drive cars. Sudan's military regime does not permit women to leave the country without permission from a father, husband, or brother.[36] In many countries, women are denied access to effective means of contraception, as well as abortion.

In the United States, women already have too many rights for fundamentalists even to imagine driving our society to such extremes. But the systematic assault on abortion rights, which has included many acts of terrorism against women's health clinics and physicians, can be described as a religious war. As I pointed out in chapter 1, much of the extreme rhetoric of the antiabortion movement is fueled by enormous anger at the very idea that a woman might decide that her own needs have precedence over those of a potential child.

An orchestrated return to traditional family values has pressured conservative men to explicitly re-valorize women who accept traditional roles. It is not incidental that the largest conservative men's group in the United States today calls itself Promise Keepers. The most endearing aspect of this movement is its emphasis on men's responsibilities as fathers. A closer look at the terms of their promise, however, makes it clear that conservative men demand leadership in return for responsibility. For all their talk of commitment, they seem to be offering women a take-it-or-leave-it deal: "Give me authority and I'll take care of you. Take away my authority, and you (and the kids) are on your own."

Of course, even a bad promise can be better than none at all. But turning back the clock is an unacceptable solution. Women deserve a better deal, one in which both leadership and responsibilities for care are shared. If democracy can work in a nation-state, it can also work in a family. If collective welfare is a responsibility in a family, it should also be a responsibility in a nation-state. Still, if we want to fend off the religious fundamentalism symbolized by the jihad, we need to resist McWorld. Globalization is forcing us to rethink both the family and the state.

On the positive side, both institutions demand commitment to the welfare of the group, binding individuals together. On the negative side, both family and state can generate oppressive hierarchies that interfere with individual rights and the full development of human capabilities. It is easy to see why the extreme alternatives of jihad and McWorld loom large. One represents a totalitarian response, the other a perfectly competitive one. Both responses require far less energy and negotiation than would a democratic attempt to collectively define and enforce responsibilities for care.

The effort to restore patriotic protectionism parallels, on a national level, the effort to restore patriarchal authority. Both moves try to stigmatize an enemy—foreigners on the one hand, gays and feminists on the other.

Ross Perot and Pat Buchanan are full of concern about ordinary Americans. They never seem to worry about the fate of ordinary non-Americans. The protectionist policies they endorse have been aptly called "beggar thy neighbor." And their consequences are far from beneficial: they often backfire because they prompt retaliation.

We don't have to choose between strict protectionism and unregulated free trade. We could, instead, devise trade policies that reflect concern for the welfare of consumers, workers, and the environment in all countries, not just our own. Surveys show that the overwhelming majority of Americans believe that trade agreements should encourage environmental protection and workers' rights. Citizens' groups from several countries have gotten together to develop guidelines.[37] College students on a number of campuses have successfully pressured their universities not to allow their logos on articles manufactured in sweatshops. We could ask all the stakeholders to agree on better rules for the game. Fair trade, not free trade. Or, to return to the analogy with feminism, fair love, not free love.

Critics of globalization have found that just using the term "fair trade" makes a difference, because it allows people to see that alternatives exist. A Harris poll conducted in April 2000 asked people to choose from among three categories of views about foreign trade. 10 percent described themselves as free traders. 37 percent described themselves as protectionist. 51 percent described themselves as fair traders.[38] In principle, at least, the invisible heart has more friends than the invisible hand.

Chicken Soup for the Global Economy

Perhaps I'm being too optimistic, making it sound as if there's easy medicine for the problems that ail us. But it can't hurt to put some chicken soup on the table. If no one wants to try it, we can pour it into the gas tank of the global economy and see what happens. A basic recipe: Start with a stock of concern for developing human capabilities, not merely increasing the size of our collective GDPs. Skim off the grease; prioritize improvements in the standard of living for the neediest of countries and the most vulnerable within countries. Develop an international system of governance in which poor countries have the same representation as rich ones.

Don't allow a race to the bottom. Impose rules of minimum taxation for all corporations within all countries. Penalize countries that refuse to guarantee basic democratic rights (including the right to organize) as well as those that fail to monitor and enforce environmental safeguards, by restricting access to our consumer markets. Insist on a basic safety net to protect workers from economic insecurity and job losses due to forces beyond their control.

It's easier to imagine solutions than to implement them. Most people occupy contradictory positions. Disadvantaged along one dimension, they are privileged along another. Lenin appreciated this when he described the "aristocracy of labor" in the advanced capitalist countries as more aligned to its national than to its class interests. Desperate Mexicans and Central Americans risking their lives to cross the hellish border zones, immigrant Turks willing to work for much lower wages than native Germans—the citizens of Global Rome are worried about barbarians at the gates. We are the lords of plenty. Small wonder we like to think that anyone with plenty has earned it.

But it is exactly this situation that globalization might change. As international markets continue to expand, most group allegiances other than those based on class will weaken. The old Marxian vision of a neatly divided society with owners pitted against workers may yet come true—unless citizens figure out ways to intervene. Even a writer for *Business Week* agrees: "The triumph of capital in the cold war has tilted the playing field against those who earn their living from work throughout the globe."[39] That old playing field again. It looks more like a pinball machine to me, or Pac Man on the loose.

Investors and citizens are at odds. From the point of view of investors, free markets are great, profits should be maximized, and regulation lowers profits. Labor is just one more cost of production. From the point of view of citizens, free markets work best in democratic countries that protect human rights, profits are one source of funds for productive investment, and regulation is crucial to protect workers, consumers, and the environment. Labor is almost everybody's everyday life, and workers are produced, educated, and maintained by families and communities.

Some citizens are investors. Many are workers. Nearly all are consumers. Some live in rich countries, some in poor ones. But all citizens of this world have something in common: a loss of control over their own economies. Imagine a supercapitalist in flight with bulging arms, Day-Glo purple gloves, and huge green wings. He wears a crown with a large green dollar sign upon it, and he sports expensive shades. His necktie is blowing in the wind. He proclaims all resistance futile. That was as far as I got with a slide show for activists at the Summer Institute for Popular Economics. At that point, the audience told me that it was too depressing a place to end. "How about having some cyborg Amazon guerrillas shoot him down?" someone asked. "No, it should be Lilliputians," others insisted, "with a large net woven from grass roots that holds him down." If we added a spoonful of kryptonite, it might work.

———————◆———————

If capitalism is now truly global, what are the global social obligations that accompany it?

—WILLIAM GREIDER,
One World, Ready or Not

DANCING IN THE DARK

Now dreams
Are not available
To the dreamers,
Nor songs to the singers.
In some lands
Dark night
And cold steel
Prevail—
But the dream
Will come back,
And the song
Break
Its jail.

—LANGSTON HUGHES

The old joke goes like this: "What's the difference between capitalism and communism?" Easy. "Under capitalism, man exploits man. Under communism, it's just the reverse." What the joke leaves out is the not insignificant fact that in both systems women have wound up doing the most important but least remunerative work. This helps explain why I've never been captivated by the Battle of the Titans. As concepts, capitalism and communism seem oversimplified to me, like Godzilla and King Kong. Still, I think we can learn from both. As E. P. Thompson puts it, "Another name for the Beast of history is experience; even the swindles have something to teach."[1]

This chapter is about alternatives to both big systems. It describes some pros and cons of Marxist theory and offers a brief explanation of the weaknesses of central planning. At the same time, it emphasizes that complete reliance on markets is no solution either. In Russia, privatization has left most people much worse off than they were before. Up and down, back and forth, ebb and flow—something is wrong with our design.

Up to now, this book has developed criticisms of our existing economic institutions, from the general ways we organize the work of caring for others to more specific features of our social policy, education finance, tax structure, and international trade. This chapter steps back to look at the larger picture, describing three directions for change which, carefully combined, could form a stable triangle of new political space. The first direction is market socialism, or, if you prefer, people's capitalism. Whether state managers or capitalist managers are in control matters less than the distribution of assets widely enough to allow everyone to play the market game. The second direction is participatory democracy. People should be enabled to govern themselves, not just within the nation-state, but within all the institutions that affect their daily lives. The third direction is shared care. Social institutions must be developed to distribute the responsibilities of caring for dependents in effective and equitable ways. Social democracy has taken some nations down this road, but we need to go much farther.

Economic theory offers us some indispensable tools for organizing our joint endeavors. That's why it's so important to get economics right—to ensure that it includes careful consideration of love, obligation and reciprocity, as well as self-interest. We must stop assuming that norms and preferences of caring for others come from "outside" our economic system and can therefore be taken as a given. We must start thinking about care as a propensity that can be defended and developed—or weakened and wasted—by economic risks and rewards. This book ends with a short list of general principles for challenging the conventional economic wisdom of the invisible hand.

Socialisms, Utopian and Scientific

The traditional opposition between the smaller words "social" and "individual" embedded in larger concepts suggests that the opposite of socialism is not capitalism, but individualism.

The origin of modern socialism is usually traced to the followers of Robert Owen, the early nineteenth-century English factory manager and self-made capitalist who led the fight for restrictions on children's labor. Owen and his followers believed that people should try to cooperate to achieve the common good. They often referred to fellow citizens as brothers and sisters, and most of them agreed that sisters should have the same rights as brothers.[2] Derided by both the left and the right, pre-Marxian socialists nonetheless had a significant impact on the evolution of so-called capitalist economies, as well as on those dubbed socialist simply because they relied on centralized state planning.

Their most conspicuous weakness was their lack of any real theory, as well as a naive confidence that good intentions usually lead to good results. In trying to remedy this weakness, however, Karl Marx and Friedrich Engels went to the other extreme, promoting a scientific approach that displaced human motives by the march of history and predicted a crisis of capitalism. In their theory, social conflict was reduced to class membership: feudal lords versus peasants and capitalist employers versus workers. An individual's interests were identical to those of other members of his class. Once class differences were eliminated by the collectivization of ownership of the means of production, they prophesied, harmony would prevail. This analysis overlooked the historical significance of patriarchal control over women.

Marx was thoroughly schooled in English political economy. But it was precisely his reliance on this tradition that led him to focus on commodities—things bought and sold in the market—and to consider all other forms of production quite literally "unproductive." He viewed the time and effort that women devoted to meeting the basic subsistence needs of workers and creating the next generation as aspects of nature, not dimensions of society. In his larger theory, labor creates all surplus, but labor itself is unproduced. Essentially, according to Marx, workers create themselves; they simply trade a portion of their wages for their means of subsistence.

Marxist theory also plays down the role of the kind of collective dynamics that cannot easily be explained in terms of control over production and extraction of a surplus—forms of domination based on nation, race, and gender, rather than class. Believing capitalism had an important historical role to play in generating technological change and alleviating economic scarcity, Marx predicted that it would eventually succumb to a falling rate of profit. In his later years, he became far more preoccupied with the direction of the capitalist crisis than the possible trajectory of socialism. His constant emphasis on material economic conditions deflected him from serious consideration of the difficulties of ensuring democratic governance.

Many books have been written about the ways that Marx disappointed his true believers. This is ironic, since he hated dogma and reputedly announced, "I am not a Marxist!" However flawed his vision, Marx painted a big picture of how ordinary people were trying to redesign their own social system and make their own history. Famously contemptuous of the Church, Marx once referred to religion as the "opiate of the masses" that substituted heavenly rewards for earthly justice.

Once, in a laundromat in New Haven, I saw some graffiti describing Marxism as the "opiate of the intellectuals." What is really intoxicating is the idea that more and better knowledge might enable us to change the social world. It makes me think not of illicit drugs but of a runner's high—the exhilaration of effort, forward movement, progress toward a finish line. But running may be the wrong metaphor, considering that Marx described history as a team sport.

Conventional economics takes rational Economic Man as a given and explains how he makes choices. Economists influenced by Marx are more likely to ask where Economic Man came from, why he wants what he wants, and whether he feels solidarity toward others. Marx's emphasis on collective action may be simplistic in its preoccupation with class, but it calls attention to the ways that people identify with members of their family, race, nation, class, or gender, and act together to pursue common interests.

If you like the cheerful story of capitalist development that stars handsome, risk-taking entrepreneurs who dream up new technological innovations, make billions of dollars, and improve all our lives in the process, don't read Marx. He won't allow you to ignore the role that organized force and violence play in the struggle for control of basic economic resources. If there is one recurrent pattern in history, it is the strong ganging up on the weak. And then—occasionally—the weak growing strong. Marx believed the proletariat would prove the best example. So far, I'd say, it's women who have clinched his point, taking advantage of economic transformation to fight for improvements in their relative position.

Planning Planning

In 1977, I joined the Venceremos Brigade, the organization that sent American activists to Cuba to help work in the fields, build houses, bridge the gap between mental and manual labor, and further the revolution. I was no fan of Cuban Leninism. But I was curious about how the Cubans had vanquished hunger and illiteracy. I had spent enough time in Mexico to be acquainted with desperate, filthy children who have to beg for food.

Unfortunately, the cadre running the brigade in my region that year became concerned about bourgeois influence. They looked particularly closely at the applications submitted by intellectual hippies. And they were unhappy with what they saw when they came to visit: women wearing cutoffs and T-shirts without brassieres, evidence of Women's Liberation. They told us that we might still be allowed to go to Cuba with the brigade if we practiced self-criticism. After some soul-searching about the relative importance of dress codes versus meeting people's basic needs, I decided that any group so confident that it understood other people's needs would be unlikely to fulfill them. I bowed out, peeved that the world seemed to offer a choice between individual freedom and social responsibility with hardly anything in between.

Most people identify socialism with the kind of central planning put into effect in the Soviet Union and China, planning that was controlled by a small political cadre of Communist Party officials. Between the end of World War II and about 1975, these authoritarian regimes delivered significant improvements in standards of living. But centrally planned, hierarchically structured institutions are slow to change and adapt; the cost of initial inefficiencies is compounded over time. The most significant problems seemed related not to the management of information, but to the management of people. These problems grew directly from the structure of power and incentives in the planning process.

Planners were accountable to none but themselves, until repressed dissatisfaction with the system began to build and spill. The ideology of scientific socialism reinforced the notion that planning was merely a technical process, and much of the economic theory that informed planning was simply wrong. My favorite example is the Soviet interpretation of the labor theory of value, which suggests that heavy industry can generate a surplus, but that the service sector and retail trade are by definition unproductive. Planners ignored the tremendous cost and frustration caused by scarcities of consumer goods, including hours spent standing in line—mostly women's hours, of course. What does Slavenka Drakulic complain of most, in *How We Survived Communism and Even Laughed*? The scarcity of sanitary napkins.[3]

Since household work did not create value, there was no need to produce items like washing machines, dishwashers, microwave ovens, or vacuum cleaners that might ease the burden.[4] Some public provision of child care and food services, planners agreed, would suffice to move women into wage employment, and that was all that mattered. What they did in their unproductive time was their own problem. Women in capitalist countries got less help with child care, but the market provided them with more choice and flexibility in the organization of family work and leisure time. At home, both men and women could invest in new consumer goods and, at least on weekends, be in charge of their own little enterprise of home.

In the traditional Marxian lexicon, consumption and leisure are relatively unimportant: people "realize" themselves in production. But what people do when not working for pay *is* an important form of production. And since people spend about as much time working outside the official workplace as inside, it's not surprising that they passionately care about the provision of goods and services that they can utilize to take care of themselves and others. The Cuban economy still largely relies on central planning. The Cubans joke that they have eliminated hunger, homelessness, and illiteracy, but they still face three major problems: breakfast, lunch, and dinner.

Marxist theory underemphasized incentive problems. The article of faith that no significant social conflict could exist within a socialist society implies that everyone will automatically do his or her best to further the common good. Not so. Apart from the fact that state ownership can be a fiction cementing the authoritarian control of a single party, it is also inefficient. If workers are paid according to predetermined rules rather than according to performance, they have little incentive to work hard. And managers have few carrots or sticks at their disposal. Perverse incentives rule: "You scratch my back and I'll scratch yours." Workers get low pay and give low effort.[5]

Probably the most serious limitation of central planning is the lack of incentives for technological innovation. State managers focus on meeting planned objectives and conforming to their superiors' expectations, rather than cutting costs or promoting new products. In capitalist countries, by contrast, the market rewards at least some productive new ideas, no matter how disruptive they threaten to be. Many years ago, Joseph Schumpeter insisted that capitalism's great virtue was its dynamism and marveled at the way it generated gales of "creative destruction."[6]

A decentralized, competitive market process holds no respect for authority, tradition, precedent, or sheer size; it can impose a harsh but impersonal discipline on even the most powerful. The dynamic forces of innovation can make up for many other sources of inefficiency, which include monopolistic power in many industries and periodic high unemployment in the economy as a whole.[7] Unfortunately, the people who benefit from innovation are not usually the same people who are hurt by inefficiency.

Centralized planning has, historically, been badly planned. But that doesn't mean that planning is a bad idea. Much depends on who the planners are. Democratic revolutions in the Soviet Union and Eastern Europe have taught us is that ordinary people can and will demand a voice. Markets can help provoke energy and discipline. They do not, however, represent a simple cure-all. Indeed, as the Russian example shows, markets can lead to the perversion of democracy and the institutionalization of theft.

The Transition to Capitalism

The Soviet Communist Party knew that things weren't working right. In 1965, Kosygin introduced changes that foreshadowed those later introduced by Gorbachev, such as encouraging competition among state-run enterprises. The managerial bureaucracy effectively resisted these changes, which would have complicated their lives. Their stubborn resistance probably also explains why Gorbachev found it so difficult to implement gradual reforms.[8]

Ironically, it was Marx who first argued that revolutions can accomplish things that reforms can never achieve; they succeed by blasting away the accretions of collective privilege that can occlude a social system, making it difficult for blood to reach the heart. It makes sense, but you can see why the patient might feel shaky afterward. You might want to put her on a special diet and monitor her life signs, including levels of poverty and unemployment. But the free-market economists who advised the most recent Russian revolution wanted to privatize as fast as possible. They boasted that their policies were economic "shock therapy."

My colleague David Kotz is one of the few economists in the United States who was critical of this policy from the outset. He served as an advisor to members of the minority faction within the Russian parliament. "Do you know what happened to Russia in 1992," he has asked rhetorically, "after they removed all price controls? Real consumer spending fell about 38 percent. Compare that to the blow to consumer spending in the U.S. between 1929–1933, during the Great Depression: 21 percent. People really suffered."[9]

In 1993, a member of the Russian parliament, Alexander Buzgalin, came to Amherst to give a talk. We took him to the Campus Center for lunch, where he exhibited a special fondness for french fries and ketchup. He explained that with a minimum wage amounting to about five dollars a month, most Russians couldn't even afford to buy newspapers. Hospitals lacked running water. The more fortunate people owned private plots of land on which they planted as many potatoes as they could, thinking simply of survival.

He told a new Russian joke, about a man who returns from a long day of looking for work and is startled by the smell of meat cooking on the stove—and even more surprised to find that the refrigerator is working again and inside it is a pitcher of juice. "What happened?" he calls to his wife. "Has communism come back?"

Markets are the new religion, Alex explained, but a lot of people sound like religious hypocrites who announce their faith and then proceed to sin. They say, "We believe in markets." Then they whisper, "But we need a plan."[10]

Markets are a method of allocating resources based on a given starting place—what people have and what they want. They don't tell you anything about what the starting place needs to look like—what people should have to begin with. Democracy is a system that allows people to govern themselves, based on rights and representation. Neither capitalism nor democracy explains how assets should be distributed. The most important question about reform in the former state socialist countries was, Who gets what? State ownership means that people collectively own the country's resources, its infrastructure, its factories. Without democratic rules, a political elite maintains tight control. Privatization could contribute to democratization—but only if ordinary people could acquire shares. That's not what happened in the former Soviet Union.

In 1993, the Soviets distributed to the adult population vouchers that assigned each person a portion of the value of state property. Every citizen had a theoretical right to a voucher in the amount of 10,000 rubles. In American dollars that was less than $50, and the sum of all vouchers did not add up to anything close to the total wealth of the country. The vouchers could be exchanged for shares, but not all enterprises put their shares up for sale, and many complicated rules and restrictions applied. The system worked to the distinct advantage of workers in potentially profitable enterprises; others, particularly those employed by schools or hospitals (not surprisingly, these were mostly women) were in a weak position.[11]

Many people couldn't afford to hold onto their vouchers until they were able to buy shares in an enterprise they thought would be a decent investment, so they sold them. Who accumulated them? Those in the know—the managers, politicians, bureaucrats involved in designing the new privatization policies. Previously known as the "nomenclatura," this class simply developed a new system of control over the economy, a less centralized form of class power. Western experts, confident that the goal of privatization was so important that it justified any means, pushed for rapid transfer of property. No serious thought was given to the need to establish or enforce rules of fair play. The results were immediately apparent to Russians themselves:

> A monstrous redistribution of wealth is taking place, as a result of which the overwhelming majority of the population is being reduced to beggary save for a few percent—by no means the most talented and competent people, but the most cunning and lacking in moral conscience or respect for laws—who are becoming unspeakably rich.[12]

Protesters carried signs featuring Russian wordplay: *Privatisatsiya = Prikhavtisatsiya*—privatization equals grabbing. By 1999, it had become clear that the new Russian owners had not used their wealth to produce more, but had simply converted it to dollars and sent it out of the country. At least $200 billion, perhaps as much as $500 billion of capital flight took place over a seven-year period. The concentration of wealth and control over the media made political democracy a farce. An article in the *New York Times* said, "At the end of a century in which Russia has been raped by Bolsheviks, the country now seems to have been raped by capitalists."[13]

Russia's GDP has steadily declined, and the standard of living of most of her people has drastically plummeted. Inflation and unemployment are endemic. Poverty and demoralization have led to significant declines in life expectancy. Even the former chief economist of the World Bank, Joseph Stiglitz, agrees that privatization took a disastrous form in Russia. He points out that, by gradually introducing markets into their still largely planned economy, China has fared much better than Russia over the past decade.

Neither central planning nor free markets can guarantee prosperity. Nor can either guarantee democracy. What seems to matter most is how we govern both planning and markets, and how our forms of democratic governance mesh with social values of love, obligation, and reciprocity. Needless to say, these are not issues that progressive economists have successfully figured out. But we have come up with some cool ideas.

———————◆———————

It is beautiful, this picture of us stretching the cloth. There is passion in the long, taut fold of it between us. Our bellies touch the edges of the table as we lean over it.

My mother is helping me make a nice blouse. She has widened the pattern and will take the darts. She marks where they go with colored tracing paper and a spiked metal wheel.

—SUSAN STINSON,
"Whole Cloth"

———————◆———————

Market Socialism

Back in 1829, the American radical Tom Skidmore declared that every man and woman had an equal right to property in the state of nature. Because the original government had failed to secure that right, he argued, it should now redistribute all property and provide both men and women with an education and an equal portion at age eighteen.[14]

In 1869, the Homestead Act bestowed ownership of western lands only upon persons who settled, cultivated, and occupied the land, not upon absentee owners (Native Americans were completely excluded from this arrangement, which could not have taken place without their dispossession).

Skidmore's proposal and the Homestead Act are two examples of rules (one merely proposed, the other implemented) regarding the distribution of assets within a market economy. The fundamental hypothesis of market socialism is that if everybody starts out in a relatively equal position, market competition will be healthy. There is a major reason why this might work better than leaving productive assets alone, and redistributing income later. If you wait until *after* the market game to redistribute things (a social democratic strategy), you will almost certainly find that the big winners in the market have so much money that they can effectively block any redistribution. For instance, if elections can be bought, rich people will buy them. Resistance to campaign finance reform in the United States is a case in point.

A gradual way of moving toward market socialism would be to make it easier for workers to buy shares in the firms they work for. The National Center for Employee Ownership estimated that U.S. workers controlled about 8 percent of total corporate equity in 1997.[15] In some cases, workers own the entire firm. One of the best-known success stories is that of a cluster of cooperatives in the plywood industry.[16] But in most instances, the extent of worker ownership is relatively modest. Public policy provides substantial tax incentives to firms that form Employee Stock Ownership Plans, or ESOPs. In 1998, about 10 million employees participated in ESOPs and other employer stock and profit-sharing arrangements.[17]

Worker ownership, however, has serious limitations. Most workers don't have the money to buy a significant number of shares, even through pension plans. Just because they own stock, workers don't necessarily have a say in management. If they do, they may be reluctant to take risks, because, unlike most investors, their eggs are all in one basket. Workers' control can create significant inequality among workers. Those who end up not only working for but owning a large successful

firm, like Wal-Mart, will prosper. Those who see their companies go
bankrupt will lose not only their jobs, but their savings and their pensions. Also problematic is the uneven distribution of good jobs. It's not
just that women and minorities are in less well-paid occupations. It's
also that many of them work for less profit-oriented companies: Stock
ownership in a daycare center is unlikely to offer the same rate of return
as stock ownership in an auto plant.

Widespread social ownership might be preferable to worker ownership. For instance, the government could purchase a substantial number
of shares and give them away, with safeguards to prevent them from
being concentrated in a few hands. John Roemer proposes creating a
separate kind of money for the purchase of ownership rights in firms.
This "stock-money," not convertible to regular money, could be distributed equally to all adults. No one would be able to buy or sell shares
with cash, but they could trade shares, which would entitle them to a
portion of the profits of the enterprise. The purpose of the restrictions
is to ensure that everyone has access to ownership, and to prevent the
kind of concentration that took place in Russia. Still, the more successful investors—those who made the best trades—would continue to
make the most money.[18]

This is a good example of how to enable competition with constraints. But not all sectors of the economy lend themselves to organization along highly competitive lines. As pointed out in chapter 3,
pressure to maximize profits can create problems with some institutions,
particularly those providing care services. We don't want hospitals to
act as though patients' rights and quality of care are less important than
the bottom line. We don't want schools to act as though nothing matters
more than test scores. We don't want nursing homes to benefit from neglecting their most expensive residents, in an effort to cut costs.

Competition may be good at serving consumers' needs, but consumers, as citizens, have principles as well as needs. These are questions that
advocates of market socialism tend to overlook, because they still think
of "the economy" as consisting of factories, stores, and banks.[19] The
Old Left line was: "Liberate the working class, then women can be
emancipated." The conventional market socialist line is a bit more

subtle: "Reorganize the really productive part of the economy, and then it will be possible to improve education, family life, health, social welfare, the environment." But which part of our economy is more vital, the cart or the horse?

The version of market socialism I like best would distribute resources directly to young people, allowing them to invest directly in their own capabilities, rather than merely buy shares of a profitable enterprise. Two lawyers, Bruce Ackerman and Anne Alstott, outline details in their book, *The Stakeholder Society*, where they argue that every American citizen who earns a high school diploma should receive a one-time grant of eighty thousand dollars upon reaching adulthood—a grant that would be financed by an annual 2 percent tax levied on the entire country's stock of wealth.[20] Their argument is that all citizens have a claim on our collective patrimony—the resources, technology, and knowledge that we have collectively inherited from the efforts of earlier generations.

———◆———

As a social system we seek the establishment of a democracy of individual participation, governed by two central aims: that the individual share in those social decisions determining the quality and direction of his life; that society be organized to encourage independence in him and provide the media for his common participation.

—TOM HAYDEN,
Students for a Democratic Society

———◆———

Democratic Governance

Reforming ownership is not enough. Democratic governance is also key. This is a principle that most Americans enthusiastically endorse when it comes to controlling our national, state, and local governments. But we don't give much thought to what it means for relations among nations or within economic institutions, such as corporations and government bureaucracies. We should.

The globalization of production is reducing the significance of national borders and, with it, the effectiveness of purely national democracy. In a world without much international governance, individual countries that maintain generous social welfare policies will be penalized (as the previous chapter emphasized). Differences in standards of living among rich and poor countries are far greater than those within most countries. Many of our most pressing environmental problems, including global warming, will require international collaboration.

These are all reasons to strengthen multilateral institutions based on democratic principles, such as the United Nations, rather than those based on financial power, such as the International Monetary Fund. We could also consider the formation of regional alliances based not merely on lowering trade barriers, but also on developing common social standards. The European Economic Community is an example of a loose confederation. The United States, Canada, and Mexico could move beyond NAFTA to develop agreements on human rights and environmental protection.

Within corporations and other economic institutions, we could increse our respect for workers' rights. Most other advanced industrial countries, including Canada, put fewer political and legal obstacles than we do in the way of workers seeking to unionize. Germany requires large enterprises to include workers on their boards of directors. We could go even further by encouraging every worker to develop professional skills and by improving access to managerial positions.

In a book called *Looking Forward*, Mike Albert and Robin Hahnel present a radical vision of decentralized, democratic planning.[21] They argue that no one should be able to specialize in one particular skill. Rather, they propose that interesting work and drudge work both be shared, by designing "balanced job complexes." Instead of choosing a job that involves just one task, people would have a choice of different sets of tasks, some menial, some skilled.

Like Albert and Hahnel, I believe that some level of participation is intrinsically good, not only because it develops important human capabilities but also because it leads to better decisions. Unlike them, however, I also believe that participation is costly and needs to be economized. I base this reservation on considerable experience with collective decision-making: twenty years of working with groups like the Union for Radical Political Economics, the Latin American Policy Alternatives Group, the Clamshell Alliance, and the Center for Popular Economics; twenty years of teaching economics in largely self-governed university departments; and twelve years of playing co-ed softball with The Bats.

Albert and Hahnel seem to assume that participation is fun, fulfilling, and functional. They talk about "bringing people's sociability to the fore."[22] Sometimes this works; sometimes it doesn't. Some groups I have worked with (the Clamshell Alliance is probably the best example) spent so much time and energy in efforts to reach consensus that they became utterly ineffective. Every political group I have worked with has suffered, to some extent, from perverse incentives fostered by participatory processes (of course, hierarchy also creates inefficiencies).

One perverse incentive could be labeled "The Dictatorship of the Sociables." Some people really like meetings. They like to talk, to negotiate, to debate. As a result, they attend meetings enthusiastically; once there, they usually prevail. The problem is, these are not necessarily the people who will get things done once the meeting is over. They may exert disproportionate influence on decision-making without really taking responsibility for it (after all, it was "the group's" decision). A direct threat (such as, "if we can't come to some quick resolution of this issue, I'm going to leave") often keeps the Sociables in check. But while it's easy to exit from volunteer political groups, it's costly if not impossible to exit from collectives governing your workplace or your home.

A second, related problem results from the "Let's Not Piss Anybody Off" principle. Participation can be a lot of fun if everybody is in a good mood. It can be really awful if even one member of the group is angry or upset. During the process of decision making, people are thinking not only about the issue at hand, but also about the collective mood. So participants often sacrifice good management to good humor. Individuals who fail to do what they promised to do are not sanctioned. Individuals who always do what they promise to do are ripped off—

especially if they are unable to pressure others to do more work by threatening to leave the group.

Carried to an extreme, democratic governance can also intrude on individual rights. In Albert and Hahnel's world, even people's personal consumption decisions (such as, "I'd like to buy a new bicycle") would be subject to collective criticism.[23] This reminds me of the Venceremos Brigade's attitudes toward my wardrobe. Nevertheless, the basic principles of participatory democracy remain compelling: some kinds of work should be equally shared, and workers themselves should have a say in determining their own pay and working conditions.

Throughout most of human history, women have changed kids' diapers and cleaned up men's messes, having been told they weren't productive enough to do other kinds of work. Virtually all traditionally female jobs are underpaid, their wages lowered not only by occupational restrictions but also by excessive confidence in the market. For the last twenty years, unions and groups of workers all around the country have been forcing their employers to sit down and reconsider the pay scales set for male and female jobs. In many cases, they have won important gains for women workers, partly by redefining "skill" and other factors that people should be rewarded for on the job.[24]

Planning Care

Social democracy is about public commitment to meeting citizens' basic needs for health, education, and social welfare. It still exists in the United States, despite the efforts that many conservatives have made to dismantle it. But the Scandinavian countries of Sweden and Norway, as well as some other European countries, such as France and Germany, are better examples. All these countries offer universal health care and provide a sturdy social safety net. Their child poverty rates—as well as their overall poverty rates—are significantly lower than those of the United States. Wealth and income are distributed more equally.

Radicals sometimes dismiss European social democracy as "capitalism with a smiley face." To me, it has always seemed like a good place to start, partly because it has immediate implications for the development of children's capabilities. But if we want to successfully extend social democracy we will need to tend to several serious problems, even beyond the one emphasized in the preceding chapter—its dependence on the nation-state. Among these problems is bureaucracy, the nameless, faceless labyrinth of rules and procedures in which centralized service delivery usually gets bogged down. Large government institutions behave like monopolies, because they are protected from any disciplinary response from the customers they serve. Their managers are directly accountable to superiors, but not to citizens. We need to create new, positive incentives for better performance and introduce more direct democratic governance.[25] We should be willing to spend the money it will take to monitor and improve the quality of public services.

A second problem relates to gender inequality. The early theorists of social democracy, including Swedish feminist Alva Myrdal, recognized that the state could make it easier for women to combine paid work with family responsibilities.[26] But they were far more eager to expand women's opportunities than to modify men's roles. It never occurred to them that a division of labor based on breadwinner dads and homemaker moms was inherently unequal. Indeed, many public pension systems remain explicitly based on the obsolete breadwinner/homemaker model.

Feminists have traditionally been divided in their attitudes toward family policies, and with good reason. Policies aimed to support family work have often been designed to keep women in the home—giving mothers, for instance, but not fathers, paid leave from work. On the other hand, policies aimed to get women out of the home—such as making public assistance conditional on work for pay—have traditionally devalued nonmarket work. We should focus instead on policies that reward family care and promote gender equality at the same time. We should encourage both men and women to combine paid work with family and community work—a new division of labor that would develop men's capabilities for care along with women's capabilities for individual achievement.

This strategy has excited debate in the Netherlands, where feminist economist Marga Bruyn-Hundt became an early, outspoken advocate

for egalitarian models of support for family care.[27] A Dutch Expert
Committee has called for the elimination of breadwinners' subsidies in
income tax and social security as well as an expansion of subsidized
child care and home care for sick and elderly people. Greater "out-
sourcing" of some aspects of family care through the market and the
state could be counterbalanced by a reduction in men's paid work time
to enable their greater participation in the care economy.[28] One policy
Alva Myrdal did suggest, years ago, was a reduction in the hours of paid
employment to six hours a day, coinciding with the hours that children
spend in school.[29]

In this country, many states are beginning to extend their public education system to meet the needs of children ages three to six. If we could
provide the same level of public support as the French, who enroll virtually 95 percent of this age group in school, both children and parents
would benefit. We also need to consider what happens to children when
they get home from school and require adult attention and supervision.
Changing school and work schedules so that they dovetail more effi-
ciently would help. But we should also make it easier for both parents to
spend less time in paid work, encouraging the kind of flexibility that
families need to decide what is best for themselves and their children.

Other countries ensure plenty of parental attention for young infants
by providing paid parental leaves. The Swedes offer a promising, if still
somewhat gender-biased, example.[30] Parents there enjoy an eighteen-
month paid, job-protected leave that can be prorated over the more extended period during which their children are under eight years of age.
One month of this leave is assigned specifically to fathers, and about 50
percent of eligible fathers actually use it.

To provide stronger encouragement for gender equity, we could insist that paid benefits be set equal to wages (so that leaves are not more
costly for higher-wage earners). Also, we could provide six months of
paid leave for mothers and six for fathers, which each must "use or
lose." Apart from that restriction, parents could distribute their leaves in
a variety of ways. For instance, both parents could work part-time for
two years at full pay.

The United States taxes families on their joint income, a practice that discourages the wife, usually a "second earner," from working more hours. Instead, we could tax individuals separately at a rate based on their individual market income, whether they are married or not. This is a much simpler approach to eliminating the so-called marriage penalty, because it would allow individuals to enjoy the benefits of pooling their income and sharing their expenses without moving themselves into a higher tax bracket. We could eliminate the tax deduction for a "dependent" who is an able-bodied adult (such as a full-time housewife or househusband) but provide a generous deduction (or allowance) for the care of a child, or an elderly, sick, or disabled person at home.[31]

A steeply progressive income tax rate on individuals would encourage people to spend less time on paid work and more on activities of direct use to their families and communities. We could also reduce the disincentives to part-time paid work by requiring companies to provide the same benefits (prorated by hours worked) to part-time as to full-time workers. At the same time, we could discourage individuals from specializing in family care by making rights to health and pension benefits conditional on some level of participation in market work. Individuals would no longer be able to gain benefits simply by marrying another adult who is covered. The costs of making these changes would partially countervail each other. For instance, the money that companies save by not automatically extending employee benefits to wives and husbands of employees could be spent on extending coverage to part-time employees.

A third problem concerns definitions of kinship. Our economic and legal system has not kept pace with changes in the types of caring relationships that individuals form. Marriage is the primary form of non-biological kinship that we recognize, yet marriage is, for many adults, a relatively short-term relationship. Rather than making divorce more difficult, which would probably discourage marriage, we could define simpler, more flexible domestic partnerships that set some guidelines for individuals who choose to live together. Gay and lesbian couples should be able to opt for these (or for marriage, if they so desire).

The state should be less concerned with the regulation of relationships between consenting adults, and more concerned with strengthening obligations to dependents such as young children and the elderly.
More than improved child support enforcement is required: we need to
rethink the ways that we define the responsibilities of kinship. Though
it may pose difficulties for some families, joint custody of children in the
absence of marriage or after divorce is far superior to an arrangement
in which one parent cares, while the other parent pays. We need to devise new ways of promoting active and engaged fatherhood.

We need also to think beyond kinship itself. One category that seems
to be entirely missing from our demographic vocabulary is "friend."
Yet many single people, especially elderly people, rely on friends or
neighbors, rather than relatives, to take them to the doctor, or to provide periodic home care. We should not limit the prerogatives of protected absences from work—such as those guaranteed by the Family
and Medical Leave Act—to occasions that involve the needs of immediate family members. Workers should have the right to define their responsibilities for the care of others in broader terms. And we should
encourage them to do so.

Extending family values to society as a whole requires looking beyond the redistribution of income to ways of strengthening cultural
values of love, obligation, and reciprocity. Current welfare state policies have done little to encourage personal contact between rich and
poor, skilled and unskilled, lucky and unlucky. Ironically, the warfare
state has accomplished more than the welfare state in this respect: military service that entailed widespread participation in the defense of important democratic ideals, such as service in World War II, created
enduring sentiments of social solidarity.

We could encourage greater civic participation, offering tax credits
and other incentives for the provision of care services that develop
long-term relationships between individuals and communities. We
could discourage residential and cultural segregation by class and ethnicity. We could defend and enlarge our public spaces. Our educational
institutions could encourage the development of caring skills and community involvement. Among other strategies, we might invite young

people to repay the money invested in them through national service rather than simply through taxes.

Policies designed to promote care for other people appear unproductive only to those who define economic efficiency in cramped terms, such as increases in GDP. The weakening of family and social solidarity can impose enormous costs, reflected in educational failures, poor health, environmental degradation, high crime rates, and a cultural atmosphere of anxiety and resentment. The care and nurturance of human capabilities has always been difficult and expensive. In the past, a sexual division of labor based upon the subordination of women helped minimize both the difficulties and the expense. Today, however, the costs of providing care need to be explicitly confronted and fairly distributed.

◆

Women today often combine breadwinning and caregiving, albeit with great difficulty and strain. A postindustrial welfare state must ensure that men do the same, while redesigning institutions so as to eliminate the difficulty and strain. We might call this vision Universal Caregiver.

— NANCY FRASER,
*Justice Interruptus: Critical Reflections
on the "Postsocialist" Condition*

◆

Taming the Beast

What have we learned from the great twentieth-century wrestling match between capitalism and communism? Most obviously, that neither system can be trusted. But rather than retreating to cynicism about the dismal science, we can roll up our shirt sleeves, boil some water, and deliver some good alternatives. We don't have to believe that markets are intrinsically bad to acknowledge that "who owns what" matters. We don't have to believe in decision-making by committee to fight for better rules of democratic governance. And we don't have to embrace the current policies of the welfare state to defend the principle that each of us has some obligation to care for others.

In this book, I've worried aloud about economists' overconfidence in that abstraction called "the market." I've argued that women, in particular, have a legacy of commitment to caregiving that should make them suspicious of the "every man for himself" principle. Throughout these pages I've sprinkled ideas about policies toward the poor, our educational system, and our tax system, and speculated about the impact of globalization and possibilities for restructuring our economic system. I've left out a number of issues, such as health care and the environment, not because I thought they were any less important, but because they were beyond my scope. I've highlighted the economic importance of family values because I believe these values are widely shared.

In closing, I offer five guidelines for efforts to bring the invisible hand of the market into better balance with the invisible heart of care:

1. *Reject claims that women should be more altruistic than men, either in the home or in society as a whole.* Women may be naturally suited to some forms of care—such as breast-feeding. That's exactly why men should hustle to make up the difference elsewhere (changing diapers comes to mind). Assigning women primary responsibility for the care of others does more than let men off the hook. It separates care from power, and therefore reduces the overall level of social and economic support for caring work.

2. *Defend family values against the corrosive effects of self-interest.* Both men and women stand to gain from strengthening values of love, obligation, and reciprocity. These values create a cultural environment in which the individual pursuit of self-interest can lead to healthy outcomes. Carried too far, however, the individual pursuit of self-interest can degrade that environment, with particularly unfortunate consequences for future generations.

3. *Confront the difficulties of establishing democratic governance in families, communities, countries, and the world as a whole.* If we are to enforce social obligations to one another, we must do so in fair and equitable ways. On every level of society we need to figure out more effective ways of coordinating our activities

without resorting to authoritarian rules or impersonal bureaucracies.

4. *Aim for a kinder and wiser form of economic development.* Calling attention to things that money can't buy doesn't require us to ignore the things it can buy. We should try to improve global standards of living, defined in broader terms than the value of market production. We need to measure our success by the improvement of our capabilities, the flourishing of our families, and the health of our environment.

5. *Develop and strengthen ways of rewarding the work of care.* Care is not just another commodity. Personal, face-to-face, emotionally rich relationships are crucial to the delivery of high-quality child care, education, health, elder care, and many other social services. Whether they take place in families, communities, corporations, or other places of work, the services of care deserve public recognition and reward.

NOTES

Introduction

1. Adam Smith, *The Theory of Moral Sentiments* (New York: Augustus Kelley, 1966).

Chapter 1

1. Rush Limbaugh, *The Way Things Ought to Be* (New York: Pocket Books, 1992), p. 146.
2. Numbers based on analysis of the General Social Survey. See Lee Badgett, Pamela Davidson, Nancy Folbre, and Jeannette Lim, "Breadwinner Dad, Homemaker Mom. An Interdisciplinary Analysis of Changing Gender Norms in the United States, 1977–1998." Department of Economics, University of Massachusetts, Amherst, MA, August 2000.
3. Sara Blaffer Hrdy, *Mother Nature: A History of Mothers, Infants, and Natural Selection* (New York: Pantheon, 1999).
4. For more discussion of this possibility see Nancy Folbre, *Who Pays for the Kids? Gender and the Structures of Constraint* (New York: Routledge, 1994).
5. Ibid.
6. August Bebel, *Women and Socialism*, trans. Daniel De Leon (New York: Schocken Books, 1971).
7. Amartya Sen, "Gender and Cooperative Conflicts," in Irene Tucker, ed., *Persistent Inequalities: Women and World Development* (New York: Oxford University Press, 1990), pp. 123–49. Feminist theorist Joan Tronto also points out

that robbing individuals of opportunities to effectively pursue their self-interest may encourage them to live through others, using caring as a substitute for more selfish gratification. See her "Beyond Gender Difference to a Theory of Care," *Signs: Journal of Women in Culture and Society* 12, no. 4 (Summer 1987), pp. 647, 650.

8. Mary O'Brien, *The Politics of Reproduction* (Boston: Routledge and Kegan Paul, 1981); Lorenne M.G. Clark and Lynda Lange, *The Sexism of Social and Political Theory: Women and Reproduction from Plato to Nietzsche* (Toronto: University of Toronto Press, 1979); John Locke, *Two Treatises of Government*, ed. Peter Laslett (Cambridge: Cambridge University Press, 1967).

9. Mary Astell, "The Hardships of the English Laws in Relation to Wives," in Vivien Jones, ed., *Women in the Eighteenth Century* (New York: Routledge, 1990), p. 225.

10. Ibid.

11. Adam Smith, *An Inquiry into the Nature and Causes of the Wealth of Nations*, 3rd ed., vol. 1 (Edinburgh: Mandel, Pig and Stevensen, 1809), p. 9. For a longer discussion of this issue, see Nancy Folbre and Heidi Hartmann, "The Rhetoric of Self-Interest and the Ideology of Gender," in Arjo Klamer, Donald McCloskey, and Robert Solow, eds, *The Consequences of Economic Rhetoric* (Cambridge: Cambridge University Press, 1988).

12. Nancy Folbre, "'The Improper Arts': Sex in Classical Political Economy," *Population and Development Review* 18, no. 1 (1992), pp. 105–21.

13. John Stuart Mill, *The Subjection of Women* (Cambridge: M.I.T. Press, 1970), p. 43.

14. Nancy Folbre, "Socialism, Feminist and Scientific," in Marianne Ferber and Julie Nelson, eds, *Beyond Economic Man* (Chicago: University of Chicago Press, 1993).

15. Catherine Beecher and Harriet Beecher Stowe, *The American Woman's Home* (New York: J. B. Ford and Company, 1869), p. 19.

16. Kathryn Kish Sklar, *Catherine Beecher: A Study in American Domesticity* (New Haven: Yale University Press, 1973), p. 87.

17. Ibid., p. 156.

18. Alfred Marshall, *Principles of Economics*, 8th ed. (London: Macmillan, 1930), pp. 685, 715.

19. David Reisman, *Alfred Marshall's Mission* (New York: St. Martin's Press, 1990), p. 210.

20. W. Pigou, *Memorials of Alfred Marshall*, "Letter to Louis Dumur, July 2, 1909" (New York: A. M. Kelley, 1966), pp. 459–61.

21. Barbara Goldsmith, *Other Powers: The Age of Suffrage, Spiritualism, and the Scandalous Victoria Woodhull* (New York: Alfred A. Knopf, 1998).

22. Jane Lewis, *The Politics of Motherhood: Child and Maternal Welfare in England, 1900–1939* (London: Croom Helm, 1980); David Kennedy, *Birth Control in America: The Career of Margaret Sanger* (New Haven: Yale University Press, 1973).

23. Rush Limbaugh, *The Way Things Ought to Be*, p. 201.

24. George Gilder, *Sexual Suicide* (New York: Quadrangle, 1973) and *Wealth and Poverty* (New York: Basic Books, 1981).

25. Allan Bloom, *The Closing of the American Mind: How Higher Education Has Failed Democracy and Impoverished the Souls of Today's Students* (New York: Simon and Schuster, 1987).

26. Connie Marshner, *Can Motherhood Survive? A Christian Looks at Social Parenting* (Brentwood, TN: Wolgemuth and Hyatt, 1990), p. 195. See also Linda Kintz, *Between Jesus and the Market: The Emotions That Matter in Right-Wing America* (Durham, NC: Duke University Press, 1997).

27. Cited in Kristin Luker, *Abortion and the Politics of Motherhood* (Berkeley: University of California, 1984), p. 163.

28. Barbara Dafoe Whitehead, "Dan Quayle Was Right," *The Atlantic Monthly*, 271, no. 4 (April 1993), pp. 47–84.

29. Sharon Hays, *The Cultural Contradictions of Motherhood* (New Haven: Yale University Press, 1996).

30. Limbaugh, *The Way Things Ought to Be*, p. 78.

31. Gary Becker, the Nobel Prize–winning economist, makes this argument explicit in an article entitled "Altruism in the Family and Selfishness in the Market Place," *Economica* 48, no. 1 (1981), pp. 1–15.

32. Elizabeth Hickey, "Mrs. Family Values: Beverley La Haye Leads Her Army of Concerned Women into the Conservative Fray," *Washington Times*, July 29, 1992, 1E.

33. Whirlpool Foundation study, *Women: The New Providers* (New York: Families and Work Institute, May 1995), p. 73.

34. Only 3 percent of women, compared with 13 percent of men, said they didn't worry at all about people caring for others. Whirlpool Foundation Study, *Women*, p. 67.

35. Linda Jordan, "Dolls versus Trucks," *New York Times*, April 19, 1993.

36. Barbara Presley Noble, "Male, Female Leadership Styles Hot Subject of Controversy," *Springfield Union*, August 18, 1993, p. 35.

37. Franz de Waal, *Good Natured: The Origins of Right and Wrong in Humans and Other Animals* (Cambridge, MA: Harvard University Press, 1996), p. 43.

38. E. O. Wilson, *Sociobiology: The New Synthesis* (Cambridge, MA: Harvard University Press, 1975).

39. In addition to de Waal, *Good Natured,* see Elliot Sober and David Sloan Wilson, *Unto Others: The Evolution and Psychology of Unselfish Behavior* (Cambridge, MA: Harvard University Press, 1998).

40. Daniel C. Batson, "How Social an Animal? The Human Capacity for Caring," *American Psychologist* 45, no. 3 (March 1990), p. 344.

Chapter 2

1. Robert Frank, Thomas Gilovich and Dennis Regan, "Does Studying Economics Inhibit Cooperation?" *Journal of Economic Perspectives* 7, no. 2 (Spring 1993), pp. 159–71.

2. A classic statement of the argument can be found in E. O. Wilson, *Sociobiology: The New Synthesis* (Cambridge, MA: Harvard University Press, 1975).

3. Robert Frank, *Passions within Reason: The Strategic Role of the Emotions* (New York: W. W. Norton, 1988).

4. The economic literature on information and transaction costs explores these issues. See, for instance, Oliver Williamson, *The Economic Institutions of Capitalism: Firms, Markets, Relational Contracting* (New York: Free Press, 1985).

5. Paula England and George Farkas, *Households, Employment, and Gender: A Social, Economic, and Demographic View* (New York: Aldine Publishers, 1986).

6. Amartya Sen long ago outlined the basic critique of economic theory that I am belaboring here. See his "Rational Fools: A Critique of the Behavioral Foundations of Economic Theory," *Philosophy and Public Affairs* 6, no. 4 (1977), pp. 317–44.

7. Elinor Ostrom, *Governing the Commons: The Evolution of Institutions for Collective Action* (Cambridge: Cambridge University Press, 1991).

8. Jane Mansbridge, *Beyond Self-Interest* (Chicago: University of Chicago Press, 1990), pp. 133–143.

9. Elliot Sober and David Sloane Wilson, *Unto Others: The Evolution and Psychology of Unselfish Behavior* (Cambridge, MA: Harvard University Press, 1998).

10. This point has been made more formally in Notburga Ott, *Intrafamily Bargaining and Household Decisions* (London: Springer Verlag, 1992).

11. Donald Parsons, "On the Economics of Intergenerational Control," *Population and Development Review* 10, no. 2 (March 1984), pp. 41–54.

12. See Douglas D. Davis and Charles A. Holt, *Experimental Economics* (Princeton, NJ: Princeton University Press, 1993) and Catherine C. Eckel and Philip Grossman, "Chivalry and Solidarity in Ultimatum Games," *Working*

Paper E92–23, Department of Economics, Virginia Polytechnic Institute, Blacksburg, VA (August 1992).

13. Two notable exceptions are Elizabeth Peters and her colleagues who have conducted ultimatum games among family members as well as among strangers, and Eckel and Grossman ("Chivalry and Solidarity"), who have explored gender differences in ultimatum games.

14. Karl Polanyi, *The Great Transformation* (Boston: Beacon Press, 1944).

15. Robert N. Bellah, Richard Madsen, William M. Sullivan, Ann Swidler, and Steven M. Tipton, *Habits of the Heart: Individualism and Commitment in American Life* (New York: Harper and Row, 1985); Amitai Etzioni, *The Moral Dimension: Toward a New Economics* (New York: Free Press, 1988). For a review of selected books on civil society and virtue see D. W. Miller, "Perhaps We Bowl Alone, But Does It Really Matter?" *The Chronicle of Higher Education*, July 16, 1999, A16–17.

16. Nancy Folbre, *Who Pays for the Kids? Gender and the Structures of Constraint* (New York: Routledge, 1994); Paula England and Nancy Folbre, "The Cost of Caring," *Annals of the American Academy of Political and Social Science* 561 (January 1999), pp. 39–51.

17. Donald J. Hernandez, *America's Children: Resources from Family, Government, and the Economy* (New York: Russell Sage, 1993).

18. Leonore Weitzman, *The Divorce Revolution: The Unexpected Social and Economic Consequences for Women and Children in America* (New York: Free Press, 1985).

19. Barbara R. Bergmann, "The Economic Risks of Being a Housewife," *American Economic Review* 7, no. 2 (May 1981), pp. 81–86. See also England and Farkas, *Households, Employment, and Gender.*

20. Jane Waldfogel, "The Effects of Children on Women's Wages," *American Sociological Review* 62, no. 2 (1997), pp. 209–217.

21. Douglas Bernheim, A. Schleifer, and L. H. Summers, "The Strategic Bequest Motive," *Journal of Political Economy* 93 (1985), pp. 1045–1076.

22. National Family Caregivers Association, "Member Survey 1997: A Profile of Caregivers," www.nfcacares.org/survey.html.

23. "Study Shows Elderly Care Costly," *New York Times*, November 29, 1999.

24. Gary Becker, *A Treatise on the Family* (Cambridge, MA: Harvard University Press, 1981).

25. Peter McDonald and Rebecca Kippen, "The Implications of Below Replacement Fertility for Labour Supply and International Migration, 2000–2050," (paper presented at the annual meeting of the Population Association of America, Los Angeles, Calif., March 23–25, 2000). See also Peter McDonald,

"Gender Equity, Social Institutions, and the Future of Fertility," *Working Papers in Demography* No. 69 (Canberra, Australia: Australian National University, 1999).

26. Arlie Hochschild, *The Time Bind* (New York: Henry Holt and Company, 1997), p. 201.

27. Francine M. Deutsch, *Halving It All: How Equally Shared Parenting Works* (Cambridge, MA: Harvard University Press, 1999); Rhona Mahoney, *Kidding Ourselves: Breadwinning, Babies, and Bargaining Power* (New York: Basic Books, 1995).

28. For more discussion of these issues see Juliet Schor, *The Overworked American* (New York: Basic Books, 1991) and Robert Frank and Phillip J. Cook, *The Winner-Take-All Society* (New York: Free Press, 1995).

29. Lee Badgett and Nancy Folbre, "Job Gendering: Occupational Choice and the Marriage Market," Department of Economics, University of Massachusetts, Amherst, MA, August, 2000.

30. Paula England, *Comparable Worth: Theories and Evidence* (New York: Aldine de Gruyter, 1992).

31. Julie Nelson, "Of Markets and Martyrs: Is It OK to Pay Well for Care?" *Feminist Economics* 5, no. 3 (Fall 1991), pp. 43–59.

32. These and related issues are discussed in an essay in Mary M. Brabeck, ed., *Who Cares? Theory, Research, and Educational Implications of the Ethic of Care* (New York: Praeger, 1989).

33. Derek Bok, *The Cost of Talent: How Executives and Professionals Are Paid and How It Affects America* (New York: Free Press, 1993).

34. Nancy Folbre, "Children as Public Goods," *American Economic Review* 84, no. 2 (1994), pp. 86–90, and Paula England and Nancy Folbre, "Who Should Pay for the Kids?" *Annals of the America Academy of Political and Social Science* 562 (May 1999), pp. 194–207.

Chapter 3

1. Richard Titmuss, *The Gift Relationship: From Human Blood to Social Policy* (London: George Allen and Unwin, 1970).

2. Associated Press, *New York Times*, July 28, 1999.

3. For a more detailed account, see Nancy Folbre and Julie Nelson, "For Love or Money or Both?" forthcoming in *The Journal of Economic Perspectives*.

4. U.S. Bureau of Labor Statistics, *Employment and Earnings*, January 1999, Table 18.

5. For a historical perspective, see Susan Reverby, *Ordered to Care: The Dilemma of American Nursing, 1850–1945* (New York: Cambridge University Press,

1987); Delores A. Gant, *A Global Agenda for Caring* (New York: National League for Nursing Press, 1993).

6. Margaret Talbot, "The Placebo Prescription," *New York Times Magazine*, January 9, 2000.

7. Robert Pear, "Few People Seek to Treat Mental Illnesses, Study Says," *New York Times*, December 13, 1999.

8. Judith J. Hibbard, "Can Medicare Beneficiaries Make Informed Choices?" *Health Affairs* (November/December 1998), pp. 181–193; Daniel Pedersen, "Is Your HMO Too Stingy?" *Newsweek*, July 26, 1999, p. 56; Suzanne Gordon, "Healing in a Hurry: Hospitals in the Managed-Care Age," *The Nation*, March 1, 1999, p. 11.

9. David Himmelstein, Steffie Woolhandler, Ida Hellander, and Sidney M. Wolfe, "Quality of Care in Investor-Owned vs. Not-for-Profit HMOs," *Journal of the American Medical Association* 282, no. 2 (July 14, 1999), pp. 159–163.

10. Sheryl Gay Stolberg, "Report Says Profit-Making Health Plans Damage Care," *New York Times*, July 14, 1999.

11. Milt Freudenheim, "More Suits Filed Against Health Insurers," *New York Times*, June 27, 2000.

12. Abigail Zuger, "Arming Unsung Heroes of Health Care," *New York Times*, November 3, 1999.

13. Alison Mitchell, "Senate G.O.P. Again Prevails on Health Care Bill," *New York Times*, July 15, 1999.

14. Peter T. Kilborn, "Nurses Put on Fast Forward in Rush for Cost Efficiency," *New York Times*, April 9, 1998.

15. Suzanne Gordon, *Life Support: Three Nurses on the Front Lines* (New York: Little Brown & Co., 1998), p. 255.

16. Todd S. Purdum, "California to Set Level of Staffing for Nursing Care," *New York Times*, November 12, 1999.

17. Deborah Stone, "Care and Trembling," *The American Prospect* 43 (1999), p. 62.

18. Robert Pear, "Reports of Abuse of Elderly Are Ignored, Panel Is Told," *New York Times*, March 23, 1999; Susan Eaton, "Beyond 'Unloving Care': Promoting Innovation in Elder Care Through Public Policy," Changing Work in America Series (Cambridge, MA: Radcliffe Public Policy Institute, 1996); *New York Times*, April 26, 1999, editorial page.

19. Lorraine Adams, "The Hazards of Elder Care," *Washington Post*, October 31, 1999.

20. Eaton, "Beyond 'Unloving Care'," p. 7.

21. "Webcams Focus on Day Care," *New York Times*, December 2, 1999.

22. Personal communication from Suzanne Helburn, Department of Economics, University of Colorado at Denver, January 2000.

23. Center for the Child Care Workforce, *Current Data on Child Care Salaries and Benefits in the United States*, www.ccw.org, March 1999; Marcy Whitebook, Carolle Howes, and Deborah Phillips, *Worthy Work, Unlivable Wages: The National Child Care Staffing Study, 1988–1997* (Washington, D.C.: Center for the Child Care Workforce, 1998), p. 20.

24. Deborah Blum, "More Work, More Play," *Mother Jones* (March 1999), pp. 1–7; Suzanne Helburn, ed., *Cost, Quality, and Child Outcomes in Child Care Centers* (Denver, CO: University of Colorado Press, 1995).

25. Marcy Whitebook, *NAEYC Accreditation and Assessment* (Washington, D.C.: National Center for the Early Childhood Work Force, 1997).

26. Helburn, *Cost, Quality and Child Outcomes*.

27. Edward N. Wolff, "Recent Trends in Wealth Ownership, 1983–1998," unpublished manuscript, Department of Economics, New York University.

28. Paul A. Armknecht and Daniel H. Ginsburg, "Improvements in Measuring Price Changes in Consumer Services, Past, Present, and Future," in Zvi Griliches, ed., *Output Measurement in the Service Sectors* (Chicago: University of Chicago Press, 1992), p. 147.

29. Data on expenditures on personal care products and services in 1995 from *Statistical Abstract of the United States, 1997* (Washington, D.C.: Government Printing Office, 1998), Table 712, p. 461. Data on the number of consumer units in that year from www.bls.gov/news.release/cesan.news.htm (accessed November 19, 1998). Data on GDP of selected countries from the *United Nations Human Development Report 1998* (New York: Oxford University Press, 1998), p. 183.

30. For more discussion of this issue, see Nancy Folbre, "The Unproductive Housewife: Her History in the Evolution of Economic Thought," *Signs: Journal of Women in Culture and Society* 16, no. 3 (1991), pp. 463–84. For a broader discussion of the omission of women's work from the national income accounts, see Marilyn Waring, *If Women Counted: A New Feminist Economics* (New York: Harper and Row, 1988).

31. Robert Eisner, *The Total Incomes System of Accounts* (Chicago: University of Chicago Press, 1989). Duncan Ironmonger's more recent estimates for Australia are methodologically superior. See his "Counting Outputs, Capital Inputs and Caring Labor: Estimating Gross Household Product," *Feminist Economics* 2, no. 3 (1996).

32. See the Web site of the National Family Caregivers Association, www.nfcacares.org.

33. On the other hand, over the same period of time we have adopted many nifty devices that increase the productivity of nonmarket work—microwave ovens, frozen dinners that are actually edible, rented videos that help entertain the children, and waterproof mascara. Failure to measure these improvements may have led to an understatement of improvements in our real standard of living.

34. John Robinson and Geoffry Godbey, *Time for Life: The Surprising Ways Americans Use Their Time* (University Park, PA: Pennsylvania State University, 1997).

35. Robert Repetto, "Nature's Resources as Productive Assets," *Challenge* (September–October 1989), pp. 16–20.

36. Ismail Seragelin, *Sustainability and the Wealth of Nations: First Steps in an Ongoing Journey*. Environmentally Sustainable Development Studies and Monographs Series No. 5. (Washington, D.C.: World Bank, 1996).

37. Herman E. Daly and John B. Cobb, Jr., *For the Common Good: Redirecting the Economy Toward Community, the Environment, and a Sustainable Future* (Boston: Beacon Press, 1994).

38. Daniel Goleman, *Emotional Intelligence* (New York: Bantam, 1994). See also Arthur Goldsmith, Jonathan R. Veum, and William Darity, Jr., "The Impact of Psychological and Human Capital on Wages," *Economic Inquiry* XXXV (October 1997), pp. 815–829.

39. For a detailed example of how education could be treated as an investment, see Dale W. Jorgenson and Barbara M. Fraumeni, "Output of the Education Sector," in Griliches, *Output Measurement*, pp. 303–341.

40. *The Ethics of Aristotle*, trans. D. P. Chase (New York: Monthly Review Press, 1963).

41. A. L. Morton, *The Life and Ideas of Robert Owen* (New York: Monthly Review Press, 1963).

42. Amartya Sen, "The Economics of Life and Death," *Scientific American* (May 1993), pp. 40–47.

43. The measures are based on the relationship of actual to minimum and maximum values of each. For an explanation of the technical details see United Nations Development Programme, *Human Development Report 1998* (New York: Oxford University Press, 1998), p. 107. Another set of interesting measures is offered by Marc and Marque-Luisa Miringoff in *The Social Health of the Nation* (New York: Oxford University Press, 1999).

44. *Human Development Report 1998*, pp. 20–21, Table 1.2.

45. *World Development Indicators, 1998* (Washington, D.C.: The World Bank, 1998), p. 253.

46. Robert Putnam, *Making Democracy Work: Civic Traditions in Modern Italy* (Princeton, NJ: Princeton University Press, 1993).

47. Robert Putnam, "Bowling Alone: America's Declining Social Capital," *Journal of Democracy*, 6, no. 1 (January 1995), pp. 65–78.

48. Robert Reich, "Do Good Fences Make Good Neighbors?" *The New Yorker*, November 30, 1998, p. 31.

49. Alfie Kohn, *The Brighter Side of Human Nature* (New York: Basic Books, 1990), p. 69.

50. On crimes in the U.S., see *Statistical Abstract of the U.S. 1997* (Washington, D.C.: Government Printing Office, 1998), Table 313, p. 201. On crimes in Japan see *Nippon: A Charted Survey of Japan 1994/95*, edited by Tsuneta Yano Memorial Society (Tokyo: Kokusei-sha, 1994), p. 333.

51. "U.S.–Japan Murder Deficit," *Time*, June 7, 1993, p. 17.

Chapter 4

1. Michael Novak, "Steeple Envy," *Forbes*, July 5, 1993, p. 46.

2. For other journalistic jibes at the nanny state, see William Bennett, "What to Do About the Children," *Commentary* 99, March 1, 1995, pp. 23–29, and Gertrude Himmelfarb, "For the Love of Country," *Current*, September 1, 1997, pp. 30–32.

3. This summary is based on the writings of George Gilder, *Men and Marriage* (New York: Pelican, 1992); *Wealth and Poverty* (New York: Institute for Contemporary Studies, 1993); Rush Limbaugh, *The Way Things Ought to Be* (New York: Pocket Books, 1993); Marvin Olasky, *The Tragedy of American Compassion* (New York: Regneny Publishing, 1995); and Newt Gingrich, *To Renew America* (New York: HarperPrism, 1996).

4. Nicholas Barr argues that many private forms of insurance are inefficient because of information problems and adverse selection. See his "Economic Theory and the Welfare State: A Survey and Interpretation," *Journal of Economic Literature* 30 (1992), pp. 741–803.

5. Nancy Folbre, *Who Pays for the Kids? Gender and the Structures of Constraint* (New York: Routledge, 1994).

6. Alva Myrdal, *Nation and Family: The Swedish Experiment in Democratic Family and Population Policy* (Cambridge, MA: M.I.T. Press, 1941).

7. Cited in Mary Ann Mason, *From Father's Property to Children's Rights: The History of Child Custody in the United States* (New York: Columbia University Press, 1994), p. 53. See also Folbre, *Who Pays for the Kids?*

8. Reva B. Siegel, "Home as Work: The First Woman's Rights Claims Concerning Wives' Household Labor, 1850–1880," *Yale Law Journal* 103, No. 1073 (March 1994), pp. 1073–1217.

9. Mason, *From Father's Property*, p. 57.

10. Theda Skocpol, *Protecting Soldiers and Mothers: The Politics of Social Provision in the United States, 1870s–1920* (Boston: Harvard University Press, 1993); Seth Koven and Sonya Michel, eds, *Mothers of a New World: Maternalist Politics and the Origins of Welfare States* (New York: Routledge, 1993); Gisela Bock and Pat Thane, eds, *Maternity and Gender Policies, Women and the Rise of the European Welfare States, 1880s–1950s* (New York: Routledge, 1991).

11. Herbert Spencer, "The Principles of Sociology," reprinted in Susan Groag Bell and Karen M. Offen, eds, *Women, the Family, and Freedom* (Stanford: Stanford University Press, 1976).

12. Beatrice Webb, *Our Partnership* (London: Longmans, Green & Co., 1948), p. 149.

13. Ibid., p. 52.

14. Theda Skocpol, *Protecting Soldiers and Mothers*.

15. Department of Labor, Women's Bureau, *State Laws Affecting Working Women*. Bulletin no. 16 (Washington, D.C.: Government Printing Office, 1921).

16. A. Holtzman, *The Townsend Movement: A Political Study* (New York: Bookman Associates, 1963).

17. Donald J. Hernandez, *America's Children: Resources from Family, Government, and the Economy* (New York: Russell Sage, 1995), p. 21.

18. Data for 1930 and 1960 are *Historical Statistics of the U.S.* (Washington, D.C.: U.S. Government Printing Office, 1976), Series A, 119–134, p. 15. Data for later years are from *Statistical Abstract of the U.S., 1997* (Washington, D.C.: Government Printing Office, 1998), Tables 14 and 24, pp. 15, 25.

19. Nor is the problem confined to intergenerational transfers of money. Assume that there is no sharing between old and young, and that individuals simply save and invest money to take care of themselves in old age. Instead of depending on their two children, the two elderly parents between ages sixty-five and eighty hire workers to take care of them. If the supply of labor in the younger generation is small relative to the demand for labor by the older generation, wages go way up. And up goes the cost of growing old.

20. George A. Akerlof, Janet L. Yellen, and Michael L. Katz, "An Analysis of Out-of-Wedlock Childbearing in the United States," *The Quarterly Journal of Economics*, CXI, no. 2 (May 1996), pp. 277–317.

21. Andrea H. Beller and John W. Graham, *Small Change: The Economics of Child Support* (New Haven: Yale University Press, 1993), p. 1.

22. Irwin Garfinkel, Sara S. McLanahan, and Cynthia K. Miller, "Trends in Child Support Outcomes," *Demography* 33, no. 4 (November 1996), pp. 483–96; Robert I. Lerman, "Child Support Policies," *Journal of Economic Perspectives* 7, no. 1 (Winter 1993), pp. 171–82.

23. Elaine Sorenson and Ariel Halpern, "Child Support Enforcement Is Working Better Than We Think," in *New Federalism: Issues and Options for States* (Washington, D.C.: Urban Institute, 1999), p. A-31.

24. Robert I. Lerman, "Child Support Policies," p. 176.

25. Elaine Sorenson, "The Benefits of Increased Child Support Enforcement," Welfare Reform Briefs no. 2 (Washington, D.C.: Urban Institute, 1995).

26. Charles Murray, "Keep It in the Family," *Sunday Times* (London), November 14, 1993, cited in James Carville, *We're Right, They're Wrong* (New York: Random House, 1996), p. 95.

27. Stuart A. Miller, "The Myth of Deadbeat Dads," *Wall Street Journal*, March 2, 1995, p. A14.

28. Lynn Smith, "Locating Deadbeat Dads—For a Price," *Los Angeles Times*, July 28, 1996, p. E3.

29. John P. Robinson and Geoffry Godbey, *Time for Life: The Surprising Ways Americans Use Their Time* (University Park, PA: Pennsylvania State University Press, 1997); Laura Shapiro, "The Myth of Quality Time," *Newsweek*, May 12, 1997, p. 65. See also James T. Bond, Ellen Galinsky, and Jennifer E. Swanberg, *The 1997 National Study of the Changing Workforce* (New York: Families and Work Institute, 1998).

30. Albert Hunt, "Democrats' Delight," *The Wall Street Journal*, September 20, 1996.

31. Susan J. Carroll, "The Disempowerment of the Gender Gap: Soccer Moms and the 1996 Elections," *PS: Political Science and Politics*, 32, no. 1 (March 1999), p. 1.

Chapter 5

1. For a good example of this point of view, see Elinor Burkett, *The Baby Boon: How Family-Friendly America Cheats the Childless* (New York: Free Press, 2000).

2. Phillip J. Longman, "The Cost of Children," *U.S. News and World Report*, March 30, 1998.

3. Robert Haveman and Barbara Wolfe, "The Determinants of Children's Attainments: A Review of Methods and Findings," *Journal of Economic Literature* XXXIII (1995), p. 1831.

4. Children's Defense Fund, Minnesota, "Family Tax Policies," www.cdfmn.org/family.htm, accessed November 19, 1999. See also Leslie Whittington, "Taxes and the Family: The Impact of the Tax Exemption for Dependents on Marital Fertility," *Demography* 29, no. 2 (1992), pp. 215–226.

5. Edward N. Wolff, "The Economic Status of Parents in Postwar America." Paper prepared for the meeting of the National Parenting Association, Department of Economics, New York University, New York, September 20, 1996.

6. Furthermore, it provides no benefits to poor families who do not pay income taxes, and is phased out for families with a taxable income of more than $110,000. For more discussion of family support issues see Sylvia Ann Hewlett and Cornel West, *The War Against Parents* (New York: Houghton Mifflin, 1998).

7. David Betson, "Alternative Estimates of the Cost of Children from the 1980–86 Consumer Expenditure Survey," Special Report 51 (Madison, WI: University of Wisconsin, Institute for Research on Poverty, 1991).

8. Irwin Garfinkel, "Economic Security for Children: From Means Testing and Bifurcation to Universality," in Irwin Garfinkel, Sara S. McLanahan, and Jennifer L. Hochschild, eds, *Social Policies for Children* (Washington, D.C.: Brookings Institution, 1996).

9. Ibid.

10. Cited in Louis Cannon, *President Reagan: The Role of a Lifetime* (New York: Simon and Schuster, 1991), p. 518.

11. Lawrence M. Mead, *The New Politics of Poverty: The Nonworking Poor in America* (New York: Basic Books, 1992), p. 23.

12. Rush Limbaugh, *The Way Things Ought to Be* (New York: Pocket Books, 1992), p. 196.

13. Mickey Kaus, *The End of Equality* (New York: Basic Books, 1992), p. 117.

14. Randy Albelda, Nancy Folbre, and the Center for Popular Economics, *The War on the Poor: A Defense Manual* (New York: New Press, 1996), p. 14.

15. For a more detailed analysis see Paula England and Nancy Folbre, "Reforming Welfare: Public Support for Childrearing in the United States," Department of Economics, University of Massachusetts, Amherst, MA, August 2000.

16. Citizens for Tax Justice, *The Hidden Entitlements*, www.ctj.org/hid_ent/part-3/part3-1.htm, part 3-1.

17. National Academy of Science, *Child Care for Low Income Families* (Washington, D.C.: National Academy of Science, 1996). Available at www.nap.edu/readingroom/books/childcare.

18. House Committee on Ways and Means, *Green Book*, 105th Cong., 1998, p. 684. Available at www.access.gpo.gov/congress/wm001.html.

19. Sandra Hofferth, "Caring for Children at the Poverty Line," *Children and Youth Services Review* 12, no. 1/2 (1995), pp. 1–31.

20. Sharon Long, "Child Care Assistance Under Welfare Reform: Early Responses by the States," testimony to House Committee on Ways and Means,

Subcommittee on Human Resources, March 16, 1999, p. 3. Available at www.urban.org/testimon/long3-16-99.html.

21. House Committee on Ways and Means, *Green Book*, p. 420, table 7–9.

22. Gary Becker, cited in Robert Pear, "Thousands to Rally in Capital on Children's Behalf," *New York Times*, June 1, 1996.

23. Mickey Kaus and others insist that Social Security only pays benefits to workers, but that's not true if you define workers as Kaus does, as those actually earning a wage. Spouses and survivors who have never worked for a wage enjoy substantial benefits. See Mickey Kaus, *The End of Equality* (New York: Basic Books, 1992), chapter 9.

24. *Social Security Bulletin*, 61, no. 4 (1998), p. 57, table 1.86. The amount of monthly benefits was multiplied by twelve to arrive at an annual estimate. Figures on total TANF spending from House Committee on Ways and Means, *Green Book*.

25. U.S. Senate, Senator Moynihan of New York, S1511, 100th Congress, 2nd Sess. 134 *Congressional Record*, S14250 (June 13, 1988), vol. 134, pt. 10.

26. Ruth Conniff, "Bad Welfare," *The Progressive* 58, no. 9 (August 1994), p. 20.

27. David Ellwood, *Poor Support: Poverty in the American Family* (New York: Basic Books, 1988).

28. The marginal tax rate (or the tax rate on the last dollar earned) is more relevant than the average tax rate, but in the simplified examples I am using here, the two are effectively the same.

29. See Albelda et al., *The War on the Poor*, p. 80.

30. See Kathryn Edin, "Making Ends Meet," and Jason De Parle, "Learning Poverty Firsthand," *New York Times Magazine*, April 27, 1997, pp. 32–35.

31. For a detailed description of effects in Baltimore, see Marc Cooper, "When Push Comes to Shove," *The Nation*, June 2, 1997, pp. 11–15.

32. Under the previous system, all but fifty dollars of child support payments was subtracted from the welfare benefit. However, welfare recipients were in a good position to bargain for under-the-table child support that could increase their total family income (by threatening to reveal their names). Under the new system, most states have eliminated the fifty-dollar pass-through, and reduced the informal leverage that mothers used to enjoy by requiring them to name the father.

33. In 1989, about 40 percent of all mothers without child support awards didn't want them. Robert I. Lerman, "Child Support Policies," *Journal of Economic Perspectives* 7, no. 1 (Winter 1993), p. 176.

34. For more discussion of the evolution of the concept of the underclass see Herbert J. Gans, *The War Against the Poor: The Underclass and Antipoverty Policy* (New York: Basic Books, 1995).

35. Ralph Vartabedian, "Unpaid Tax Total Put at $195 Billion a Year by IRS," *Los Angeles Times*, May 2, 1998, p. A1.

36. Peter Gottschalk, Sara McLanahan, and Gary Sandefur, "Dynamics of Poverty and Welfare Participation," in Sheldon Danziger, Gary Sandefur, and Daniel Weinberg, eds, *Confronting Poverty: Prescriptions for Change* (Cambridge, MA: Harvard University Press, 1994), p. 96; La Donna Pavetti, "Who Spends Longer Periods of Time Receiving Welfare?" in R. Kent Weaver and William T. Dickens, eds, *Looking Before We Leap: Social Science and Welfare Reform* (Washington, D.C.: Brookings Institution, 1995), p. 40.

37. Michael Ybarra, "Getting Off Welfare Is a Point of Pride to Nominee's Sister," *Wall Street Journal*, July 19, 1991, p. A7. See also "The Judge Who Judged His Sister," *Christian Science Monitor*, July 30, 1991, p. 13.

38. David van Biema, "The Storm over Orphanages," *Time*, December 24, 1994, p. A23; Charles Murray, "The Coming White Underclass," *Wall Street Journal*, October 19, 1993, p. A14.

39. Frank Furstenberg, Jr. and Andrew J. Cherlin, *Divided Families: What Happens to Children When Parents Part* (Cambridge, MA: Harvard University Press, 1991); Deborah A. Frank, Peri E. Klass, Felton Earls, and Leon Eisenberg, "Infants and Young Children in Orphanages: One View from Pediatrics and Child Psychiatry," *Pediatrics* 97, no. 4 (April 1996), pp. 569–577.

40. Douglas J. Besharov, "Orphanages Aren't Welfare Reform," *New York Times*, December 20, 1994, p. A23; Nina Bernstein, "Deletion of Word in Welfare Bill Opens Foster Care to Big Business," *New York Times*, May 4, 1997, p. A1.

41. Steven A. Holmes, "G.O.P. Sees Shift in Child Welfare," *New York Times*, March 13, 1995, p. A7; Bernstein, "Deletion of Word."

42. James Heintz and Nancy Folbre, *The Ultimate Field Guide to the U.S. Economy* (New York: New Press, 2000), pp. 123, 133.

43. Greg Duncan and Jeanne Brooks-Gunn, eds, *Consequences of Growing Up Poor* (New York: Russell Sage Foundation, 1997).

44. Jeanne Ellsworth and Lynda J. Ames, "Introduction" in Ellsworth and Ames, eds, *Critical Perspectives on Project Head Start: Revisioning the Hope and Challenge* (Albany: State University of New York Press, 1998), p. x.

45. For a brief history of Head Start and a general review of evaluations of its effects, see Lisbeth B. Schorr, *Within Our Reach: Breaking the Cycle of Disadvantage* (New York: Doubleday, 1988).

46. Kathryn Kuntz, "A Lost Legacy: Head Start's Origins in Community Action," in Ellsworth and Ames, *Critical Perspectives on Project Head Start*, p. 1.

47. Schorr, *Within Our Reach*, p. 191.

48. Carol H. Ripple, Walter S. Gilliam, Nina Chanana, and Edward Zigler, "Will Fifty Cooks Spoil the Broth?" *American Psychologist* (May 1999), p. 327.

49. *A Welcome for Every Child III* (New York: The French American Foundation, 1999).

50. *A Welcome for Every Child III.*

Chapter 6

1. Kay Hollimon, "Rich School Districts Set Up Foundations to Raise Funds," *San Antonio Express*, December 8, 1991.

2. Robert B. Reich, "Big Biz Cuts Class; Firms Talk Loud, Do Little for Schools," *Washington Post*, April 21, 1991, B1.

3. It is also important to note that many of the legal victories of the civil rights movement were dismantled in the 1990s, contributing to increases in racial and ethnic segregation in major school districts across the country. See Gary Orfield, Susan E. Eaton, and the Harvard Project on School Desegregation, *Dismantling Segregation: The Quiet Reversal of Brown v. Board of Education* (New York: New Press, 1996).

4. Amy Gluckman, "Tests and Money," *Dollars and Sense* (March–April 1998), pp. 11–13; John Chubb and Erik Hanushek, "Reforming Educational Reform," in Henry J. Aaron, ed., *Setting National Priorities: Policies for the Nineties* (Washington, D.C.: Brookings Institution, 1990), pp. 213–247. It is important to note that studies have found a positive relationship between measurements of school quality and students' future earnings. See David Card and Alan B. Krueger, "Does School Quality Matter? Returns to Education and the Characteristics of Public Schools in the United States," *Journal of Political Economy* 100, no. 1 (1992), pp. 1–40.

5. Caroline Hoxby, "How Teachers' Unions Affect Education Production," *Quarterly Journal of Economics* 111 (1996).

6. For an excellent summary of the legal and legislative history of the school funding fights, see Gregory G. Rocha and Robert H. Webking, *Politics and Public Education: Edgewood v. Kirby and the Reform of Public School Financing in Texas* (Minneapolis/St. Paul: West Publishing Company, 1992).

7. Louis Dubose, "Twenty-One Years Before the Bar," *Texas Observer* 81, no. 20, October 13, 1989, pp. 3–4.

8. A sample of over a hundred Texas districts showed that the wealthiest ten spent about three times as much per pupil as the poorest four: Jonathan Kozol, *Savage Inequalities* (New York: Crown Publishers, 1991), p. 214.

9. Roberto Suro, "Texas Court Rules Rich-Poor Gap in State School Spending Is Illegal," *New York Times*, October 3, 1989, p. A1.

10. "Texas Board Approves Teaching of Evolution," *New York Times*, November 13, 1990. William L. Taylor and Dianne M. Piché, "A Report on Shortchang-

ing Children: The Impact of Fiscal Inequity on the Education of Students at Risk," report prepared for the Committee on Education and Labor, U.S. House of Representatives (Washington, D.C.: U.S. Government Printing Office, 1990), pp. 5, 23.

11. Jana Rivera, "An Equal Chance at Education," *Hispanic Outlook in Higher Education* 5, no. 6, November 15, 1994, p. 1.

12. On Boston, see K. Jackson, *Crabgrass Frontier: The Suburbanization of the United States* (New York: Oxford University Press, 1985), p. 76. On San Antonio, see Rocha and Webking, *Politics and Public Education*, p. 20.

13. *Snapshot '91: 1990–91 School District Profiles* (Austin, TX: Texas Education Agency, 1992), p. 60.

14. Douglas S. Massey and Nancy A. Denton, *American Apartheid: Segregation and the Making of the Underclass* (Cambridge, MA: Harvard University Press, 1993).

15. The figures for instructional expenditure per student are based on figures from Texas Research Institute; for test scores, see Texas Education Agency, *Snapshot '91*, p. 56.

16. Based on a conversation in 1996 with Charles Slater, then superintendent of the Alamo Heights Independent School District.

17. "A Parable for Legislators," *Texas Observer*, September 28, 1990, p. 1.

18. Rocha and Webking, *Politics and Public Education*, p. 108.

19. Gene Koretz, "Economic Trends," *Business Week*, April 5, 1999. For great summaries of educational finance issues, see *Funding for Justice: Money, Equity, and the Future of Public Education* [not dated]. It is available from Rethinking Schools, 1001 East Keefe Avenue, Milwaukee, WI 53212. See also the special education issue of *Dollars and Sense*, March/April 1998.

20. Kozol, *Savage Inequalities*, p. 220.

21. Fabio Silva and Jon Sonstelie, "Did Serrano Cause a Decline in School Spending?" *National Tax Journal* 48, no. 2 (June 1995), pp. 199–215.

22. Walter Tschinkel, "Poverty, Not Bad Schools, Hinders Learning," *Miami Herald*, April 25, 1999.

23. Ibid.

24. Bob Peterson, "Teacher of the Year Gives Vouchers a Failing Grade," *The Progressive*, April 1997, p. 22.

25. Thomas Toch, "The New Education Bazaar," *U.S. News and World Report*, April 27, 1998, p. 34.

26. Amy Wells, *Time to Choose* (New York: Hill & Wang, 1993); D. Moore and S. Davenport, "School Choice: The New Improved Sorting Machine," in W. Boyd and H. Walbert, eds, *Choice in Education* (Berkeley: McCuthan, 1990).

27. Massey and Denton, *American Apartheid: Segregation and the Making of the Underclass.*
28. Noreen Connell, "Under-Funded Schools. Why Money Matters," *Dollars and Sense* (March-April 1998), pp. 14–17, 39.
29. Thaddeus Herrick, "Private Group Creates a School Voucher Plan," *Houston Chronicle,* April 23, 1998.
30. Thaddeus Herrick, "Edgewood: After the Money," *Houston Chronicle,* November 24, 1998.
31. *University of Massachusetts Fact Book, 1996–1998* (Amherst, MA: University of Massachusetts, 1999), p. 47.
32. Ibid., p. 45.
33. Jeffrey A. Miron, "No Reason for State Universities," *Boston Business Journal,* July 13, 1992.
34. Todd Mason, *Perot: An Unauthorized Biography* (Homewood, IL: Business One Irwin, 1990), p. 122.
35. Michael S. McPherson and Morton Owen Schapiro, *The Student Aid Game* (Princeton, NJ: Princeton University Press, 1998).
36. Thomas Mortensen, report to the National Council of Educational Opportunity, cited in Sondra Beverley, "Rich Kids, Poor Kids: The Education Gap Is Widening," *St. Louis Post-Dispatch,* April 29, 1997.
37. Kian Ghazi, *Emerging Trends in the $670 Billion Education Market* (New York: Lehman Brothers, March 17, 1997), p. 69.
38. Gordon C. Winston, "Subsidies, Hierarchy, and Peers: The Awkward Economics of Higher Education," *Journal of Economic Perspectives* 13, no. 1 (Winter 1999), p. 20.
39. James K. Boyce and Thomas W. Hutcheson, *17 Questions on the Budget Cuts and Public Higher Education in Massachusetts* (Amherst, MA: Institute for Economic Studies, 1990), p. 17.
40. McPherson and Schapiro, *The Student Aid Game*; Mary Jordan, " 'Need-Blind' Admissions Policy at Top Private Colleges Losing Favor to Wealth," *Washington Post,* April 26, 1992, p. A1; Ali Crolius, "MHC Building Occupation Ends," *Daily Hampshire Gazette,* April 19–20, 1997, p. 1.
41. *University of Massachusetts Fact Book, 1984–85* (Amherst, MA: University of Massachusetts, 1986), p. 50, table 25. The percentage was tabulated to the exclusion of students who did not respond, for consistency with the later figures.
42. Maureen Turner, "Beyond Race Relations," *The Valley Advocate,* March 13, 1997, p. 8.

Chapter 7

1. Richard A. Easterlin, "Does Money Buy Happiness?" *Public Interest* 30 (Winter 1973), pp. 3–10.

2. Robert Lane, "Does Money Buy Happiness?" *Public Interest* 113 (Fall 1993), pp. 56–65.

3. *United Nations Human Development Report 1998* (New York: United Nations, 1999), p. 30.

4. United for a Fair Economy (UFE), *Born on Third Base: The Sources of Wealth of the 1997 Forbes 400.* Available from UFE, 37 Temple Place, Fifth Floor, Boston, MA 02111 or www.ufe.org. See also Ann Marsh, "Meet the Class of 1996," *Forbes,* October 14, 1996, p. 108.

5. Thomas Piketty, "Social Mobility and Redistributive Politics," *Quarterly Journal of Economics* CX, no. 3 (August 1995), pp. 551–584.

6. Quoted in Lionel Robbins, "Economics and Political Economy," *American Economic Review* 71, no. 2 (May 1981), p. 5.

7. Jim Goldberg, *Rich and Poor* (New York: Random House, 1985).

8. For more scholarly discussion of the implications of efforts to avoid cognitive dissonance, see Jon Elster, *Ulysses and the Sirens: Studies in Rationality and Irrationality* (Cambridge, UK: Cambridge University Press, 1979) and Robert Frank, *Passions Within Reason: The Strategic Role of the Emotions* (New York: W. W. Norton, 1988).

9. Marvin Minsky, *The Society of Mind* (New York: Simon and Schuster, 1985), p. 276.

10. In 1987, for instance, total tax revenues amounted to $1,678 billion, and total corporate profits before tax, $266.7 billion. See Department of Commerce, *Statistical Abstract of the United States, 1990,* p. 273, table 455 and p. 429, table 696.

11. Official Web site of the Libertarian Party, www.lp.org/issues/platform/taxation.html, accessed October 18, 2000.

12. Bruce Bartlett, "Should We Abolish the Estate Tax?" Brief Analysis No. 202, National Center for Policy Analysis, January 27, 1997. Available at www.ncpa.org.

13. Joseph A. Pechman, *Federal Tax Policy,* 5th ed. (Washington, D.C.: Brookings Institution, 1987), p. 236; Roy L. Prosterman and Tim Hanstad, "Fight the Deficit with Estate Taxes," *Washington Post,* September 5, 1990, p. A19; Citizens for Tax Justice, "Should Congress Phase out the Estate Tax?" www.ctj.org, July 1999.

14. Phillip Stern, *The Rape of the Taxpayer* (New York: Random House, 1973), pp. 323, 325–326; see Alan Murray, "Senate Panel Democrats Opposed Gains-Tax Cut but Voted for Giant Loopholes in Estate Levies," *Wall Street Journal,* October 13, 1989, section E, P A16.

15. Pechman, *Federal Tax Policy,* p. 236. On comparison with Japan, see Prosterman and Hanstad, "Fight the Deficit."

16. The Gallup Organization, "Haves and Have-Nots: Perceptions of Fairness and Opportunity—1998," Section 5, *Social Audit* (www.gallup.com/poll/socialaudits/resource_distribution.asp).

17. Sam Pizzigatti's *The Maximum Wage* (New York: Apex Press, 1992) is a wonderfully readable history of progressive taxation that makes a case for more radical reform.

18. Sandra Block, "Inheriting a Nightmare," *USA Today*, January 8, 1999. See also Nick Ravo, "A Windfall Nears," *The New York Times*, July 22, 1990, p. E4.

19. *Statistical Abstract of the U.S. 1999*, p. 474, table 742.

20. This argument is often attributed to Arthur Okun's classic book *Equality and Efficiency: The Big Tradeoff* (Washington, D.C.: Brookings Institution, 1975). However, Okun's treatment of this issue is far more balanced and humane than most textbook interpretations of it. He never argues that efficiency should be our primary social goal.

21. Sam Bowles and Herbert Gintis, "Efficient Redistribution: New Rules for Markets, States, and Communities," *Politics and Society* 24 (1996), pp. 307–42. See also Louis Putterman, John Roemer, and Joaquim Silvestre, "Does Egalitarianism Have a Future?" *Journal of Economic Literature* XXXVI (June 1998), pp. 861–902.

22. Okun, *Equality and Efficiency*, p. 1.

23. Bowles and Gintis, "Efficient Redistribution."

Chapter 8

1. John Gray, *False Dawn: The Delusions of Global Capitalism* (New York: New Press, 1998).

2. Peter Stalker, *The Work of Strangers: A Survey of International Labour Migration* (Geneva: International Labour Office, 1997).

3. *Business Week*, July 5 1999, p. 16.

4. Ibid., p. 244.

5. Nancy Folbre, "Business to the Rescue?" *The Nation*, September 21, 1992, pp. 281–282.

6. Peter Dicken, *Global Shift: Transforming the World Economy*, 3rd ed. (New York: Guilford Press, 1998), p. 397.

7. *Business Week, Preparing Your Business for the Global Economy* (New York: McGraw Hill, 1997).

8. Ibid., p. 22.

9. Cited in William Greider, *One World Ready or Not: The Manic Logic of Global Capitalism* (New York: Simon and Schuster, 1997), p. 98.

10. Elisabeth Rosenthal, "In China, 35+ and Female = Unemployable," *New York Times*, October 13, 1998.
11. Greider, *One World Ready or Not*, p. 98.
12. Sam Dillon, "Sex Bias Is Reported by U.S. at Border Plants in Mexico," *New York Times*, January 13, 1998.
13. Cece Modupe Fadope, "Production vs. Reproduction," *Multinational Monitor* 17, no. 10, October 1996, p. 8.
14. Cited in Stalker, *The Work of Strangers*, p. 149.
15. For a wonderful elaboration of this point, see Arlie Russell Hochschild, "The Nanny Chain," *The American Prospect* 11, no. 4, January 3, 2000.
16. Warren Cohen, "Home Wreckers: Congress's Roles in the Au Pair Tragedy," *The New Republic*, November 24, 1997, p. 18.
17. Cited in Eric Schmitt, "Crying Need; Day Care Quandary," *New York Times*, January 11, 1998.
18. *Business Week*, May 14, 1990, p. 98.
19. Gray, *False Dawn*, p. 62.
20. See Dicken, *Global Shift*, chapter 3.
21. Dani Rodrik, *Has Globalization Gone Too Far?* (Washington, D.C.: Institute for International Economics, 1997).
22. Ron Scherer, "Eye on Firms That Use Cheap Labor Abroad," *Christian Science Monitor*, November 14, 1997.
23. Rodrik, *Has Globalization Gone Too Far?*; Sara Anderson and John Cavanaugh with Thea Lee and the Institute for Policy Studies, *Field Guide to the Global Economy* (New York: New Press, 2000), p. 43; Nancy Folbre and the Center for Popular Economics, *The New Field Guide to the U.S. Economy* (New York: New Press, 1995), Chart 5.11.
24. William Greider, *One World, Ready or Not*, p. 360.
25. The Economic Policy Institute, *The Failed Experiment: NAFTA at Three Years* (Washington, D.C.: June 26, 1997), p. 25.
26. Al Franken, *Rush Limbaugh Is a Big Fat Idiot* (New York: Delacorte Press, 1996), pp. 177–178.
27. Gene Koretz, "Downsizing's Economic Spin," *Business Week*, December 28, 1998, p. 30.
28. House Committee on Education and Labor, Subcommittee on Labor-Management Relations and Subcommittee on Employment Opportunities, *Hearings on H.R. 1616*, 99th Cong., 1st sess. (Washington, D.C.: Government Printing Office, 1985).
29. Michael C. Jensen and Perry Fagan, "Capitalism Isn't Broken," *Wall Street Journal*, March 29, 1996.
30. Russell Baker, "The Market God," *New York Times*, March 23, 1996, p. A17.

31. Robert Sullivan, "A Letter from Dad," *The New Yorker* 72, no. 5, March 25, 1996, p. 17.

32. Patrick Buchanan, *The Great Betrayal* (New York: Little, Brown & Co., 1998), p. 106.

33. Ibid., p. 325.

34. *International Herald Tribune*, June 11, 1998, p. 1.

35. Benjamin R. Barber, *Jihad vs. McWorld: How Globalism and Tribalism Are Reshaping the World* (New York: Ballantine, 1995), p. 29.

36. Lisa Beyer, "Life Behind the Veil," *Time*, November 8, 1990. See also Jan Goodwin, *Price of Honor: Muslim Women Lift the Veil of Silence on the Islamic World* (New York: Penguin, 1995).

37. For more discussion of this issue see William Greider, "Global Agenda," *The Nation*, January 31, 2000, pp. 11–16.

38. Anderson and Cavanagh, *Field Guide to the Global Economy*; "Globalization: What Americans Are Worried About," *Business Week*, April 24, 2000, p. 44.

39. William Wolman and Anne Colamosca, *The Judas Economy: The Triumph of Capital and the Betrayal of Work* (New York: Addison-Wesley, 1997), p. 1.

Chapter 9

1. E. P. Thompson, "Outside the Whale," in *The Poverty of Theory and Other Essays* (New York: Monthly Review Press, 1978), p. 243.

2. Nancy Folbre, "Socialism, Feminist and Scientific," in Marianne Ferber and Julie Nelson, eds, *Beyond Economic Man* (Chicago: University of Chicago Press, 1993), pp. 94–110.

3. Slavenka Drakulic, *How We Survived Communism and Even Laughed* (New York: HarperPerennial, 1993), p. 30.

4. Gail Lapidus, *Women in Soviet Society: Equality, Development, and Social Change* (Berkeley: University of California Press, 1978).

5. For a more detailed discussion of incentive structures, see John Roemer, *A Future for Socialism* (Cambridge, MA: Harvard University Press, 1994).

6. J. A. Schumpeter, *Capitalism, Socialism and Democracy*, 3rd ed. (New York: Harper and Row, 1950).

7. For a discussion of the relationship between competition and efficiency, see Oliver Williamson, "Contested Exchange Versus the Governance of Contractual Relations," *Journal of Economic Perspectives* (Winter 1993), pp. 103–108.

8. Edward A. Hewitt, "Reforming the Economy," *The Nation*, June 13, 1987, pp. 803–804.

9. David Kotz, "Russia in Shock," *Dollars and Sense* (June 1993), pp. 9–11, 17.

10. Personal communication with Alexander Buzgalin, April 13, 1993.

11. Oleg Bogomolov, "Who Will Own 'Nobody's Property'? The Perils of Russian Privatization," *Dissent* (Spring 1993), pp. 201–208.

12. Ibid., p. 208.

13. John Lloyd, "The Russian Devolution," *New York Times*, August 15, 1999.

14. See Sean Wilentz, *Chants Democratic: New York City and the Rise of the American Working Class, 1788–1850* (New York: Oxford University Press, 1984).

15. James Heintz, Nancy Folbre, and the Center for Popular Economics, *The Ultimate Field Guide to the U.S. Economy* (New York: New Press, 2000), p. 29.

16. Len Krimerman, "Why Economists are Wrong about Co-ops," *Dollars and Sense* (September 1998), pp. 44-9.

17. Heintz and Folbre, *The Ultimate Field Guide to the U.S. Economy*, p. 29.

18. Roemer, *A Future for Socialism*.

19. Thomas Weisskopf provides an eloquent defense of market socialism in "Toward a Socialism for the Future in the Wake of the Demise of the Socialism of the Past," *Review of Radical Political Economics* 24, no. 3–4 (Winter 1992), reprinted in Victor Lippit, ed., *Radical Political Economy: Explorations in Alternative Economic Analysis* (Armonk, NY: M. E. Sharpe, 1996).

20. Bruce Ackerman and Anne Alstott, *The Stakeholder Society* (New Haven: Yale University Press, 1999).

21. Michael Albert and Robin Hahnel, *Looking Forward* (Boston: South End, 1991). Albert and Hahnel provide a more technical and mathematical defense of their proposals in *The Political Economy of Participatory Economics* (Princeton, NJ: Princeton University Press, 1991). Another helpful proponent of this point of view is Pat Devine, *Democracy and Economic Planning* (Boulder, CO: Westview Press, 1988).

22. Ibid., p. 94.

23. Ibid., p. 48.

24. For a great description of an actual bargaining process, see Joan Acker, *Doing Comparable Worth: Gender, Class and Pay Equity* (Philadelphia: Temple University Press, 1989).

25. David Osborne and Ted Gaebler, *Reinventing Government: How the Entrepreneurial Spirit Is Transforming the Public Sector* (New York: Plume Books, 1993).

26. Alva Myrdal, *Nation and Family: The Swedish Experiment in Democratic Family and Population Policy* (London: Kegan Paul, Trench, Trubner and Co., 1945).

27. Marga Bruyn-Hundt, "Scenarios for a Redistribution of Unpaid Work in the Netherlands," *Feminist Economics* 2, no. 3 (1996), p. 129.

28. Ina Brouwer and Eelco Wiarda, "The Combination Model: Child Care and the Part Time Labour Supply of Men in the Dutch Welfare State," in J. J.

Schippers, J. J. Siegers, and J. De Jong-Gierveld, eds, *Child Care and Female Labour Supply in the Netherlands: Facts, Analyses, Policies* (Amsterdam: Thesis Publishers, 1998).

29. Alva Myrdal and Viola Klein, *Women's Two Roles: Home and Work* (London: Routledge and Kegan Paul, 1956).

30. Clare Ungerson, "Gender, Cash, and Informal Care: European Perspectives and Dilemmas," *Journal of Social Policy* 24, no. 1 (1995), pp. 31–52; Sheila B. Kamerman and Alfred J. Kahn, "Child and Family Policies in an Era of Social Policy Retrenchment and Restructuring," unpublished paper presented at the Luxembourg Income Study Conference on Child Well-Being in Rich and Transition Countries, September 30–October 2, 1999.

31. Julie Nelson, "Feminist Theory and the Income Tax," in *Feminism, Objectivity, and Economics* (New York: Routledge, 1996), pp. 97–117.

INDEX

Abortion, 15, 205
Affluence, 32
African Americans, 129
Agreement, implicit, 30
Aid to Families with Dependent Children
    (AFDC), 90, 97, 113, 114, 118
    child support enforcement, 124
    implicit tax and, 121–122, 123
    work requirement, 123
    See also Welfare state
Altruism, xiv, 5, 11, 12, 14, 15
    caregiving and, 46
    child-rearing and, 34–35
    competitive disadvantage of, 25–26
    distribution of, 33
    empathy, 19–20
    feminism vs. patriarchy, 20–21
    kin-based, 19, 25
    reciprocity and, 25–26
    self-interest and, 29–30, 33
    virtue and, 37
American Federation of Labor, 93
Astell, Mary, 8
At-Risk Child Care, 118

Bargaining power, 5–6
Becker, Gary, 119

Beecher, Catherine, 12
Bergmann, Barbara, 18
Besant, Annie, 13
Birth control, 9–11, 101, 104
    abortion, 15, 205
    Comstock Law, 13
    fertility decline and, 13–14
    individual autonomy and, 14
    legal repression of, 13, 204
    sex and motherhood, 13
Blood donation, 53–54
Bloom, Allen, 14
Bottom line. *See* Market economy
Bradlaugh, Charles, 13
Brown, Helen Gurley, 4–5
Brown v. Board of Education, 142–143
Bruyn-Hundt, Marga, 227
Buchanan, Pat, 203, 206
Bull market, 3
Burke, Edmund, 11

Capital mobility, 193–194, 202
Capitalism, 11–12
    bad vs. good, 186
    families and, 89–91
    market-based society, 20–21
    multinational corporations, 196

Capitalism (*continued*)
  See also Communism; Corpornations;
    Globalization; Marx, Karl; Nanny
    state
Care penalty, 22–25
  elder care, 36–38
  fairness and care, 30–32
  love/commitment and, 38–41
  Nice Person's Dilemma, 28–30
  parenthood costs, 33–35
  rat race effects, 42–44
  reciprocity and contracts, 25–28
  short-term strategies, 22–24
  spillover effect, 49–51
  trends in caring, 32–33
  women's employment, 44–46
Caregiving:
  commodity of, 48–49, 51–52
  competition and, 24
  costs of, 55–57
  economic value of, 66–68, 230
  emotional support vs. bottom line, 57–60
  income for, 45–46
  labor trends and, 37–38, 43–44
  nature of, 24–25
  outcomes of, 37
  quality of, 41–42, 48–49, 50
  shared, 18–20, 39–40, 42, 210
  spillover effect, 49–51
  Universal Caregiving, 230
  See also Care penalty; Caring labor;
    Opportunism; Success
Caring labor, xi–xii
  costs of, xv, xvi, xx
  egalitarian models of, 227
  feminine definition of, 17–18
  market forces and, xii–xiii
  patriarchy and, 20–21
  responsibility for, 8, 10–11
  rewards of, 24–25, 51
  sharing of, 18–20, 39–40, 42
  subordination and, 7, 8–9
  women and, xiv–xv, 4–5, 10–11
  See also Child care; Coercion; Work

Carnegie, Andrew, 172
Central planning. *See* Communism
Child care, 5–6, 8, 44
  nanny importation, 190–193
  quality in, 62–63
  tax credits, 117–118
  See also Motherhood; Parenthood
Child Care and Development Block Grant,
  118
Child and Dependent Care Tax Credit, 118
Child Labor Deterrence Act of 1995, 194
Child support, xvi, 34, 39, 86
Child support enforcement, 104–107, 124
Children:
  child labor, 194, 211
  child-rearing cost subsidies, 111–113
  cycle of disadvantage, 130
  European public policy, 135
  Head Start, 130–131
  infant mortality, 129
  parental ineptitude and, 129–130
  poverty and, 128–131
  productivity of, 92–93
  See also Aid to Families with Dependent
    Children (AFDC); French policy;
    Temporary Assistance to Needy
    Families (TANF)
Choice, 7, 8
  abortion and, 15
  implicit contract and, 30, 39
  individuals and competitive markets, 32
  work and values, 47–48
Citizens for Tax Justice, 172
Civil rights movement, 142–145
Civilized behavior, 12, 14–15
  civic participation, 74–77, 229–230
  civic virtue, 32
Clamshell Alliance, 224
Coercion:
  division of labor, 5
  maternity, forced, 38–39
  property rights, male, 6, 8
  violence against women, 6–7

Commitment to care. *See* Care Penalty; Caregiving
Communism:
  capitalism, transition to, 216–219
  central planning in, 213–216
  household work and value, 214
  incentives, work/innovation, 215
  privatization, 216, 217–219
  revolution and, 216
  See also Market socialism
Community, xx
  evolving forms of, 32–33
  globalized economy and, 202, 203–204
  market economy stabilization, 24–25
  membership in, 29
Compensation:
  caring labor and, xi–xii
  See also Money
Competition, xi
  altruism and, 25–26
  caregiving and, xiv–xv, xvi, 24, 55–57
  individual choice and, 32
  male vs. female, 17–18
  patriarchal power structure and, xiv
  rat race and, 43–44
  supply and demand, xii–xiii
  technology/economic growth and, xiii
  See also Capitalism; Globalization
Comstock law, 13
Consumer Expenditure Survey, 66
Contraception. *See* Birth control
Contracts, 7–8
  emotions and, 27–28
  implicit, 30, 39
  reciprocity and, 25–28
Coontz, Stephanie, xx
Cooperation, 28
  altruism/self-interest and, 33
  Nice Person's Dilemma, 29–30
  social capital and, 74–77
  socialism and, 211
Corporations, 185–186
  capital mobility, 193–194, 202
  cyberspace and, 188

downsizing, 196–200, 201
  female production workers, 189–190
  immigration and, 186–188
  McWorld vs. religious fundamentalism, 203–206
  nanny importation, 190–193
  overseas labor, 188
  social conservatism and, 203–206
  state policies and, 194–195
  See also Globalization
Cost/benefit ratio, xiv, 5, 24
  care services, professional, 55–57
  education and, 136–137
  human capital development, 71–73
  personal services and, 27–28
  taxes and, 170–172
  treatment limitation, 58–60
  See also Success
Crowding out, 86–87
Cultural norms, 4
  caregiving and, 51–52
  motherhood and, 17
  self-image and, 6

de Waal, Franz, 19
Deadbeat dad, 107
Declining marginal utility, 161–162
Deming, R. Edwards, 78
Democracy, 210, 222–223
  bureaucracy in, 226
  civic participation, 229–230
  decentralized planning/participation, 223–225
  gender inequity and, 226–228
  globalization of production and, 223
  individual rights, 225
  kinship definitions in, 228–229
  public education, 227
  social democracy, 225–230
  women's work and, 225
  workers' rights, 223
Dependency, 5, 6
Desegregation, 142–145
Dewey, John, 136

Division of labor, 5
Divorce. *See* Marrriage
Domestic violence, 7, 124
Douglas, Paul, 95
Dow Jones Industrial Average, 55, 64
Downsizing, 196–200, 201
Downward mobility, 162

Earned Income Tax Credit (EITC), 113,
      117, 175
Easterlin, Richard, 160–161
Ecological niches, unselfishness, 29–30
Economic dependency, 5, 6
Economic growth, xiii, xv
   health of, 64–65
   Human Development Index (HDI),
      73–74
   nonmarket work and, 66–67
   personal relationships and, 32
   self-interest and, 9
   specialization and, 5–6, 39
   See also Corpornations
Economic segregation, 76
Economics:
   care and, 210, 227
   caring jobs, wages for, 45–46
   child-rearing and, 34–35, 39
   crowding out, 86–87
   elder care and, 36, 37
   ethics and, 24
   happiness, 161
   health/education expenditures, 72
   human capital, 71–73
   income inequalities, 47–48
   nonsatiation, 161–163
   perverse incentives, 85–87
   quality of care and, 63–64
   rent-seeking, 87–88
   resources, control of, 213
   reward structure, 54–55
   trust/respect and, 26–27
   welfare measurement, 68–71

   See also Market economy; Marx, Karl;
      Nice Person's Dilemma; Social
      ecology; Success
Edgewood legal case, 143–145
Edin, Kathryn, 122–123
Education, xv
   charter/magnet schools, 150–151
   child productivity and, 92–93
   civil rights movement and, 142–145
   cost/benefit ratio, 136–137
   equal opportunity, 157–158
   equalization, 145–149
   expenditures for, 72, 138–139
   extended day, 227
   funding inequities in, 142–145
   higher education, 152–157
   human capital theory and, 140–141
   measures of, 137–138
   outcomes, 139–140
   separate-but-equal, 142–143
   standardized testing, 140, 141
   teaching, 141
   voucher programs, 149–150, 151–152
Efficiency, 16, 26, 39, 85, 180–181
   See also Sustainability
Egalitarian societies, 5
Ehrenreich, Barbara, 104
EKCO Corporation, 196–198
Elder care, 36–38, 60–62
Emotions, xii
   care penalty, 38–41
   contracts and, 27–28
   economic success and, 72–73
   love and coercion, 38–41
   quality of care, 49
   social capital and, 77
   therapeutic force of, 57–58, 60
Empathy, 19–20, 31–32, 39
Employee Stock Ownership Plans
      (ESOPs), 220–221
Employment. *See* Work
Engels, Friedrich, 211
England, Paula, 45
Equal opportunity, 157–158, 226–228

Equal rights, 4, 10–11
Equity, 180–181, 227
European Economic Community, 223
Exclusionary rules, 6

Fairness, 30–31, 43–44
Families:
  child productivity, 92–93
  democratic bureaucracies and, 226–228
  destructive factors, 89–91
  economic systems of, xv, 94–96, 201–
    202, 227
  individualism and, 89–91
  market economy and, 12, 24–25
  self-interest and, xvi
  solidarity/generosity and, 29
  stability of, 93
  values in, xii, 1, 16, 50–51, 79, 205, 229
  wage employment and, 89–90, 93–94
  See also French policy; Nanny state;
    Welfare state; Women
Family allowance, 112, 116–120, 132
Family and Medical Leave Act, 229
Family wage, 93, 94–95, 97
Family-state, xvi, 108
Federal housing assistance, 116
Fee-for-service insurance, 58
Feminism, 4, 9
  anti-abortion activism and, 15
  democratic bureaucracies and, 226–228
  equality vs. difference, 17–18
  individualism and, 20
  self-sacrifice, 15–16
  social, 18
Fertility rates, 6, 37, 71, 85, 95, 102
Food stamps, 117, 120
Foot-binding, 6
Frank, Robert, 47
Fraternal Order of the Eagles, 97
Free markets. See Corporations;
    Globalization
Freeman, Sonya, 5

French policy:
  child care centers/maternal schools,
    132–134
  family allowance, 132
  family policies/national health
    insurance, 132
  maternal leave, 131–132

G.I. Bill, 101
Game theory, 30–31, 32, 43–44
GATT (General Agreement on Tariffs and
    Trade), 193
Gender:
  achievement and, 3–5
  democratic institutions and, 226–228
  double standard and, 4, 10, 20
  political disputes and, 107–108
  work choice and, 47–48
General Agreement on Tariffs and Trade
    (GATT), 193
Genital mutilation, 6–7
Gilder, George, 14
Gingrich, Newt, 127
Globalization, xv, xvi
  community and, 202, 203–204
  competitive pressures and, 57
  democratic governance and, 196
  fair trade, 206
  safeguards in, 207–208
  See also Corpornation
Good Child's Dilemma, 36, 50–51
Good Parent's Dilemma, 30, 50–51
Good Person's Dilemma. See Nice Person's
    Dilemma
Gorbachev, Mikhail, 216
Government:
  birth rates and, 41
  child-rearing subsidies, 111–113
  European public policy, 135
  family support policies, 116–120
  federal housing assistance, 116
  nation-states in, xv, 194, 203, 205
  plant closing regulation, 199–200
  welfare state and, xv–xvi

Government (*continued*)
  See also Corpornations; French policy;
    Nanny state; Welfare state
Great Depression, 96
Greed, 16
Gross Domestic Product (GDP), xii, 18
  defined, 64–65, 66, 67
  economic valuing, 68–71, 230
Group solidarity, 19, 29

Happiness, 160–161
Haveman, Robert, 111
Head Start, 130–131
Health care services, xv, 72
Health maintenance organizations
    (HMOs), 56, 58–59
Hightower, Jim, 64
Hispanics, 129, 143–144
Hochschild, Arlie, 42
Home health workers, xii, 63
Homestead Act of 1869, 220
Honesty, xiv, 7
Human capital:
  cooperation, 74–77
  development index, 73–74
  education and, 140–141
  investment in, 71–73
  Total Quality Management (TQM) and,
    78–79
Human Development Index (HDI), 73–74
Human Rights Watch, 189

Immigration, 186–188
Implicit agreement, 30
Implicit tax, 121–122
Incentive to work, 176, 215
Income:
  benefits and, 227–228
  caregiving and, 45–46
  family wage, 93, 94–95
  inequity in, 112, 129
  parenthood and, 34
  women and, 34–35, 44, 47–48
  See also Money

Individualism, 14, 20
  choice and, 32
  competition for wealth and, 24–25
  family weakness and, 89–91
  socialism and, 211
Inequality, 183
  democratic institutions and, 226–228
  See also Equality
Infant mortality, 129
Institutionalization, xv
International Monetary Fund, 223
International trade. *See* Corpornation;
    Globalization
Internet:
  resources on, 61, 62
  virtual immigration, 188
Investment:
  human capital, 71–73
  human development, 73–74
Invisible hand/handshake, xii–xiii, 1, 27,
    210, 231–232
Invisible heart, xiv, 1, 231–232
Islamic purdah, 6
Italian birth rate, 41

Japan:
  birth rate, 41
  economic cooperation, 78
Jevons, Stanley, 167
Jihad, 203–206

Kinship:
  altruism and, 19, 25
  democratic definitions of, 228–229
  economic systems and, xv

Labor market, 34–35
  caregiving and, 37–38, 45, 48–49
  immigrants in, 186–188
  nanny importation, 190–193
  overseas labor, 188
  rat race effect, 42–44
  slavery, 90
  strikes and, 40

women in, 44–46, 47–48
See also Market economy
Labor theory of value, 214
Lane, Robert, 161
Liberal feminism, 4, 9
Life expectancy, 101–102
Limbaugh, Rush, 3, 14, 16, 198
Locke, John, 7–8
Long-term success, 23–24

MAI (Multinational Agreement on
    Investment), 193
Malthus, Thomas Robert, 9–10, 85
Mansbridge, Jane, 29
Market economy, xi
    asset distribution, 220
    bull market, 3
    caregiving and, xiv–xv, 48–49
    efficiency in, 16, 26
    family as stabilizer, 12
    impersonal society in, 20–21
    individual choice in, 32
    nonmarket production, xi–xii
    parenthood and, 34–35
    reward structure in, 54–55
    stabilization of, 24–25
    supply and demand in, xii–xiii, 45
    transactions in, xii–xiv
    See also Invisible hand/handshake;
        Success
Market socialism, 210
    asset distribution, 219–220, 222
    competition and, 221–222
    social ownership, 221
    worker ownership, 220–221
    See also Communism; Socialism
Marriage, 9, 27, 42, 92, 93, 228–229
Marshall, Alfred, 12
Marshner, Connie, 15
Marx, Karl, 196, 211–213, 214–215, 216
McFarlin Oil Company, xvii–xix
McWorld, 203–206
Measures of Economic Welfare (MEWs),
    68

Medicaid, 56, 60, 117
Medicare, 59, 61, 100, 117
Men:
    caregiving and, 18–20
    civility of, 12, 14–15
    division of labor and, 5
    ideals of, 17–18
    Lockian economic principles and, 7–8
    property rights of, 6, 8
    selfishness of, xiii–xiv, xvi, 15
    See also Patriarchal power; Women
Mexican American Legal Defense and
    Educational Fund (MALDEF), 144
Middle class, 177–180
Milk metaphor, 3–4
Mill, John Stuart, 10–11, 166
Mobility, 32, 162, 193–194
Money, xvii
    distribution of, 166–168, 174
    happiness and, 160–161
    luck/effort and, 164–166
    moral dissonance and, 169–170
    nonsatiation, 161–163
    satisfaction, 166–167
    self-esteem and, 168–169
    See also Income; Taxes
Morality. *See* Social norms
Motherhood, 13
    abortion and, 15
    cultural contradiction of, 17
    forced, 38–39
    labor market and, 34–35
    See also Birth control
Moynihan, Daniel Patrick, 119–120
Multinational Agreement on Investment
    (MAI), 193
Myrdal, Alva, 91, 226, 227

NAFTA (North American Free Trade
    Agreement), 193, 198, 223
Nanny state, 3, 83–84, 108
    child support enforcement, 104–107, 124
    crowding out, 86–87
    Daddy state and, 93–96

Nanny state (*continued*)
emergence of, 84–89
family weakening, 89–91
market/family failures, 91
parenting support, 94–96, 116–120
patriarchal political authority and, 91–93
perverse incentives, 85–87
rent-seeking, 87–88
subsidized homemaking, 96–99
See also Children; Social Security
National Alliance for Caregivers, 37
National Association for the Education of
Young Children, 63
National Blood Data Resource Center, 54
National Center for Employee Ownership,
220
National Center for Policy Analysis, 173
National Center for Women and Aging, 37
National Family Caregivers Association, 37
National Labor Committee, 190
Nation-states, xv, 194, 203, 205
Nice Person's Dilemma, 24–25, 29–30, 43,
50–51
Nietzsche, Friedrich, 48
Nonmarket production, xi–xii, 66–68, 92,
226–227
Nonsatiation, 161–163
North American Free Trade Agreement
(NAFTA), 193, 198, 223
Novak, Michael, 83
Nursing, xii, xiv, 40, 44, 60
Nursing Home Compare, 61
Nursing homes. *See* Elder care

Obligations:
moral, 12, 13
rules of, xx
Opportunism, 24–25
long-term relationships and, 75–76
Prisoner's Dilemma, 28
Owen, Robert, 11–12, 73, 211

Parenthood:
direct costs of, 33–34
indirect costs of, 34

ineptitude in, 129–130
love and, 38–39
public support of, 94–96
Pareto, Vilfredo, 166–167
Participatory democracy, 210, 223–225,
229–230
Patient Bill of Rights, 60
Patriarchal power, xi, xiv
caring and, 20
division of labor and, 5, 6
feminist individualism and, 20–21
male property rights, 6, 8
paternalism, benevolent, 97, 103–104,
204–205
political authority, 91–93
religious fundamentalism and, 203–205
See also Coercion
Pay. *See* Income
Perot, Ross, 203, 206
Personal relationships, 27–28, 32, 86–87
Perverse incentives, 85–87
Pink-collar employment, 44–46
Polanyi, Karl, 32
Political action, xx, 16
Poor Law (England), 85
Population growth, 9–10, 12
Positive externalities, 49–51
Poverty, 128–131, 166
Prisoner's Dilemma. *See* Nice Person's
Dilemma
Productivity:
care and, 230
family unit and, 89
human capital and, 71
Lockian principle of, 7–8
women and, 6–7
Progressive taxes. *See* Taxes
Pro-life perspective, 15
Promise Keepers, 205
Property rights, 6, 8
Prostitution, 10, 13
Public assistance. *See* Welfare state
Putnam, Robert, 75, 77

Quality of care, 41–42, 48–49, 50, 51
    child care, 62–63
    economic pressure and, 63–64
    elder care, 60–62

Race, 95
    civil rights movement, 142–145
    welfare programs and, 119–120
Rat race effect, 42–44, 45
Rathbone, Eleanor, 94–95
Reciprocity, 25
    agreement, default on, 30
    caregiving and, 50, 51
    enforcement of, 26
    Good Parent's Dilemma, 30
    Nice Person's Dilemma, 29
    personal relationships and, 27–28
    standardized products and, 26
Relationships:
    long-term, 75–76
    personal, 27–28, 32
Religious fundamentalism, 203–205
Rent-seeking, 87–88
Reproduction, 10, 13
    legal/political activity and, 13–14
    See also Birth control
Responsibilities:
    enforced, 86–87
    familial/social, xvi
    motherhood, 13
    rules of obligation, xx
    shared, 7, 18–20, 39–40, 42, 210
    See also Caring labor; Obligations
Rewards of care, 24–25
    caregiving and, 51–52
    cooperation and, 29
Risk pooling, 86
Rodriguez, Demetrio, 143–144
Rules of obligation, xx
Ryan, John, 93

Sanger, Margaret, 13, 14, 38
Schroeder, Patricia, 105

Self-determination, 7–8
Self-interest, xiii–xiv, 9–11, 24
    altruism and, 29–30, 33
    child-rearing and, 34–35
    long-term relationships and, 75–76
Selfishness, xiii–xiv, xvi, 15
    market-like behavior, 32, 51–52
    See also Unselfishness
Self-sacrifice, 10–11, 12, 15–16
Sen, Amartya, 28
Separate spheres doctrine, 11–13
Separate-but-equal education, 142–143
Sex:
    motherhood and, 13
    See also Prostitution; Reproduction
Sexual harassment, 45
Shared care, 18–20, 39–40, 42, 210
Shaw, George Bernard, 94
Sheppard-Towner Maternity and Infancy
    Protection Act, 96
Short-term care strategies, 22–24
Skidmore, Thomas, 219–220
Slavery, 90
Smith, Adam, xii–xiv, 9, 24, 32
Social capital, 74–77
Social democracy. See Democracy
Social ecology, 24
Social feminism, 4, 18
Social insurance programs, 86–87
Social norms, xiii–xiv, 4
    care, 32, 60
    choice and, 7
    fairness/reciprocity, 30–32
    moral dissonance, 169–170
    moral principles, 79–80
    paternal child-rearing, 39
    sex and parenthood, 13
    See also Caring labor; Coercion;
        Reciprocity
Social obligations. See Nanny state
Social programs, 159
    See also Money; Taxes
Social safety net, xv, 113

Social Security, xx, 36, 86, 88, 90, 108
  elderly population and, 101–103
  family structure and, 98–99
  intergenerational reciprocity in, 98,
    99–100, 101, 102–103
  maternalism vs. paternalism, 103–104
  medicare, 100
  pension system of, 97–98
  spousal/life insurance, 98
  Survivor's Insurance, 119
  women and, 100–101
Social Security Act of 1935, 96–97
Social welfare programs, xx, 40
  See also Nanny state
Socialism, xii, 3, 210, 211–213
  See also Communism
Solidarity, 19, 29
Sorenson, Elaine, 106
Southern Baptists convention, 203–204
Soviet Communist Party. See Communism
Specialization, 5–6, 39
Spencer, Herbert, 94
Spillover effect, 49–51
Sports, team, 33
Steuerle, Eugene, 111
Stowe, Harriet Beecher, 12
Strober, Myra, 18
Subordination, 7, 8–9, 93
Subsidies, 56, 61, 96–99, 111–113, 116–120
Success, xvii
  bottom-line care, 57–60
  caregiving economics and, 55–57
  economic health, 64–65
  economic welfare measurement, 68–71
  human capital, investment in, 71–73
  Human Development Index (HDI),
    73–74
  long-term, 23–24
  measurement of, 53–55, 64
  moral principles and, 79–80
  nonmarket work, 66–68
  quality of care, 60–64
  self-centeredness and, xx
  social capital and, 74–77

  Total Quality Management (TQM) and,
    78–79
  See also Economic growth
Supply and demand competition, xii–xiv,
    45
Sustainability, 23, 186, 192
Sustainable Economic Welfare (SEW),
    70–71

Talbot, Margaret, 57–58
Tax Freedom Day, 170, 172
Taxes:
  cost/benefit analysis, 170–172
  Earned Income Tax Credit (EITC), 113,
    117, 175
  employee stock ownership plans and,
    220–221
  estate taxes, 172–174
  implicit, 121–122
  incentives to work and, 176
  marriage penalty, 228
  multinational operations, 195
  progressive income tax, 174–176, 228
  Reagan Revolution, 173, 175
  regressive, 175
  social programs and, 159, 195
  Victory Tax, 175
  See also Money; Social Security
Teaching, xii, xiv, 40, 44, 141
Team sports, 33
Technological development, xiii, 6
Temporary Assistance to Needy Families
    (TANF), 106, 113, 116–117, 118, 119
Texas educational inequities, 143–145
Thatcher, Margaret, 3
Thomas, Clarence, 127
Titmuss, Richard, 53
Total Quality Management (TQM), 78–79
Townsend Plan, 97
Transactions, xiii–xiv
  burden of proof in, 125–127
  good behavior score and, 126–127
  institutional/foster care, 127

punishment and, 125
welfare reform and, 120
Transitional Child Care, 118
Trickle-down theory, 9
Trust, xiv, 19, 27

Ultimatum game, 30–31, 43–44
Union of Japanese Scientists and
  Engineers, 78
United Nations, 223
Universal Caregiving, 230
Unselfishness, 29–30, 51–52

Values:
  civic virtue, 32
  families and, xii, 1, 16, 50–51, 79, 205,
    229
  job choice and, 47–48
  women's work and, 45
  See also Social norms
Venceremos Brigade, 213, 225
Violence. See Coercion
Virtue, 37, 51
Voluntary Simplicity movement, 162

Wage employment, 89–90, 93–94, 121
Wages. See Income
Webb, Beatrice, 94
Welfare Queen, 113–114
Welfare state, xv–xvi
  families in, 201–202
  female problem of, 114
  mothers in, 40
  personal interactions in, 229
  recipient reduction, 124–125
  reform of, 120–125
  self-interest and, 9
  social insurance programs, 86–87
  social safety net programs, 113
  subsidies, 56, 61, 96–99, 111–113
  See also Nanny state; Social welfare
    programs
Wells, H. G., 94
Whitehead, Barbara Dafoe, 15

Wolfe, Barbara, 111
Wolff, Edward, 111
Wollstonecraft, Mary, 9
Women:
  care services and, 55–57
  caregiving responsibilities and, xiv, 3–4,
    35
  civilizing influence of, 12, 14–15
  corpornational employment of, 189–190
  employment discrimination, 93–94
  male domination of, 6, 204–205
  motherhood, 34–35, 38–39
  productivity of, 6–7, 8, 66
  rights of, xiv–xv, 10, 14
  self-interests of, xix–xx, 4, 14
  self-sacrifice and, 10–11, 12, 15–16
  separate spheres doctrine and, 11–13
  specialization and, 5–6, 39
  status of, 6
  subordination of, 7, 8–9, 93
  success, definition of, 79
  work and, 34–35, 42, 44–46, 47–48, 73,
    225
  See also Coercion; Feminism; Men
Woodhull, Victoria, 13
Work:
  caregiving and, 37, 48–49
  efficiency in, 16
  female productivity, 6–7, 8, 225
  incentives to work, 176, 215
  Lockian economic principles and, 7–8
  nonmarket, xi–xii, 66–68, 92, 226–227
  parenthood and, 34–35
  pink-collar, 44–46
  plant closing regulation, 199–200
  rat race effect, 42–44
  values and choice of, 47–48
  wage employment, 89–90, 93–94, 121
  See also Corpornations
Worker Adjustment and Retraining Act of
  1988, 200
World Trade Organization (WTO),
  194–195